RECOLLECTIONS OF A
NORTHUMBRIAN LADY

BARBARA, AGED EIGHTY-TWO, DRESSED FOR THE
QUEEN'S LAST DRAWING-ROOM

THE RECOLLECTIONS
OF A
NORTHUMBRIAN LADY
1815-1866

The Memoirs of Barbara Charlton
of Hesleyside, Northumberland

Edited by
L. E. O. Charlton

THE SPREDDEN PRESS
STOCKSFIELD
1989

First published by Jonathan Cape, 1949
Reprinted 1950.

Reprinted 1989,
with new preface and introduction, by
The Spredden Press,
Brocksbushes Farm, Stocksfield, Northumberland NE45 7W3

© M. Craig and S. Higgens, 1989
Preface © The Spredden Press, 1989
'Hesleyside and the Charltons' © Country Life, 1989

ISBN Hardback   1 871739 04 7
Paperback   1 871739 05 5

Printed and bound by
SMITH SETTLE
Ilkley Road, Otley, West Yorkshire LS21 3JP

PREFACE TO SECOND EDITION

I am pleased that the Spredden Press is publishing another edition of my great-grandmother's memoirs and I am grateful for the opportunity to write its introduction. The *Recollections* were originally published in 1949, being edited by my uncle, Air Commodore L. E. O. Charlton, a gifted writer who had led an eventful life. He was born in 1879, nineteen years before the death of his grandmother Barbara Charlton, and I believe that it was his admiration of her that prompted him to edit her diaries and to have them published. He originally intended a second instalment but, at the age of fifty-one, 'an ordinary routine of life had succeeded to the liveliness and sparkle of (Barbara's) younger married state' and he must have decided that this was the time to say a final goodbye.

Before he was twenty-one my uncle had been awarded a Royal Humane Society medal for risking his life to save that of another man, and had won the D.S.O. for gallantry at Spion Kop. Later he received other awards and a mention in despatches for his services in the Boer War. He joined the Royal Flying Corps before the Great War, being made a Commander of St Michael and St George in 1916 and an officer of the Legion of Honour, and served as Air Attaché in our Embassy in Washington from 1919 until 1922.

He resigned from the RAF on a matter of principle and took up writing. I remember him with affection as being kind and modest, with a deep historical and geographical knowledge of his grandmother's North Tyne Valley.

Changing surnames seems to be a family trait as the reader will find. Barbara's second son (the delicate Ernest who lived to be eighty-seven) changed his name to that of Anne in order to inherit her brother's estate of Burghwallis, six miles north of Doncaster. The latter was sold in 1943 by Ernest's son George Anne, whose second son I married. After my father died in 1950, my husband changed his name back to that of Charlton. So today there are Charltons twice over at Hesleyside.

I wonder what Barbara would find most strange in her valley now. Might it be the absence of her husband's railway line and its replacement by motor cars and buses travelling at, to her, incredible speeds over tarmac roads which in her day were little more than cart tracks?

She would be astonished to find many of her husband's farms planted with spruce trees, the result of a national timber shortage caused by the Great War. She would wonder why some 2,600 acres of valley had been flooded and she would search in vain for Mounces, the sporting lodge of the Swinburne family. Like other irreplaceable stone buildings it lies under the biggest man-made lake in Europe.

Barbara would find the changes in her household equally remarkable. She would find no butler or housekeeper with their retinues and their attendant problems; no chain of house-maids climbing the back stairs with their loads of coals and brass hot-water cans, descending with buckets of ashes and slop pails. The gardeners and grooms have gone; she would find their places taken by machines and the motor car. Hot and cold water from taps would undoubtedly intrigue her, as would the marvels wrought by electricity which is the main substitute for the maids. There is no need for a 'bell-pull' to summon someone to replenish the fire: oil-fired central heating and a thermostat do all that is necessary. She would be surprised to find that young ladies no longer learn the arts of deportment, embroidery and music but have a huge variety of occupations open to them. A higher proportion of women ride horses than in her day, but what would she think of their doing so astride?

Barbara would find Hesleyside itself almost unchanged. Only the courtyard over which she and her husband put a roof in order to build a billiards room is back to its early state. Hindley's eighteenth-century clock still chimes the hours and the iron entrance gates and park railings, put up by her father-in-law when he moved the public road down to the riverside, are in reasonable repair. She would find it hard to recognize the small, stone-built village of Bellingham that she knew though the Town Hall and the workhouse (now the county library as well as a restaurant), both built by her husband's efforts, are in good repair. The Tyne Bridge and Bonomi's Catholic Church, the work of her father-in-law, stand as solid as ever.

She would be delighted to find that many of the local families she knew and visited are still in their houses and farms, and that in the Upper North Tyne Valley the four 'graynes' are well represented. Also she would be pleased to know that her great grandson, my husband, is President of Bellingham Agricultural Show, like her own husband who founded it in 1847.

Mamie Charlton, 1989

HESLEYSIDE AND THE CHARLTONS
by Giles Worsley

The miseries of life in remote country houses have seldom been more evocatively described than by Barbara Charlton writing of Hesleyside as she had known it in the first half of the nineteenth century: 'the long passages had no heat, the outside doors were never shut, the hall and corridors were paved with flagstones, while, to complete the resemblance of Hesleyside to a refrigerator, the grand staircase, also of stone, and the three large old-fashioned full-length windows halfway up with their frames warped by excessive damp . . . contrived to make the downstairs space a cave of icy blasts. Even in my early years at Hesleyside funguses grew on passage woodwork.'

But at least by the nineteenth century the Charltons were no longer in danger of 'Buckleughe' coming raiding across the border in search of members of the family on whom he could slake his thirst for revenge. The border valley of Tyndale, which runs north-west from Hexham, has always been one of the most isolated parts of England, and before the accession of James I it was one of the most notorious. Its remoteness, and the roughness of its terrain, where bogs made approach by horse extremely tricky, meant that the writ of central government could only be cursorily applied. The papers of Tudor monarchs are full of irritated complaints about the lawlessness of the valley, and of the Charltons, the largest of the four 'graynes' or 'surnames' that accounted for most of its inhabitants.

And of course there was always the threat of violence from the north. As late as 1595 the Governor of Berwick was forced to write to Lord Burghley about a raid by three hundred Scots led by the Laird of Buccleugh searching for Charltons who had

had the temerity to claim back property stolen in a previous raid. Buccleugh also complained that in an earlier raid the men of North Tyndale had captured his grandfather and taken his sword which they had never returned (it is still at Hesleyside). He found four Charltons, 'able and sufficient men', and slew them.

It was to give some protection from such raids that the leading branch of the Charltons built a pele tower at Hesleyside, where they had owned land since at least the mid-thirteenth century. This was described by Sir Robert Bowes in 1542 as 'ane lytle towre'. In fact, in the face of superior forces the inhabitants of the valley preferred to use their knowledge of the bogs to avoid the threat. The tower does not survive, but according to Edward Charlton who wrote within living memory of its demolition, it resembled those at Cockle Park and Halton.

The events of 1603 slowly brought peace to the valley, and by 1631 William Charlton felt secure enough to build a two-storey range to the east of the tower. That this was a building of some distinction is revealed by traces of Classical arcading (and a datestone) that survive in the courtyard. The effect must have been similar to the contemporary arcade at Chillingham Castle, north-east of Alnwick.

If its remoteness is one key to understanding Hesleyside, the other is the religion of its owners. The Charltons are an old rescusant family, but despite all the disadvantages that adherence to Roman Catholicism brought, they managed to carry out two major rebuildings in the eighteenth century. According to the *History of Northumberland*, Hesleyside was damaged by fire in 1738 and the damage apparently not made good until the very end of the century. It is unclear whether William or his son Edward, who succeeded in 1736, was primarily responsible for laying out the avenues centred on the house, shown in an estate map of 1776.

Edward Charlton died in 1767 and was succeeded by his son William, then aged fourteen. He must have felt that Hesleyside, with its pele tower, courtyard entrance, old-fashioned facade and only two small rooms on the ground floor, needed improving, but it was nearly thirty years before he took action. When he did, he demolished the pele tower, improved the kitchens and offices and added a new south front in a simple Palladian style which would have been fashionable when he succeeded, but distinctly old-fashioned by the mid 1790s. This again was only one room thick, with a central three-bay hall flanked by a large room on either side and a fine Imperial staircase directly behind the hall.

William Charlton did not live to see his work completed for he died in February 1797, leaving a fourteen-year-old heir, William John Charlton. Although it has been suggested that the architect Ignatius Bonomi did work for the younger William after 1800 and possibly around 1812, it is clear from the accounts that no important work was carried out on the Hall until William's death in 1846.

It was during William John Charlton's time that Barbara Charlton, his daughter-in-law, suffered so dreadfully at Hesleyside. Not only was the house appallingly cold and damp, but the table manners were revolting and the food disgusting. Apart from excellent mutton it was mainly 'bad beef, unsound bread, mostly of the barley cake variety, salt butter and diseased potatoes . . . and undressed lettuce always occupied the middle of the table, at which each member of the family would dab in turn, tearing off a leaf, sprinkling salt on the dirty tablecloth . . . Water, drunk out of black glass, was the family beverage'.

That her parents-in-law were not the complete savages that Barbara made them out to be can be seen from the accounts which include substantial payments to the furniture makers

Gillows between 1811 and 1820, as well as a payment of £110 to Miller, cabinetmarker, on February 16, 1811, and of £19 8s for 'drawings, etc' to John Varley on June 14, 1813.

Barbara and her husband, William Henry Charlton, lost no time in making the house more comfortable, and according to her memoirs she summoned Ignatius Bonomi to Hesleyside 'to plan alterations in order to make the house warmer and more habitable for William and me'. Bonomi, who was based in Durham, was the natural architect for the Charltons to call upon. Not only did he have an extensive practice among Northern Catholic families, he had also built the new Catholic chapel largely financed by the Charltons at Bellingham, the neighbouring village. There were also family links, and indeed his sister Justina had spent a long convalescence at Hesleyside.

Bonomi's works were limited to creating a new entrance on the north side of the house, sheltered by Newton's Ionic porch, with a narrow lobby to reduce draughts. He also built a screen to disguise the courtyard, with a handsome Italianate clock-tower, and made a small extension to the dining room, to the left of the new front door. He must also have been responsible for the gates at the end of the new drive and for the balustrading in front of the east wing.

To modernise the interior the Charltons turned to the otherwise little-known Thomas Worthington. Barbara Charlton describes him as the foreman for Crace, the well-known firm of interior decorators, but as the bills were all sent out in his name, and from York not London, it would seem that he had set up on his own account. The Charltons had come across Crace's work a couple of years earlier when they had rented Brandsby Hall in Yorkshire from 1845 to '47. This was the seat of William Charlton's first cousin Charles Cholmeley, who had just moved into the neighbouring house, Gilling Castle, where he engaged Crace to decorate the gallery.

This was not the Charltons' final work at Hesleyside. In 1861 central heating was installed in the passages and gas put in all the rooms except the dining and drawing rooms. Then in 1863 the courtyard was covered over and a billiard room formed. Unfortunately, this was badly built and damp soon got in, even affecting the books. It was finally demolished by the present owners.

William Henry Charlton lived well but left innumerable debts. He had been dead only three months when all the contents of Hesleyside were auctioned, down to the gas brackets on the halls, the napkins in the drawers and the azaleas in the garden. The house was then let. This did not solve the problem, and in October 1887, at a time of severe agricultural depression, the house and the entire estate, estimated at approximately 20,000 acres, were put up for sale. Despite controlling a rent roll of £5,000, bidding failed at £119,000, well below the reserve of £150,000.

The house remained let until 1919 when Mrs Charlton's father (another William Henry Charlton), who had married in 1914, moved back, taking advantage of the buoyant land market to sell some of the land that nobody would take in 1887, so clearing the debts on the estate.

The publishers are grateful to *Country Life* for permission to print this abbreviated version of an article that first appeared in *Country Life* (18 May 1989).

CONTENTS

X The Course of True Love (1839)   102

The Charltons of Hesleyside. The Course of True Love.
Letter from a Lover. Family Squabbles. A Plot is framed.
Gretna Green. Re-marriages in London. Barbara's Mother-
in-law. Sisterly Correspondence. Maria Augusta signs a
Deed and departs for ever from Burghwallis. A.D. 1839.

XI Arrival at Hesleyside (1839)   121

Hesleyside and Its Surroundings. The Bride's Arrival. Miss
Catherine Fenwick. Survey of Past. Teresa Charlton and
Sir Francis Delaval. The Capheaton Gallopers. The Dixons
of Mantle Hill. *Une Maitresse Femme*. Barbara's Father-in-
law when Young. Halfway over Europe. Famous Lawsuit.
The Family of Cholmeley. A Mother's Caution disregarded.
Old Days on North Tyne. The Spirit-breaking Hags. Per-
secution. Brutality. A Doctor intervenes. The Place of
General Interest. Diphtheria. Kindness unrequited. The
Miss Berrys. A.D. 1839.

XII Account of the Home Scene (1839–42)   149

Hesleyside, the House. Mary and Kate Charlton. Lady
Jane Swinburne and the Boy Algernon. Story of Lost Heir
of Capheaton. Maria Augusta pays a visit. Barbara's first
Child. A Miserable Time. Mrs. (Cholmeley) Charlton's
Mental State. Death of Henry Charlton. Death of Barbara's
First Child. Schwalbach. Wright's Bank Breaks. Brussels.
Old Mrs. Blount. Living in a *bouge*. Place Verte. A Dream
and its consequences. A.D. 1842.

XIII Barbara Reigns Supreme (1842–49)   169

They reign supreme at Hesleyside. A Family *décousue*.
Death of Fanny Heneage. Burghwallis revisited. Durham.
Frank Charlton. Death of Maria Augusta Roselia. Two
Years at Brandsby. Birth of a Daughter. Death of Thomas
Charlton. Life as lived at Hesleyside. Death of William
John. Mary and Kate Charlton go Abroad in Search of
Health. Death of Little Eddy. Bellingham Agricultural
Show. London. The Standard of Hesleyside. Kate Charlton
marries a Sicilian Baron. Teaching Village Scholars
French. The Derwentwater Estates and Greenwich Hos-
pital. Unedifying Clergy. A Poaching Raid. A.D. 1849.

LIST OF ILLUSTRATIONS

Thomas Fitzherbert of Swinnerton = Mary Teresa, d. of Sir Robert Throckmorton, Bt., of Caugnton

4 sons.

9 daus.

Thomas = Mary Anne Smythe,
(eld. son),   widow of Thos. Weld.
d.s.p.   She subsequently m.
              George, Prince of
              Wales.

George Tasburgh of Bodney,   =   BARBARA
Co. Norfolk. d.s.p., making it   d. 1805
conditional that his widow's
2nd husband and heirs should
take the name and arms of
Tasburgh.

2ndly George Crathorne
of Crathorne and Ness.
b. 1761, d. 1825. He
assumed the name and
arms of Tasburgh.

George Anne of Burghwallis.   =   .2ndly Mary, d. of Robt.
b. 1717, d. 1785.   Needham of Histon,
                                   Co. Mon.

Frances Editha, dau.   =   Michael Anne of Burghwallis,   =   Maria Augusta Rosalia.
and co-heir of Wm.   b. 1777, d. 1853. He assumed   d. at Crathorne, 1844.
Gage of York   the name and arms of Tasburgh.
(AUNT ANNE).

George Anne
(eld. son). b.
1775, d.s.p.
1802.

Mary,   =   Charles Fairfax
d. 1861   of Gilling Castle,
            Yorks. d.s.p.
            1871.

Frances   =   George Heneage
(FANNY).   of Hainton.
d. 1842.   d. 1864.

George Anne of
Burghwallis, b.
1813, d. unm.
1882. He re-
tained the name
of Anne.

Edward Charlton   =   Teresa, d. of Sir
of Hesleyside. m.   John Swinburne
1746.   of Capheaton.

William Charlton   =   Margaret, d. of
of Hesleyside. m.   John Fenwick.
1778.

William John Charlton   =   Katherine, d. of Francis
of Hesleyside m. 1809.   Cholmeley of Brandsby.

BARBARA.   =   William Henry Charlton of Hesleyside.
b. 1815,   N'land. b. 1810, d. 1880.
d. 1898.

PREFACE

WHEN memoir-writing takes, as in this case, the form of an autobiographical record it is usually undertaken to relieve the tedium of the passing hours in advanced old age. So did it happen here. The old lady, decked out to do homage to the Queen at Victoria's last Drawing-room, whose portrait is inserted as a frontispiece to this volume lived the last years of her life in a gloomful Ebury Street lodging with her two unmarried daughters in attendance on her. In such circumstances ennui was the enemy to beware. She was therefore happily inspired to commit to paper the recollections of a long life, aided by a retentive memory and, in further support, a formidable array of closely inscribed diaries, each accounting for a single year, which it had been a life-long habit to accumulate.

It is not pretended that there is any great literary merit in her writing, nor is it claimed that what she had put down deserves to rank her among notable writers of the sort. Nevertheless she has achieved, probably for the mere reason that she could not help it, something in the nature of a veritable period piece, charged with a special interest for those who like to read a human document and particularly addressed to the many who are still curious about the social background of the recent past, more especially in its relation to the old Catholic families of northern England. For the family from which the writer sprung, as also that into which she married, were of those who adhered all through history to the Church of Rome.

The curtain rises on a picturesque variety of scene. Childhood in a Yorkshire home; an educational interval in Paris;

the return from thence as a marriageable Victorian miss to lead the life of thoughtless gaiety, both rural and metropolitan, prescribed for such; marriage to a young Northumbrian squire of large property and territorial importance; motherhood, bringing with it an increasing weight of maternal cares. Such would be a conspectus of the book which, in this its first instalment, is brought to a finish with the approach to womanhood of the writer's elder daughters and the adolescence of her sons.

The atmosphere is Catholic throughout the book, though this arises naturally from the writer's birth and family associations, not from a religious trend. She herself devoutly practises her faith and so do those about her, but she allows herself full licence to criticise, and even to deplore, a weakness where she finds it, and is especially outspoken on the subject of the education of Catholic youth. This is in no sense to inveigh against the religious side of things; on the contrary, it is an honest endeavour, the outcome of a long experience, to face contemporary facts as she conceived them. She is talking of what happened a hundred years and more ago when the shadow of persecution had only recently been lifted, when social life was much more primitive than now, the viewpoints of behaviour more narrow, and when, in Catholic eyes, apostasy was an unimaginable crime.

The writer died in harness, so to speak; her memoirs not quite complete.

INTRODUCTION

THE writer of these memoirs was Barbara, wife of William Henry Charlton, Esq., of Hesleyside in the county of Northumberland and daughter of Michael Tasburgh, Esq., of Burghwallis in the county of Yorkshire: born May 31st, 1815; married June 20th, 1839; widowed June 15th, 1880; died January 30th, 1898. Her life of eighty-three years thus tallied with the nineteenth century and corresponded with the whole Victorian Era. It was lived under four sovereigns during a period of vital change at home and much turmoil abroad, and was coeval with the birth pangs, growing pains, and adolescence of England as she is to-day.

Barbara's own family, as also that into which she married, were both of old descent and in neither case had they changed faith at the Reformation. They both belonged to that cohesive Catholic community, emancipated by the Act of 1829, the various members of which possessed entailed estates, the dignity conceded to a landed class, and the rightful enjoyment of a position in Society corresponding to their territorial prestige.

A convent education abroad at the hands of French nuns was a normal education for Catholic girls of good family a hundred years or more ago, and Barbara, following in her mother's footsteps, received her early teaching in the Paris of The Restoration under Charles X from that source. Her parents for a time resided there and, received as was their right in the best Parisian society, acquired an extensive circle of friendship and acquaintance among the leading families of France. Barbara learnt to speak French perfectly as a convent child, while the widening effect on her mind of her parents' social way of life, at a particularly impressionable age among a people noted for their vivacity and intelligence, joined to her own sharp faculties of perception, contributed to keep her interested all her life in movements and events and in touch with burning questions of the day.

It also happened that her husband, although born and bred in a remote part of the country within a stone's throw of the Border, and in many respects a traditional country squire, was himself a man of intellectual ability, with the experience of a German university behind him, and not without a fair degree of scholarly attainment.

Instead, therefore, of following neighbourly example and lending themselves to a vegetable existence entirely preoccupied with the domesticities of life, and well content therewith, Barbara and her husband identified themselves with the community at large and seemed to have been perpetually in motion, taking frequent trips to foreign parts, running south to London both in and out of season, and staying with friends and relations at their houses in the country.

Although fervently a Catholic herself, while her husband lived, at any rate, in strict observance of the precepts of his Church, they did not confine their social interests, as was then too much the wont with Catholics, to the company of co-religionists, but mixed with people irrespective of their creed. Born, however, as they were, and marrying as they did, the background of their lives partook inevitably of Catholicity, and Barbara's early pages forcibly recall a day, now belonging to a well-forgotten past, when adherents of the Roman Church were somewhat eyed askance and were apt, in consequence, to set themselves conspicuously apart.

The Catholic Relief Act of 1829, passed in the reign of

George IV during the Duke of Wellington's administration, did remove in one sweep, it is true, the many disabilities undergone by Catholics up to then and which, following on the 'Popish Plot' of 1678, had been increased during the Restoration period. As a result of that Act Roman Catholics were admitted to Parliament and to all but a few of the highest posts, civil or military, in the service of the Crown.

In its legislative operation the Act was instantly effective, but it did not alter at the time to any great extent a prejudice against the Church of Rome entertained by the Protestant and Dissenting sections of the population, long inured to look on 'Popery' as subversive and outlandlish. The English Catholics, therefore, in the years subsequent to their emancipation continued to be thrown back largely on themselves, and it was in this atmosphere of antipathy on the one hand and of proud estrangement on the other that Barbara's youth and early womanhood were passed. As some offset to the social conditions thus obtaining it may be stated that the landed class of Roman Catholics in England was politically in fashion. They formed a fairly numerous community possessing wealth and considerable local influence, and in this way assumed an importance in the eyes of politicians which caused them to be courted at election times previous to 1867, in which year the borough franchise was extended to all ratepayers.

Apart from the above-mentioned tendency towards clannishness, a legacy of the abrogated penal laws, and apart from a system of cousinly intermarriage, necessitated by the matter of religion and in some respects unfortunate, the Catholic county families did not differ greatly from their neighbours of an equal social status. It was on the younger sons that the recent disabilities had rested more heavily. For with these a long exclusion from the liberal professions, the services, the public schools and universities, had had the not unnatural effect of restraining ambition, restricting outlook, and developing a policy, with all its attendant disadvantages, of stay-at-home.

Barbara, for all her gadding about, was never careless of her matronly responsibilities or impatient of the burden that motherhood exacts; indeed, she performed her duty conscientiously in both respects as an admirable hostess and a devoted parent of her children. These qualities appertain, of course, to the Northumbrian years of her life and those pages of her memoirs that report the scene at Hesleyside go to make a social document which excitingly portrays the ups and downs of a countrified existence on the Border a hundred years ago, where conditions were very different from those prevailing in the Midlands and the South, where the long-established families of squirearchal repute were held in reverence by the people roundabout, where the tenant farmers had been for generations on the land, and where something of a feudatory nature was in the bearing both of man and master.

L. E. O. C.

THE RECOLLECTIONS
OF A NORTHUMBRIAN LADY

BIRTH AND PARENTAGE OF BARBARA

BEFORE commencing on the memoirs certain matter of a preliminary nature related to Barbara's birth and parentage must be submitted for the reader's better understanding.

In mid-December, 1814, Mr. and Mrs. Tasburgh of Burghwallis Hall, near Doncaster, aged respectively thirty-seven and twenty-two years, sailed by packet from Ramsgate to Calais for the purpose of a sojourn in Paris. Mr. Tasburgh, who previous to his marriage in 1810 was Mr. Michael Anne, may be accepted as a well-to-do Yorkshire squire of aristocratic bearing and, in most respects, typical of his generation, the owner of extensive lands in the West Riding which had descended from father to son, without intermission, since the days of the Plantagenet kings.

His wife, Maria Augusta Roselia, was also of Yorkshire origin, being the sole surviving child of George Crathorne of Crathorne, Co. Yorks, who also, for reasons that will soon be given, changed his ancient name to Tasburgh on his marriage. Maria's childhood and early youth were spent perforce in France under circumstances that follow: When the Peace of Amiens was concluded with Napoleon in 1802 her father, imagining it to be of long duration, took his wife and child with him to France for foreign travel, only to be caught on enemy soil when hostilities were renewed a few months later. For several years they were interned at

Verdun by the French, Maria, meanwhile, receiving education in Paris at *Le Couvent des Dames Anglaises*. When she was seventeen years old an attempt was made to transplant her to England for the purpose of a fitting marriage, but the French authorities refused her permission to embark. A permit had however been given for the conveyance home for burial of a dead English nun, and the difficulty of Maria's passage was very simply overcome by the substitution of herself in the crated coffin thus placed at her disposal. In such manner did this young lady, heiress to a considerable estate, return to the land of her birth.

Mr. Tasburgh kept a diary while in Paris, one entry in which describes a visit to the Catacombs. It took place on February 14th, 1815, and the diary reference ends with these words:

'I was under a good deal of anxiety for my wife during this disagreeable but curious promenade, both from the nature of the thing itself, the naturally unpleasant feelings it aroused, and the great distance traversed and the consequent fatigue. But she bore it without any ill effect, though in the seventh month of her pregnancy. Certainly there was no great thanks due to my prudence, but I was unaware of the extent or horribleness of these mansions of the dead.'

It is Barbara who is thus indirectly referred to, and on the 23rd of the same month Mr. Tasburgh and his wife make an excursion to St. Cloud where Napoleon principally resided when in Paris. It was an ill-omened jaunt. Six days later the abdicated Emperor reappeared in the south of France, and on March 20th with his arrival at the capital the Hundred Days began. But at the first whisper of the landing Mr. Tasburgh and his wife made all speed back to England. Maria Augusta had already undergone internment and was determined not to risk a repetition. It thus came about that

Barbara was born in a London suburb instead of Paris, as was perhaps originally planned. And having got as far, let her now introduce herself.

'I, *née* Barbara Tasburgh, was born at Hampstead on the 31st of May, 1815, during *les Cent Jours*; my mother having been hurried away from Paris on Napoleon's return. I am the 4th child and 3rd daughter of Michael Anne of Burgh-wallis, Co. York, and of Maria Augusta Roselia, only surviving child and heiress of George Crathorne Tasburgh, born at Nice in 1792.

'As it has always been a puzzle to friends, and even to my own family, how we came to have three surnames and three estates it may not be out of place here to elucidate this intricate point.'

The point is indeed intricate, but so far from elucidating it Barbara's explanation makes confusion worse confounded. The facts, as plain as can be stated, were as follows: Barbara's grandmother on the female side was another Barbara, a Miss Fitzherbert of Swinnerton in Staffordshire, who married George Tasburgh, Esq., of Bodney Hall, Co. Norfolk. This George Tasburgh predeceased his wife, dying without issue, leaving to his widow his estates, and enjoining on her to take a second husband. In doing so, however, he laid down a condition – namely, that the man of her choice in the case of a remarriage should bear the name and arms of Tasburgh and should pass them to whatever children there might be. The widowed lady took unto herself George Crathorne of Crathorne, Co. Yorks, whose elder brother Thomas was the present head of that ancient family, the sole surviving child of their union being Maria Augusta Roselia, mother of our Barbara, who, in comformity with the above-mentioned condition, bore the name of Tasburgh from her birth. Her father, however, relinquished it on the death of his elder brother Thomas, and reassumed the name of Crathorne, which, it may be stated, died out with him. Maria Augusta thus became a double heiress and eventually succeeded to the two estates of Bodney and Crathorne.

The circumstances of Maria's upbringing have already been described. Shortly after her arrival in England, posing as a dead nun on the journey, she married Michael Anne of Burghwallis, Co. Yorks, and on his marriage it was necessary for Mr. Anne, as in the case of Mr. Crathorne, to assume the name and arms of Tasburgh. So we are brought to the writer of the memories, who was, as stated by herself, the fourth child of that marriage, her own name being Tasburgh, her father's Anne, and that of her grandfather, Crathorne.

We now return to the memoirs, asking for the reader's indulgence while Barbara directs attention to her Anne and Crathorne forbears.

'The first record of my Crathorne ancestry according to the old pedigree, now almost effaced, dates from Humphrey of that name who in 1066 held certain hides of lands in the lordship and town of Baynard, lying upon the Water of Leven. A vague beginning, and written in very vague language. In the old Crathorne pedigree few but eldest sons are recorded in the long line of decent from the Conquest down to my mother's time, but to some of the younger sons must be awarded credit for deeds of valour. The shell, for example, surmounting the coat of arms, is evidence that scions of the family fought in the Crusades. In the chancel of the old church at Crathorne, over the vault in which my mother lies, and in a recess of the north wall within the altar rails, there is a freestone effigy of William de Crathorn, evidently a younger son as he does not find place on the bare family stem, who fell at the battle of Neville's Cross in 1346. It is possible that his body was brought back to Crathorne, though much more likely that he was buried amongst the slain on the field of battle. Before joining the King's forces he made a verbal will in the presence of the Blessed Sacrament with the priest and villagers as witness, which was proved in the Court of the Archbishop of York and which can still be seen in the York Diocesan Registry.

'The Crathornes must have latterly possessed much land, a fact indicated by an eighteenth century marble tablet in Crathorne church the inscription on which reads as follows: "Underneath lieth the body of Ralph Crathorn, Lord of Crathorn, Ness, Plowland, Welwick, and Thorp juxta Welwick, who died April 19th, 1755." Ralph is eventually succeeded by his nephew who married Isabella, daughter of Sir John Swinburne, Bart. of Capheaton in the County of Northumberland, and had issue Henry, Francis, Thomas, George and Isabella, the last two being twins.

'Tradition relates that this Isabella Swinburne, whose sister Teresa married Edward Charlton, Esq., of Hesleyside, Northumberland, was not the most sensible person to bring up a family of five children. The daughter died at seventeen, but the four boys grew to manhood without a profession in life. No wonder the estate could not bear such a strain. True! the cruel penal laws debarred Catholics from the liberal professions, but they could still become doctors, or consuls, or take to literature, or even enter foreign military service. Alas! they chose to look on themselves as unconformable, to congregate as such, and to drown injustice in strong liquors, while their oppressors looked on with delight to see the buds of the best Catholic families imbrue themselves with the waters of destruction.

'Henry, the eldest of Isabella's children and generally spoken of as Harry – *l'enfant gâté des Dames* – left a very large debt on the estate. He is said to have been the

handsomest man of his day. He went to China with Lord
Macartney on the latter's appointment to the Pekin Court
as first British envoy in 1792 and probably had a hand in
the writing of Swinburne's Travels; it is at any rate certain
that he bore the whole expense of publishing them. Harry
Crathorne was born in 1757 and never married. There can
hardly be a doubt that he inherited his beauty, wildness of
disposition, and ill-regulated mind from his flighty mother,
for he lost his father at the tender age of seven. The sole
redeeming point of his unsettled career was a faithfulness,
throughout a life of dissipation, to a certain lady of his love
by whom he had two sons, one of whom became the Abbé
Campbell, for many years priest at Spetchley. The other son
went into the Army. He came on a visit to Burghwallis when
I was a girl, and I remember him as being straight and tall
with very aristocratic features.'

All this about the wild Harry is by no means beside the
point, for he was in fact Barbara's great-uncle. He was
succeeded by his brother Thomas who, dying childless,
passed on the property to another brother, George, Barbara's
grandfather and the inheritor of an impoverished estate.

'My grandfather and grandmother generally lived in
Italy, mostly at Nice where my mother was born on January
19th, 1792, the sponsors at her baptism, represented of
course by proxy, being George Augustus Frederick, heir
apparent to the throne, and Mrs. Fitzherbert, the infant's
aunt by marriage, who was secretly his wife. My mother at
the age of ten was put to *Le Couvent des Dames Anglaises,
Rue des Fossés, Quartier St. Victor, Paris*, where she was
evidently not taught English and never afterwards learnt to
speak or write it properly. Her Italian accent never left her.
My dear mother had the head, face, and features of a well-
cut cameo, with a profusion of light auburn hair, but she

was a little too tall and her figure had been sadly neglected
by the nuns.

'When she was seventeen years old her godmother, Mrs.
Fitzherbert, wished to take charge of her and present her in
society, but this intention was frustrated. Her father, who
had been for long a *détenu* at Verdun and without the means
of ascertaining how far the reports, unfavourable to Mrs.
Fitzherbert's character, which casually reached him while in
durance, were true, preferred to accept his brother's tittle-
tattle version of the case and forbade all intercourse between
his young daughter and her aunt. Further to enforce this
interdiction he authorized his brother Thomas, who was the
head of the family and then lived in York, to get the girl
married to the first Catholic gentleman of good family who
should present himself. Thus did my poor mother fall a
victim to vile calumny, while her sudden transplantation and
her broken English did not help matters. In 1809, therefore, at the age of seventeen, after having been for seven
years strictly cloistered in a convent, she was married to
Michael Anne of Burghwallis, Co. Yorks, who thereupon
assumed the name and arms of Tasburgh by royal licence.
My brother George, born in 1813, retained the name of
Anne, but my two elder sisters and myself were always
known as the Misses Tasburgh and subsequently became
equal sharers in the Crathorne property.

'Of the family of Anne of Burghwallis Mr. Hunter, the
well-known genealogist, has remarked that it is a single
instance of the male line being maintained in its ancient
post and rank out of all the gentry of the Deanery of Doncaster summoned to appear before the Heralds in 1584.
The pedigree dates from Sir William de Anne, Constable of
Tickhill Castle in the time of Edward II, who married the
coheiress of Haringel and thus acquired the Manor of

Frickley which was sold in the latter part of the eighteenth century. Burghwallis came from the heiress of Fenton in the reign of Elizabeth. Mr. Hunter observes: "The Annes, like too many other families, have not been careful of preserving their ancient evidences, and theirs was not one of the muniment rooms to which our diligent antiquary Dodsworth had access." '

EARLY CHILDHOOD AT BURGHWALLIS

THE curtain now rises on a scene of home life at Burgh-wallis. There are four children in the nursery, the difference in age between the youngest and the eldest being four and a half years. Mary the first-born, a seven-months child, came into the world in December 1810; Fanny followed after an interval of eleven months; the boy George first saw the light in July, 1813; finally, Barbara, so named for her grandmother on the Tasburgh side, was born at the end of May, 1815.

A word about Burghwallis. It was, and still is for that matter, a many-gabled, rambling, and interesting structure, and occupies its site with a certain dignity and grace. In the distant past it must have grown undoubtedly from a home-stead to a mansion by a process of accretion, the last of which occurred in Barbara's infancy and consisted of the five-gabled east front somewhat overshadowing in importance the older parts behind it. Until the middle of the eighteenth century the Anne family was seated at Frickley and, prior to the sale of that extensive property, Burghwallis was used alternatively as a dower-house, when a widow was available, or as a residence for the son and heir on reaching man's estate. That it was, in the full meaning of the term, a 'country-house' finds proof in the diary of one Nicholas Blundell, from which the following short entries are ex-tracted: '1714. *July 1st.* My wife and I came to Burghwallis, where we lodged. *July 2nd.* Cousin Anne of Frickley and his wife dined at Burghwallis. *July 3rd.* Edward Fletcher, the fiddler, played to us. My Lady Smithson and I danced country dances.' (Lady Smithson, by the way, who married Sir Hugh Smithson, Bart., and thus became grandmother to the first Duke of Northumberland, was originally Elizabeth, daughter of Marmaduke Lord Langdale. Her sister Jane married in 1654 Michael Anne of Frickley and was Barbara's great-great grandmother.)

But now let Barbara tell us something of her childhood.

'Of my early years at Burghwallis I especially remember having *soi-disant* pet animals in our nursery which was for night as well as day, the old day nursery having been turned into a school-room. In this large room, formally the Chapel and now (1892) a billiard room, there were then only two windows, with old-fashioned sills, which faced each other at the end furthest from the door. One overlooked the yard and was our popular look out, while the other gave on to the front entrance which seldom presented to us children a scene of delirious excitement. On one sill was a cage containing a pet squirrel, let loose at times for our diversion, and on the other was a canvas box enclosing caterpillars of every procurable variety. This was by way of instructing us in natural history and to this day I can smell the fetid odour of corruption and decay that emerged from that detestable collection. Considering that four children and two nurses slept, ate, and had their being in this one room these animals were certainly *de trop*, and in all probability we owed our universal dislike of pets to the disgust we had imbibed for them in early life.

'For playthings we had a stand-up barrel organ and a large rocking-horse, but no toys whatever except those given to us by stray visitors, gifts that were few and far between. In particular I remember a doll, a present from Aunt Anne who made periodical visits to Burghwallis in the

Bodney Hall, Norfolk, the property of Barbara's grandmother, lent to French Benedictine nuns at the time of the Revolution (see p. 59). The house was destroyed in the early nineteenth century.

Burghwallis Hall, near Doncaster, from the east. Barbara's childhood home. Both sketches are by Barbara's mother, Maria Augusta Rosalia Tasburgh.

company of her sister Miss Gage. Aunt Anne, as we always called her, was the widow of my father's eldest brother George, who died without issue in July, 1802, of scarlet fever after only five days' illness.

'From my earliest to my latest recollection I remember having been my dear mother's favourite child, with never an unkind thing either said or done to me. I fancy her partiality arose from the fact that I resembled her father, so much so that I used to be called *little grandpapa*, and also, it may have been, because I bore her own mother's name. It was an acknowledged understanding among us children that if a favour had to be asked of my mother, then *little grandpapa* was sent as spokesman. But though I was my mother's favourite I certainly was not my father's, who, though most kind at times of illness, thought a third daughter a superfluous addition to his family.

'On Christmas Days we had the honour of dining late with our parents. How cold it was with our white frocks and short sleeves! And when the mummers came in afterwards, fantastically dressed, to act a play in the servants' hall, ye gods! how I used to shake in my little shoes. We were allowed so few enjoyments as children that to dine downstairs on Christmas night, with grandpapa, Aunt Anne, and Miss Gage at table also, was an unforgotten landmark in our lives. Above all I must not forget our dear, kind old friend Billy Morritt, brother to the Squire of Rokeby the friend of Sir Walter Scott, who was very fond of us poor caged-up children, especially of my sister Fanny. He would pretend that he had chosen her for his future wife, but being the fattest and reddest-faced man I ever remember to have seen his advances were not received with acclamation. Fanny was the most delicate among us and a universal favourite with friends and strangers. To improve our figures we were made to lie for half an hour every day reclined on boards, and then to walk up and down the passage with weights on our heads. The latter exercise was fun and quite the most effective for the formation of a good carriage, as shown by the Italian contadine who carry themselves in such a stately manner.

'I remember when I was not quite five seeing my mother dressed for a grand ball given by Mr. and Mrs. Bacon Frank of Campsall. Great fear was entertained that her dress would not arrive from London in time. It was black and jet, probably on account of mourning for George III. Soon after the ball there was a sale at Campsall, and I have a vivid recollection of our going over, nurse and nursery-maid and all, carrying a large covered clothes-basket to bring away a peacock that had been given to us. The rooms were all quite bare of furniture, excepting a small one where sat Mrs. Bacon Frank and the old blind grandmother, a quakeress, dressed in the faultlessly neat attire of that people. The family left Campsall the next day and, for forty years, the mansion was let to strangers. At that time the Rev. Mr. Yewbank of Burghwallis Rectory used to take pupils and we often met the two boys, Rodolphus and Aspinall Bacon Frank, going from Campsall to the rectory on their ponies. Those were the only children we ever spoke to. Their sister Jessy, not famed for her beauty, married an Italian whose name appeared, not greatly to his credit, at the trial of Achilles versus Newman.

'When my sisters were old enough they had a nursery governess, a Miss Perkins who was sister to Aunt Anne's maid. She may have helped me with my letters, but what I best remember is that she let me play in her room, even when my sisters' lessons were in progress, and I felt very grateful towards her for releasing me from the smelly caterpillar atmosphere. How keenly does a child feel gratitude!

I cried when Miss Perkins left. Her's was such a sad position at Burghwallis, too low to keep us company in the drawing-room and too high for association with the servants. No wonder, poor woman, she liked having Mr. N—— the priest to converse with after evening prayers, and to have a little supper with him later in her room. The higher powers, however, did not approve of her little goings-on and she had to leave. Soon after the priest left as well and Mr. Best, who was a great favourite with us and used to go coursing with my brother George, came in his place. George, I may mention, displayed a great talent for drawing at a very early age.'

It is not surprising that Barbara's young brother drew so well, for both parents had strongly developed artistic taste. Mrs. Tasburgh's drawings of Crathorne and Bodney are rough sketches only it is true, but her self-portrait is truly a work of art, well-drawn and exquisitely coloured. As for Mr. Tasburgh, his skill was such that only recently a British Museum official suggested to their present owner the propriety of bestowing a collection of French drawings, chiefly of an architectural nature but in no sense draughtsmanship, on that venerable institution as specimens of late eighteenth-century pencil-work.

So much for the Burghwallis scene of childhood. It is now the year 1821. Barbara is six years and eight months old; Mary, the eldest child, is eleven. Mr. Tasburgh is about to uproot himself and family and resort to France for a stay of some duration. The reason of this flitting is not precisely known, but Bodney, the estate in Norfolk, had been on the market and was sold, a portion of the purchase price going to the erection of the east wing at Burghwallis to which attention has been drawn. It is highly probable that a means was sought of escaping the acute discomfort of living in a house largely given over to the builders, and hence a flight to Paris.

THE FAMILY REMOVES TO PARIS

'THE first intimation we children had of leaving England was on an afternoon when George was busy copying one of Bewick's birds. My father came in to the room and in his never very cheerful tone suddenly gave my brother the option of going with the family to France or to school at Ushaw.

'It is hardly credible that a father should have presented an only son of seven years with such a choice, and at a time, moreover, when the most rapid journey from Paris to Durham could not have occupied less than a week or ten days. In those days all schools and colleges were inhuman and rough, and those farthest north were naturally the least civilised. The sons of many Catholic squires were educated at Ushaw, including all the Charltons of Hesleyside of that generation, and for the reason that Mr. and Mrs. Charlton promised to look after George, and have him home for the holidays with their own sons, he did ultimately go there. But at the time of asking the boy of seven years was wiser than his father and plumped for Paris.

'Just before our emigration to the Continent Mrs. Fairfax of Gilling Castle, with her two daughters Lavinia and Harriet and her son Charles, came to stay, and we had much fun and games. Sixteen years later, almost to a day, my sister Mary became the wife of this same Charles.

'How vividly I recollect the exodus to France early in February, 1821! I can still see, as if it were only yesterday, the large yellow family coach being trundled to the front entrance to be stowed with all our belongings, and all the bustle and excitement on that bright February morning is still ringing in my ears. We children were exhorted to keep quiet and watch proceedings from the nursery window, those obnoxious caterpillars having already been done away with. Then came the four horses and postilions and, when all was ready, we were bidden to go down and get in. All the servants, and most of the villagers, clustered in the driveway to have a last look at us and wave farewell, many of them bathed in tears. Going abroad in those days was really a parting, and affectionate and attached servants and retainers were not yet out-of-date. Our family coach had two dickeys in addition to the box-seat, the one in front being occupied by the man-servant Ryecroft and Nurse Glaisby. Nurse Glaisby, who had come to us when I was an infant in arms, remained in the family for forty-eight years. She died at eighty-two and was buried in the Burghwallis church-yard, begging before her death that she should be laid alongside Monsieur le Roux, the priest, and so rise on the Last Day hand in hand with a co-religionist. In the hind dickey rode my father and, with him, each of my sisters in turn as his *compagnon de voyage*. Inside sat my mother, brother, one of my sisters, and myself, and when all were settled in their respective places off we started. My mother was crying bitterly; not on account of leaving Burghwallis for which she cared little, but at the affection shown to her by the people left behind.

'While in London we occupied lodgings in Green Street kept by my grandfather's foreign valet, Monsieur Lamoureux, and his maiden sister. For some reason or other we remained a fortnight or more in London. My father had his saddle-horse sent up from Yorkshire and used to ride in the Park. It must have been a very early season that

C

year, probably on account of the coronation, for I well remember being in the Park one Sunday afternoon when rows of carriages passed slowly by, as in a funeral procession, with my father riding among them on his celebrated mare Georgette.

'We poor children were taken to see no sights whatsoever. My mother never left the house and as often as I saw her she was lying either on the sofa or her bed. *Pour tout divertissement* a glass-blower came once to the house to display his craft and left behind him some Lilliputian bottles and glasses, but having no doll, nor the fraction of a doll, to go with them in our play we soon gave them away.

'I had a good sleep crossing over to France and the sailing boat that carried us arrived at Calais as the sun was rising. Ryecroft carried me from the boat to Quenet's Hotel and as the fisherwomen passed to go out with nets for shrimp or crabs my astonishment was great to see their queer caps, long earrings and remarkably short skirts.

'We children were delighted with the journey from Calais to Paris. There was a courier who rode on ahead in order to have a relay ready at each post; such broad-backed, sturdy horses they were, with plaited tails tied up with gaily coloured ribands, bright trappings, and bells tinkling on the harness. The postilions with their enormous jackboots, ornamented short roundabout jackets, and little round black hats with coloured trimmings, pleased us beyond measure, while the incessant cracking of whips *en l'air* was a sheer novelty. Still more amused were we to watch the postilions, at the end of a stage, washing out the nostrils of their steeds with brandy from a black bottle for fear lest the strongly built quadrupeds had been put to more exertion than their nerves could stand.

'I do not remember the French inns on the road, though

probably they were small and dirty. Each morning we set off with fresh food for the day, but we got so sick of frangipane each day that our first act on arrival in Paris at the Hotel Radstadt, Faubourg St. Germain, was to bury the remainder of the cake in the garden. But before leaving that same hotel something else was very nearly buried, not in the garden but in the cemetery of Père-Lachaise, and that something was myself. The way of it was this:

'As my two sisters were soon going to school at the Fossés, the convent where my mother had been educated, she, with her foreign ideas and her enthusiasm for convent discipline, thought it best to accustom them, and me as well, to school fare. And as the only form of supper at the Fossés for the *internes* all the year round was cold meat, salad, hard-boiled eggs, and Gruyère cheese, our hotel suppers, it was ordained, should henceforth consist of that extremely indigestible diet. Time went on, and then one night Nurse Glaisby, who slept in my room, heard me groan in my sleep and, coming to my bedside, found me in a high fever. Home remedies were applied, but to no avail; inflammation rapidly set in and very nearly extinguished poor little me.

'Even when almost *à l'article de la mort* I was quite conscious of what went on about me; of my bed being surrounded, my father sitting on one side of it and my mother, in great distress, sitting on the other. There were two doctors there as well, one a tall and stately Englishman, who bled me and put leeches on me. But after that my mind became a blank until one day my mother told me I was out of danger, and that if I was a good girl and took my medicine I would soon be well again. How can I tell how long my illness lasted? But this I do know: that no toys were given me to make the time pass. Greatly did I long for a doll, however rubbishy, to dress and undress, but no one dared to gratify my wish for fear of my father, who looked on toys with horror.

'After my recovery from this severe illness I remember my mother, very smartly dressed, taking us three girls, also very smartly dressed, to the Fossés Convent, where she was to stand godmother to Miss Brodrick, the Sister Mary Stanislaus of my day, on her becoming a novice. I was frightened when I saw three figures crawling with their bodies prone towards the altar clad in what appeared to me as winding-sheets, having previously been denuded of all their worldly finery.

'A comical scene took place about this time at the Hotel Radstadt where we occupied the best apartments *au premier*. We were about to leave for Versailles, where it had been settled we would spend the summer, and my parents had gone over on the day in question to see that all had been prepared in accordance with instructions. They had not long been gone when a Bishop of some renown drove up to the door in a carriage and four, and demanded rooms. I should mention that the Radstadt was famous for its loyalty to Church and State, and that this very same Monseigneur had always been lodged *au premier* on his previous visits. The good landlady, therefore, anxious to please the high dignitary of the Church, and remembering that she would only have us with her for a few more days, decided then and there that we should be dispossessed. Accordingly, everything appertaining to the family of Tasburgh was at once removed to the storey above, a proceeding which Ryecroft and Nurse Glaisby, not understanding a single word of French, had no power to resist. Poor landlady! Little did she know my father, who became livid with rage when he returned from Versailles to discover what had been going on during his short absence, and imperiously insisted on the restoration of his rights. The landlady begged for forgiveness, but forgiveness minus his apartments was no good to my father. The uproar on the staircase was such that at last Monsieur l'Évêque put his head out to inquire what the noise was all about, and gave up the rooms as soon as he had been informed, his opinion being that the landlady had not acted rightly towards either party.'

This episode brings the earlier part of Barbara's childhood to a natural conclusion. She is now established in Paris with her parents and her sisters, there to remain, on and off, for the ensuing nine and a half years, her stay at the end of that time only being terminated by the Revolution of 1830 by which Charles X was deposed and Louis Philippe enthroned.

Barbara's extended stay in France falls into several parts which will be dealt with *seriatim*. The first comprises a period of three years during which she lives with her parents at Versailles. The second part relates her experience as a pupil-boarder at the Fossés Convent until she is withdrawn for unstated reasons. The third part includes the continuation of her education at the hands of governesses under the parental roof. Next comes the Chantilly interlude, in reality a divagation from the main subject. Finally, there is a renewal of convent life until revolution breaks out.

So far she has not succeeded in depicting a particularly happy childhood, the impression that she conveys being of a family, the wife included, held in thrall by a stern male parent who holds original and distinctly repressive ideas on the upbringing of his children.

Barbara writes with a vivid recollection of this girlhood period of her life and has some interesting things to say. She has therefore been given, so to say, her head, and only pure irrelevances have been excerpted from her manuscript. In its later pages memories crowd so thickly on her mind that the material she handles becomes at times unwieldy, giving an editor some work to do. But she was at her most impressionable age during the years spent in Paris, a period moreover of much historic interest, and even at the cost of a certain copiousness of detail her full record of that 'Restoration' interlude appears worthy of preservation.

IV

EDUCATIONAL BEGINNINGS

'SHORTLY after the brabble over the apartments *au premier* we flitted to Versailles and lived there, at No. 12, Boulevard du Roi, for the next two years. My two sisters were transferred as boarders to the Fossés Convent, leaving my brother George as my only playfellow and very good companions did we become. Behind our house was a narrow courtyard and the stables, and beyond that a good-sized garden with a summer-house. Unfortunately no flowers grew, for the trees therein were old and tall with a heavy leafage overhead and spreading roots below. George and I spent many a happy hour climbing up in them and sitting in the forks. I was strictly forbidden to loiter in the yard on my transits from house to garden; nevertheless I managed to get several lessons in the art of grooming horses, my special ambition being to rub down my mother's white pony and make up its straw bed myself.

'On my seventh birthday, May 31st, 1822, I was sent for by my mother who announced with all due solemnity that I had now come to the use of reason, and I wondered what she meant seeing that there were many unreasonable people about much older than myself. However, the upshot was that some few days later I was dispatched with nurse to the abode of a decrepit, dirty, snuffy old Irish priest, over eighty years old, a Reverend Mr. Sheridan, who lived a long way off and who was to teach the religious duties which it was necessary for me to fulfil now that I had attained the age of seven. This old priest's *bonne*, who cooked and did for him, had a mania for canary-birds, cats, and small dogs, and the sickening animal smell of his close room so effectually brought back to mind that terrible caterpillar cage on the nursery window-sill at home that all the veneration and devotion I should have been feeling, but for my over-sensitive olfactory organ, was smothered at birth. This poor octogenarian had gone through all the horrors of the Revolution, and used to tell me how he saw, in the days of the Terror, the rabble biting at their bread, both it and their hands red with the blood of their victims.

'In those days society kept very primitive hours at Versailles. My mother, who had a large acquaintance, gave dinners and *soirées* and I was allowed to appear at the latter festivities, always keeping close to Mrs. Wiseman or Miss Mostyn or Miss Stannix, special friends of my mother and good friends to me as well. An old Monsieur de Lauzun, an offshoot of the historical family of that name, used to visit us often in the winter evenings, and my mother, who spoke French like a native, found him exceedingly good company. And so passed the winter of 1822 which I remember to have been bitterly cold. I did some not very serious lessons, French with my mother and English with my father, who himself was also learning German.

'In May the next year my mother gave a luncheon to her Paris friends on the occasion of *Les Grandes Eaux*, when all the fountains of Louis XIV in the palace grounds are set playing at once, and when everyone was busy at table my brother and I slipped quietly from the house to see the fun. We roamed about the park, mixing among the sauntering crowd, and had the time of our lives. Nurse Glaisby, who was helping with the lunch behind the scenes, concluded we had been taken in hand by some among the party, but when the waters ceased to play and there was yet no news of our whereabouts, tired as she was, she sallied forth in great distress of mind to look for us. Eventually she found us stretched out on the grass in front of dragoons blissfully regaling ourselves with comfits, having threaded our way most dexterously through the surging crowd so as not to miss *le Bouquet*, the final and most splendiferous of all the *jets d'eau* there had been. Never in after years did I so throughly enjoy seeing *Les Grandes Eaux* as on that happy afternoon. The French are famed for sobriquets. At that time there was living in Versailles an English family named Waters, each member of which was tall and stout. They were known locally as *Les Grandes Eaux*.

'I have omitted to say that I had a younger brother, Michael, who was born at Burghwallis in June, 1818, and who died the following January at the age of seven months. And now again, at Versailles, in October, 1823, a second little Michael was brought forth, a seven months' child as was the eldest of us, Mary. A Madame Henri came as nurse to baby.

'My life was quiet and dull during the cold winter of 1823. Thanks to the sociable instincts of English nurses in a foreign capital, I got to know the children of the Horace Smiths, their father being a co-author with his brother of that witty poetic parody, *Rejected Addresses*. He had also married his deceased wife's sister. His daughter by the first wife was very plain but very highly educated, and four or five years older than me. So utterly neglected had my own education been that I took no pleasure in reading, quite failing to understand why Miss Smith always had her button-nose buried in a book. The sole book in my possession was an old edition of the *Hundred Wonders of the World*, which she did not disdain to borrow. Mrs. Smith gave no end of childrens' parties to which I was always allowed to go; indeed most of the English children living round-about went to them, and it was only the prejudice against a man marrying his first wife's sister that prevented all the parents from being on visiting terms with the Horace Smiths.

'In May, 1824, we left No. 12, Boulevard du Roi for an even worse dampery in the Boulevard de la Reine. It was the last house at one end of the row and had a garden the gate of which opened on to meadows; but it was a dark, gloomy abode. My father was older than my mother by fifteen years and a man of fads and theories which he adhered to with great tenacity, and among other things he delighted in dark houses smothered in the gloom of tree-planted boulevards. My mother, born and reared in the sunny South, suffered in consequence from a sort of ague and reclined for a great part of the day on the sofa. Walking in the walled garden there one day, Harriet Fairfax, my sister-in-law to be, told me the story of the Sleeping Beauty, and such an impression did it make on my young mind that evermore I connected that aguish house with the fairy-tale. It had also this drawback: that we now lived so far from the Park that I lost sight of all my young friends.

'At the end of that year's summer holidays I went back with my sisters to the Fossés Convent, my age being nine and three months.'

So ends, for the time being, Barbara's home life, and for the ensuing six years her education, secular and religious, is in the care of nuns. This early portion of her chronicle is, of course, written from memory alone after a lapse of time longer than the biblical span of life. Actually she was seventy-seven when she wrote it down and yet her narrative is clear and consecutive, and not at all the rambling recollection so often typical of great age. The rest of her experience in Paris is equally a feat of memory and, though much that she has to say of eminences and personalities comes of later knowledge, it is instructive to notice how her worldliness increases with her youthful years and how, while yet a mere child, her social sense develops.

V

EARLY MEMORIES

A SHORT description of this once celebrated convent of
Les Dames Anglaises to which Barbara, following in the
footsteps of her mother and her sisters, and of many female
forbears, is now sent should on no account be omitted. In
her mother's time, some thirty years previous to Barbara's
admission as a pupil, it was recognized as the most fashionable religious house of education in Paris and the daughters
of the French aristocracy were largely educated there. In
1817 George Sand, less well known as Madame Dudevant,
went to this convent of the English Augustinians in her
thirteenth year. In her biography, *Histoire de ma Vie*, one
of the best books ever written of its sort, she relates the
story of her conversion one evening in the convent chapel
and graphically describes the straggling, irregular plan of
the building with its prison-like exterior.

It was founded about the middle of the seventeenth
century by the Right Reverend Dr. Smith, Bishop of
Chalcedon, and the Venerable Lady Mary Tredway, serving
thenceforth as a peaceable retreat for numerous religious
members of the foremost Catholic families of England. A
list of the religious dead whose bodies had been interred on
convent soil includes, not counting lay sisters, about a
hundred well-known names and forms a miniature Catholic
Directory in itself of the days of religious persecution.

Several distinguished lay Catholics were also buried in
the convent grounds at different times, as, for instance, Sir
Edward Chancellor Hales in 1695 and William Howard,

Earl of Stafford, who died there suddenly in 1734. The exiled princes of the House of Stuart, when residing at the Court of St. Germain, used to come to the convent very often. The Ratcliffe family had become much attached, also, to the institution, the third Earl of Derwentwater having decreed before his execution in 1716 that his heart should be deposited in the convent church, and the community has religiously observed the anniversary of his death ever since.

'There were two separate and distinct classes at the Convent, *la grande Classe* adjoining the refectory for those pupils who had made their First Communion, and *la Classe des Petites* for those who had not yet had that happiness. Only sixty pupils could be accommodated, so that parents wishing to send their daughters to the English nuns had to inscribe their names almost at birth. In my mother's time the Superioress was Mrs. Canning, who died four years before it was my turn to go, a person of great beauty, refinement of mind, and charm of manner, besides being endowed with a superior intellect. Napoleon gave her his promise to protect the convent provided she allowed him to walk sometimes in its gardens, a promise which, in those uncertain days, she was only too willing to accept and always received him with courtly etiquette on the rare occasions of a visit. It was to the regret of the *pensionaires* that the Emperor did not come more often, for they were given a holiday whenever it happened. But the Superioress was quite content, for the mere fact that he had the *entrée* to the garden constituted in itself protection.

'My sister Fanny, three and a half years my senior and well grown for her age, was also in *la Classe des Petites* and, of a very sweet disposition, naturally protected me.

'The nuns were forced to employ secular teachers as their

rule forbade them to be away from their refectory at meals or to be absent when the Office was being recited, and they seem to have had the peculiar knack of engaging the most objectionable, low-caste women, whether French, Belgian or German. When I went there a Mdlle. Gilbert was installed as secular mistress of the little class; a woman of vile disposition. She did not dare try her tricks on me, although I was the youngest in the school; Fanny would have seen to that! But *elle se faisait un plaisir de taquiner* a poor little sickly girl, Armande de Gallifet, who had very sore eyes and often a *vésicattoire* on her arm. This cruel woman used to give poor Armande, who was only nine years old, the most difficult handwriting to copy, well knowing her inability to do so. The fiend would then delight to decorate the child with *les oreilles d'ânes et les écriteaux* and suchlike asininities, as described by the young Princesse Elène Massalski, who afterwards become Princesse de Ligne, in her memoirs. But the Superioress of the *Abbaye aux Bois* had the good sense to stop all such proceedings. It has always been a puzzle to me how our nuns allowed this disgraceful bullying to go on, especially as it was common knowledge that Armande's father, and her elder sister Valentine, behaved brutally to her at home because she was possessed of a large *dot* and was not dependent on her family. With all her wickedness, Mdlle. Gilbert possessed *l'art de raconter* in a most forcible manner, but the nuns stopped her from doing so for some unknown reason.

'Among those in the *première classe* with my sister Mary was Valentine de Serrant, who married Prince de la Tremöille, and who was famous as a linguist, knowing seven languages when she was sixteen years old. There were also four Mdlles. Perron, two in the high class and two in the low, whose father is mentioned in Bourienne's memoirs as money-lender to Napoleon. His daughters had all the manners and appearance of *des parvenues*, in spite of which they married among *la haute noblesse* whose purses required replenishing. There were likewise at the Convent the four daughters of Thérèse de la Rochequelin, the heroine of La Vendée. The youngest was quite the most interesting child in our class, a girl of genius, with a perfect disposition, high spirited, very independent, and thoroughly generous. She had one of those remarkable memories, needing only to read once over a long piece of prose or poetry to repeat it word for word.

'The convent building, which was in a crumbling condition, was as cold as ice in winter and the most dangerous abode for delicate girls at that season of the year. I have often thought that my poor sister Fanny, who died at the early age of thirty-one, had her constitution ruined by the bitter cold and the low diet of those winter months. Fanny made her First Communion in the autumn of 1824, together with Julia Canning, Catherine Fitzwilliam, Alix de Mortemart, and Bresilia Sumpter, a Brazilian girl, the fairest of the fair, with flaxen hair and a milk-white skin, all of whom were accordingly promoted to the first class, so that my favourite sister and I were henceforth completely separated.

'Not long after we three sisters spent a day with the Rokewood Gages to see a royal procession on the occasion of the coronation of Charles X. It was a pouring wet day and we were driving in an open carriage. We were all thinly clad and Sister Marianne, who had charge of our wardrobes, had, if you please, sent me out in my thin yellow dancing shoes. The nuns had an iron routine about dress. Whatever might be the weather, our summer dresses stayed on our backs from Easter Sunday till the Feast of All Saints on November 1st. It would certainly appear that in respect of common sense and worldly wisdom nuns are not well gifted.

'In the winter Louisa Riddell of Felton, Northumberland, died. She was in the first class and the particular chum of my sister Mary, who felt her death keenly. Early on the morning of the funeral the coffin was exposed in the cloisters, the church was darkened and hung with black for the Office of the Dead, and all the English, Scotch and Irish priests in Paris attended the solemn requiem. In the middle of the Service Mary had a swooning fit and was carried out of church. Sister Mary Austin – Poulette, we called her – who had been Mama's *petite Mère* and was ours likewise, wrote to my father, who came at once and took Mary away from the Convent, never to return.

'At the end of 1824 Fanny and I left the Convent, she for good and I until September, 1827, when I returned for a short time, of which more anon, to be prepared for my First Communion. The dampery in the Boulevard de la Reine had been given up and my poor mother, after three years of gloom and suffering, was now located at No. 9, Place d'Armes where a bright sun shed its lustre on her bedroom and drawing-room. We found her quite another being. Being a large family, we occupied the *rez de chaussée*, with Nurse Glaisby and the manservant, in addition to ourselves, on one side of the courtyard, and Madame Henri, in charge of baby Michael, the cook, housemaid, coachman and English groom opposite. A governess was sent for from England.

'Where my father procured us our governesses I know not, but whoever selected them was most unfortunate in their choice. After great difficulty and delay, an elderly lady arrived, an Irishwoman with a first-class brogue of the name of Sheridan. Miss Sheridan was both good and kind-hearted, but there was something very peculiar about her and about her teaching method. On the first day of lessons she set my sisters to spell and learn the meaning of the words in Dr. Johnson's *Dictionary* slap-dash through, beginning on page 1; useful, perhaps, but hardly a judicious proceeding. I was not yet ten myself. But Miss Sheridan helped me with all kindness and never bullied me, and encouraged me to play with my baby brother by saying, "Family affection is the foundation of all religious education." And it was the truth she spoke! Our music master, Monsieur Bodin, came from Paris once a week to give us each a lesson, and Miss Sheridan always helped me to make myself ready for his visit. At breakfast she and my father warmly discussed the relative merits of their sister countries and the wrongs of the poor Irish Catholics, Miss Sheridan contending that the Irish spoke better English than the English did themselves.

'In April we went to Dieppe for a six months' change of air, travelling in the large yellow family coach which now carried, additional to its load when we left Burghwallis, Madame Henri, my baby brother, and Miss Sheridan, not to count Carafe, my mother's pet dog, which was sick from time to time with the motion of the stuffy carriage, so further increasing my dislike of pet animals. The sea air was not advantageous to poor Miss Sheridan's health, and another governess had to be sent for in her place. The day the poor woman left to take ship to Dover she filled a green baize bag with shingle, and my mother, uneasy on her account, recommended her to the captain's care. Some months later the news came that she had been admitted to an asylum, there supposedly to end her days. It was very sad!

'The next governess sent over was an Englishwoman, much younger than her predecessor; she might have been

D

about thirty. It was her first situation. She was not bad looking, but disfigured by smallpox. It was rumoured that she had been engaged to be married, but that the smallpox had intervened, with a consequent souring effect on her disposition, which was the opposite of Miss Sheridan's. This new governess, Miss Begg was her name, disliked children and was unkind to them. I never really got to know anything she did like, except dress and gossipy talk of men and husbands to my sisters. She was not unbalanced, like Miss Sheridan, but if gross ignorance and a total incapability for teaching be a pledge of sanity then Miss Begg certainly possessed it in a high degree. She could not construe a line of her own language, much less any other. Child as I was, I used to wonder how she so managed my sisters' Italian lessons that they taught her in lieu of she teaching them. Miss Begg was totally incompetent for the situation of governess, even in a lower social rank, and would have been best suited teaching ABC in some village school. Under her I learnt the Catechism like a parrot, for she was unable to explain its meaning to me. My father must have guessed the truth, for he was most particular about religion, and got the *curé* of the *Paroisse de Dieppe* to come twice a week to give us instruction in the Faith. And yet, to do Miss Begg full justice, she did get me on with my music and plain sewing.

'A long time after I remonstrated with my father for having kept such an incompetent person as governess, and he retorted that it was necessary at the age my sisters were, and surrounded by unprincipled foreigners, for a conscientious Englishwoman to be in charge of them. I understood and accepted his reason, but how low Catholic education must have been at that time to produce nothing better than Miss Begg.

'In July Grandpapa Crathorne arrived at Dieppe, bringing

with him my brother George from Ushaw for the holidays. George was much altered and no longer the *bon camarade* of earlier days, but in any case my jailer was far too heartless and wrapped up in self to encourage family affection in her pupils. Both my father and grandfather had their English horses at Dieppe and rode a great deal. George had only three weeks of holiday and when his time had expired my father took him back to school, leaving Grandpapa behind at Dieppe. Only a few days later Grandpapa was seized with a fit of apoplexy. He recovered consciousness and received all the rites of the Church, but he expired on the afternoon of August 19th, 1825, at the age of sixty-four. In the absence of my father Count Henri d'Orfeuille made the necessary funeral arrangements and the coffin was kept in the cathedral pending my father's return, when it left for England under the care of my grandfather's manservant, Mark. On September 9th, three weeks exactly after he had died, my grandfather's body was laid in the family vault at Crathorne. Knowing that the Crathorne property must come to her eventually, he had begged my mother, before his fatal illness, to provide handsomely out of it for her younger children, leaving the estate itself to little Michael if she liked. He never succeeded to it himself, as his second brother Frank was in possession until his death in 1833.

'My Great-uncle Frank, who came next to Henry, *l'enfant gâté des dames*, was evidently of no bright intellect, having received some injury in his youth which had probably affected the brain. When jilted by a lady to whom he was engaged, and much attached, he shut himself up at Crathorne and forbade his house to women. A priest was always with him and the household work was conducted solely by men, as in a monastery. For the last thirty years of his life it is a well-known fact that he never spoke to a woman, even refusing to see his own niece, my mother. Presumably he was quite daft and though he lived at Crathorne it was my grandfather who administered the estate, and after him my father. Frank died at the age of seventy-four, having lived a healthy, frugal life and, except for a deep-rooted belief that woman was the Devil incarnate, is said to have been the sweetest-tempered and most amiable of men.

'Our stay at Dieppe was drawing to a close when my father came one morning into the school-room, asking if we had in our possession any religious books belonging to the *curé* who instructed us, as a person had just arrived to announce his death. The poor old man, it seemed, had gone for an evening bathe and had not returned. He had probably been overtaken by a cramp and sank, and his body had been washed ashore.

'We left Dieppe in September, this time for Paris where we took possession of a spacious but luckless apartment, *au premier*, in the Rue Royale. The old Duchesse de Laval Montmorency occupied the *rez de chaussée*, and *quel beau monde du vieil régime* used to visit her, whose carriages and liveried servants standing in the courtyard gave us a lively scene to look out on. The Church of la Madeleine was at that time in process of being built, and from early morning to eventide the sound of chisel and hammer reached our ears. The small Church of the Assumption in the Rue St. Honoré was our own place of worship. When the cold weather came again how I used to envy the old women sitting over their *chaufferettes*, offering roasted chestnuts and hot coffee for sale, as we tramped to church in the early morning.

'My father had bought a French pony of about fourteen hands so that one or other of my sisters could go riding with him. On November 1st it was Fanny's turn, and no sooner was she seated on this brute than, *pour cause de rien*, it reared straight up as in a circus, throwing my poor sister with such violence that she rebounded from one side to the other of the narrow entrance way. One of my father's senseless fads was the propriety of ladies riding in small soft, fur caps, that were no protection to the head in case of accident. My mother and I were looking from a bedroom window when this most unfortunate incident occurred, and she rushed below to meet Fanny being carried upstairs, where they laid her on a bed unconscious and for a long time so. The English surgeon and physician who had saved my life at the Hotel Radstadt in 1821 were sent for, and the first time I ever saw a man in tears was when the doctors told my father they feared the case would have a fatal end. But they either underrated Fanny's constitution or their own powers of healing, for although it was a long illness, and perhaps never quite overcome, my dear sister did recover. Before 1826 came in she was pronounced well enough to be removed to our previous apartments in the Place d'Armes, Versailles. Only, however, to have a relapse and her head again shaved and blistered. But, as before, youth was on her side and gradually she got well enough for the school-room to take lessons in music and dancing, spending the rest of the time much as she pleased. Fanny was passionately fond of reading and, together with Mary, had learnt Italian very well from an Italian master at the Fossés. Now her knowledge came in well, for she got a copy of *I promessi Sposi* and translated it for Miss Begg's benefit, so ludicrously reversed were the roles of governess and pupils in our ill-appointed school-room.

'How hateful at that time was my daily exercise. I was only ten years and eight months old and should have been running on ahead with a hoop, like other children of my age. But no! instead I was pinned to my jailer's side and forced to listen to her inane chatter about dress and people. Thank God! chilblains, French chilblains, came at last to my rescue and for many weeks I was spared those odious outings. The school-room sofa was mine exclusively, they were such bad chilblains, and a French doctor came frequently to dress them.

'During the Lent of 1826 a Mission was given in the Church of St. Louis, though to what Religious Order the missionaries belonged I was too young to inquire. But whatever it was their zeal was stretched too far to bear good fruit. A morning and an afternoon Conference were held each day while the Mission lasted, with two pulpits opposite each other one of which was occupied by the Propounder of the Faith and the other by the Devil's Advocate. During the Conferences the church was darkened so that Faith and Heresy might wrangle in an atmosphere of gloom. *Les Dames du monde* usually went to the afternoon Conference and it happened on one occasion that Faith lost the thread of his argumentative discourse and attempted to recover balance by personally abusing his opponent, on which the fashionable congregation, their spirits cowed by the dim light, took fright and rose as one to leave the church. This produced vociferations from both pulpits of *Femmes, asseyez-vous*, and resultant screams from the panic-stricken congregation, so that the Conference was abandoned for that afternoon.

'In May, 1826, the King and his Court came to Versailles to show himself to his liege subjects there and, in common with the rest of the family, I too was presented. The presentations took place in the *salle de bal* of the Palace and my heart beat fast for fear I should make a wrong reply if

I were good-naturedly spoken to. In after days, as will be
seen in its place, that early presentation served me a good
turn.

'As Sir Astley Cooper had recommended seaside air, my
father took Fanny to Boulogne for a month, sending not
only for his own horse but also for the very brute that had
been the cause of all the mischief. He said it would
strengthen her nerves to ride again. What a mistake!
Although she had not ridden since her accident a year and
eight months ago, she obeyed in fear and trembling, and
mounted the vicious brute once more. It was a quiet ride
through the town, but once on the grass the ill-conditioned
animal set off at a wild gallop among the whirling windmills
at full sail, poor Fanny being far too weak to hold it. When
it was at last stopped she all but fainted. The animal was
then sold and, when the month was up, Fanny went back
to Versailles in much better health.

'In those days there was a considerable English colony in
Versailles and we children had plenty of dances and picnics,
and private theatricals. But my two sisters always preferred
to anything else a visit to Mrs. Wiseman and her daughter,
who afterwards became Comtesse Gabrielli. Miss Wiseman
particularly, though much older than they, was a companion
to them. I remember their son and brother, the future
cardinal, coming to Versailles, a thin, delicate-looking
youth, who even then, when he must have come straight
from Ushaw, was made much of by the Catholics as a
young man of extraordinary ability and promise. Ushaw,
though a rough school, was always celebrated, before and
after the vice-presidency of Lingard, for turning out the
best-informed Catholics. There was no espionage, no en-
couragement for boys to tell tales of one another, and so the
spirit of the school was good. I never saw Wiseman from

the day he dined with my parents at Versailles in 1826 until he was a cardinal and dined with us, my husband and myself, in Eaton Place twenty-five years later, on which occasion I got Gunter to make a cake in the shape of a cardinal's hat that amused him highly. At that time he was hugely stout and coarse-looking, bearing a strong resemblance to his good and kind mother.'

VI

CHANTILLY AND THE LA FEUCHÈRES

In the autumn of the year 1827 Mrs. Tasburgh yields to the persuasion of its royal owner and, for the first time since the family's arrival in France six years since, accompanies her husband to Chantilly for the festival of St. Hubert, patron saint of the chase and dogs, which is observed each year on November 3rd. Mr. Tasburgh has been accustomed to pay a yearly visit, unaccompanied by his wife, as the feast came round, to the magnificent mediaeval home of the Princes de Condé, situated some twenty miles to the north of Paris. The reason for his intimacy with the owner of the château, Louis Henry Joseph, Duke of Bourbon, then just past his seventieth year, is told at some length by Barbara in the memoirs, although she approaches the subject in somewhat of a side-stepping fashion, and there is no need to anticipate what she has to say. A preliminary note or two on the interesting story may, however, not be thought amiss.

This Duke of Bourbon was the father of the ill-fated Duc d'Enghien who was executed by Napoleon in 1804, and with whom the house of Condé ended. The Duke, with very many other members of the French nobility, 'emigrated' after the fall of the Bastille, and it was while in exile that he met, and was promptly captivated by, the notorious Sophie Dawes, later Baroness de Feuchères, who at that time was a domestic servant in London.

Sophie, the daughter of a drunken fisherman named Dawes belonging to St. Helens in the Isle of Wight, was

born in 1795 and was thus forty years younger than her
royal ducal paramour. He had his youthful mistress educated
and, after the Restoration, took her back with him to France.
To avoid scandal, he had her married, representing himself
as her father, to de Feuchères, then a major in the Royal
Guards, providing a substantial dowry, making her husband
his aide-de-camp, and bestowing on him the title of baron.
The rest of Sophie's career does not concern these memoirs;
suffice it to say that her husband had obtained a legal
separation from her not long before Mrs. Tasburgh's visit to
Chantilly, having discovered the nature of the Duke's relations with his wife, that she was allowed great freedom of
behaviour at the château by her besotted lover, and that her
presence there in such an equivocal position had heretofore
constrained Barbara's mother from accepting the ducal
hospitality.

And now for Barbara's somewhat confused and, in
places, diverting account of her parents' connection with
Chantilly.

'When in 1896 the *Jerningham Letters* were published I
was calmly told by one of the cousinhood that the Bodney
estate belonged to Lord Petre. "I beg your pardon," I said
to my informant, Lady B., "Bodney has always belonged to
the Tasburghs, but it became Crathorne property owing to
the marriage of my grandfather George Crathorne with the
widow of George Tasburgh, and it was my grandfather,
then residing at Nice, who lent Bodney Hall to some French
Benedictine nuns who fled from France at the time of the
Revolution." My words only called forth a reiterated state-
ment from Lady B., and after she had gone I was left in
dreamland, unable rightly to adjust my recollection. Who
was right, and who was wrong? And how to probe the truth
of this century-old affair?

'In my perturbation I sat down and indited a letter to Princethorpe where the Bodney nuns now had their convent, for, long ago as it was, who should know better than they the facts about their flight from France and the hospitality they received in England? I received very soon the following reply:

'✠ Pax.
'Benedictines of Our Lady of the Angels,
'Princethorpe
'12, December, 1896.

'DEAR MADAM, – Our Reverend Mother has given me the pleasing task of answering your letter, and I hope I shall be able to afford you some gratification by my replies to some of your questions.

'Our Community was founded at Montargis, near Orleans, and was obliged to leave France in 1792. Madame de Mirepoix was then the Mother Prioress. She had amongst her Children a few English subjects, one of whom was Mère de Sainte Felicité Swinburne, whose nephew Mr. Tasburgh generously lent Bodney Hall to the poor exiles. They remained there until 1811, when they removed to Heath Hall.

'The Princesse de Condé, sister of the Duc de Bourbon, did reside with our Community as a lady boarder from 1805 to 1814, that is for about six years at Bodney and about three years at Heath Hall.

'Abbé Louis le Roux was Chaplain to the Community from 1802 till about 1811; he did not to go to Heath Hall.

'I am sorry I cannot give you any information concerning the Poor Clares; no one here has heard of any of that Order having been at Bodney.

'We shall be delighted at any time, by further information, to give pleasure to the grandchild of our benefactor. Our mother always retained the most grateful

recollection of her first English home. I am sorry Bodney
Hall has been pulled down, as that prevents any possibility of our getting a photograph of it.

'Yours sincerely in J.C.

'Sr. M. Mechtilde, O.S.B.

'This letter was just what I wanted to put myself in the
right, and it was nice, moreover, to know that the nuns were
grateful for the nine years of shelter, free, gratis and for
nothing, given to them by my grandfather.

'As for the *Clarisses*, or Poor Clares, I asked about they
stayed on at Bodney for years after the Benedictines had left.
But my father was then administering the estate. He was
not very receptive on the subject of nuns and priests, and I
expect the Poor Clares, their poverty notwithstanding, had
to pay rent. In 1851 I went with a French lady to visit the
said *Clarisses* in the Avenue de Saxe, Paris. I told them who
I was and put many questions to the fossillized nun behind
the curtain. She told me they had still four in their community who had been at Bodney, but, do all I could, I was
not allowed to speak to them.

'And now to relate her royal brother's gratitude for the
hospitality shown to his sister, Sœur Marie Joseph de la
Miséricorde otherwise La Princesse Louise de Bourbon,
who, the family estates being confiscated, comes to England
well-nigh penniless and is given asylum at Bodney, with
nothing to pay, for six years. A few of her letters from there,
with Bodney wrongly spelt Rodney, are quoted in Crétineau-
Joly's *Histoire des trois derniers Princes de la Maison de
Condé*, from which it may be gathered that some of the rules
or offices differed a good deal from those in force at the
Varsovie convent where she had been before. The royal
lady, a person of undoubted piety and almost delirious

religious enthusiasm, the sister of the last Duc de Bourbon, sallies forth in 1795, at the age of thirty-eight, in search of a religious order to suit her ardent zeal. In vain she tries Carmelites, Trappistes, Capuchins – it is all to no purpose. In my own humble opinion the craving for religious power, more than a spirit of real piety, runs through her correspondence with her father, the Prince de Condé, as with her much-loved brother, the Duc de Bourbon, and very probably this same love of religious power was a natural consequence of her appointment by Louis XVI, in 1786, as Abbesse de Remiremont in the Vosges district, where only princesses of the Empire were qualified for such a post, and which was suppressed in the Revolution. Finally, she pronounces her final vows, in 1802, as a Benedictine nun in a convent of Perpetual Adoration at Niewictz near Warsaw, with the future king, Louis XVIII, and his daughter-in-law, the Duchesse d'Angoulème, as her sponsors, so taking the name of Sœur Marie Joseph de la Miséricorde. At the murder of her nephew, the Duc d'Enghien, she leaves Niewictz and comes to England to join her brother in exile and to comfort him on the cruel death of his only son, living at Bodney for the first six years and for the next three at Heath Hall, Co. Yorks, not far from Burghwallis. When about five years old, I remember being taken to Heath Hall to see the *clothing* of Mary and Eliza Needham, cousins of my father. Sister Marie Joseph proceeds from Heath Hall to Chelsea in 1814, where she stays two years. After the return of the Bourbons to the throne of France she is recalled to Paris in 1816 and is settled once for all by the King at the Temple with full power over the religious under her. And only then does her restless heart find itself at ease, for at last she has obtained a position of authority so dear to a Condé. She dies in 1824 at sixty-eight years of age.

'How much better it would have been had she remained near the brother she loved so well, and had been his safeguard against the infamous Feuchères and his assassins. Hanging sleeves à la Feuchères would then not have come into fashion about 1830.

'As soon as the Duc de Bourbon heard of my parents being in France the grateful old man sent them a general invitation to Chantilly for the hunting season, and especially for *St. Hubert* which in those days was kept in great style at the Château. His invitation mentioned that my mother should always have the seat of honour by his side in *la voiture des Princes*, a delicate hint that Madame de Feuchères would not obtrude her presence, and he added that his stables were wholly at my father's command.

'In 1827, however, a very touching appeal was sent to her from the Duke, and she yielded to persuasion. We were all, I remember, in my mother's room looking on at the packing of her smart frocks for that year's St. Hubert when my father entered to announce the death of the Duke of York, and now, because it was a visit to royalty, the rule about Court mourning had to be complied with. Great was the consternation! The time was short! How the necessary black was produced I know not. But it was produced and Father and Mother disported themselves at Chantilly for the week of St. Hubert. The old Duke received my mother with the effusion of feeling belonging to a brother who still mourned a beloved sister to whom, by the father of his guest, a great kindness had been done.

'To Chantilly French princes flocked, but few princesses on account of Sophie Dawes. A few women of high birth and a higher sense of decorum had never abandoned the Duke in his dark days, and to the care of these my mother was consigned. Madame de Feuchères, coarse, vulgar and bad, made her presence conspicuous and her influence felt in every way she could, but she had received a royal command to keep her distance from my mother, and such an order she could not but obey. Madame de Feuchères had always a reinforcement of profligate Dawes at Chantilly. She organized the private theatricals and was disgustingly coarse in her acting. Of course she gave the *ton* to the *société théâtrale*, which was a chosen corps made up largely from her own kith and kin. The princely guests in no way objected to my mother having the seat of honour in the royal carriage, for was she not the daughter of the Duke's benefactor; but they did not see my father in the same light and were apt to resent the cockering up he got.

'Before the end of the week one of the princely guests, of high degree and a very deaf old man, had taken a fancy to my mother's cameo-cut face. Sitting one night next to her at dinner, and imagining that he whispered in a soft, lover-like undertone, he yelled out *"Madame, lequel est le numero de votre chambre?"*; to which my mother, who was as sharp as a needle, answered in an equally high voice: *"Demandez à mon mari, Prince."*

VII

LES FOSSÉS AND LE SACRÉ CŒUR

BARBARA, now twelve years old, has yet three more years to complete in France before she sees her Yorkshire home again, during the last two of which she again becomes a boarder-pupil in the care of nuns. For her parents, taking her two sisters with them, return to England in the spring of 1828, and all home life ceases for her. Her narrative of this educational period, thus isolated from her family, is clear and connected, and throws a highly revealing light on the convent system of those days as applied to the upbringing of young girls.

A word or two about the two high-born ladies who patronize the convent pupils may not be thought amiss. The Duchess of Angoulême was the King's daughter-in-law, wife to Louis-Antoine, last Duke of the name, who invaded Spain in 1823 at the head of a powerful army and restored Ferdinand VII to his throne. The Duchess of Berry was also the daughter-in-law of Charles X, a widow since 1820. She it was, after the King had been deposed in 1830, who made an abortive attempt with an armed following to secure the throne of France for her son, and who subsequently deprived herself of the sympathy of her supporters by marrying in secret an obscure Italian count.

The Count of Chambord, also mentioned by Barbara, was the son of the Duchess of Berry, born seven months after his father's death by violence and on that account christened, among his other names, Dieudonné, and hailed by the populace as the *'enfant du miracle.'* The death of his grand-father, Charles X, in 1836, and of his uncle, the Duke of Angoulême, in 1844, left him the last male representative of the elder branch of the Bourbon family.

'In the winter of 1827 my sisters Mary and Fanny, at the respective ages of seventeen and sixteen, made their débuts in Paris and went to many balls, including those given by Lady Granville, our Ambassadress, and those given by the Duke of Orleans. They also went to the opera now and then. Late hours were not the rule in those days, so that the dissipations of the evenings did not interfere with lessons the next day. During that winter, also, my French chilblains reappeared and I was again laid up with them.

'How little did I guess on the evening of our last romp together that my dear little brother Michael and I were so soon to part. My father was at Chantilly when he sickened, and again the English doctor came, but only to declare after a few days that it was water on the brain and that my father ought to be sent for in all haste. On the twenty-first day of the illness our little angel left us, aged three and a half. On the morning of his death there was not a dry eye in the entire house excepting one, my jailer's, and yet she had known him and lived with him for nigh on two years of his short life, though without showing him much of either attention or affection. Of we three sisters, I naturally felt the wrench of parting most.

'We remained in Paris till the beginning of June and then went back to Versailles to a detached house in the Quartier St. Cloud, with a pretty garden and a little lodge, the memory of baby Michael preventing us from returning to our old quarters in the Place d'Armes. But I must say I was astonished that we left Paris without visiting his grave at Père-Lachaise.

E

'Latterly in Paris my sister Mary was very much run down; her blood had become impoverished and she came out in spots, all of which was brought on, according to the doctor, by city life, too much society, and lack of country air. The celebrated French doctor, Dupuytren, was sent for and, I suppose, ordered a change of scene and habit, for after his visit we were taken out a great deal more in the carriage and enjoyed whole day excursions in the country. My jailer, be it mentioned, was as strong as a horse and always did the Black Lent with the utmost scrupulosity.

'She had very few scruples, however, on my account, for it was just about this time that the family's Father Confessor felt obliged to speak his mind out about the total lack of religious instruction I had received from her. She had known of his opinion for some time, but had taken no notice of it. The result was that in September I was sent back to the convent to be prepared for my First Communion, being now twelve years old. Mrs. Stoner was the Superioress at the Fossés, a woman of weak mind and eaten up with selfish, soul-saving scruples. It was doctor's orders that I should only do *maigre* once a week, but Mrs. Stoner, in her folly, refused to comply with this direction, saying that her own soul would be imperilled if any child under her charge failed to observe an abstinence enjoined by the Church. In consequence of this deadlock, I was sent instead to the Convent of the Sacré Cœur, Rue de Varennes, Paris, at that time quite a newcomer among religious houses.

'The Sacré Cœur that I went to was certainly a refinement on other convents of that day, although the English girls at it suffered somewhat from neglect and were, perhaps, regarded as incumbrances. It was housed in the princely domain of the Hôtel Biron whose long suites of rooms, gilded salons, the avenues of trees, and the grounds in

Maria Augusta Rosalia Tasburgh (née Crathorne). A self-portrait in the costume of Marie Antoinette.

general, impressed me vastly. The *règlement* was perfect; no regiment of the line could have had a better discipline or been more smartly drilled. Madame Barat was the head, or general, of this establishment, and her brother, a Jesuit of course, was its Chaplain. *La première maitresse*, answering to the colonel or the second-in-command, was Madame de Gramont, a hunchback dwarf. Her face was typical of that deformity, but hers was a sad expression rather than a disagreeable one, and her beautiful, deeply sunk, keen, dark eyes seemed to pierce through and through whoever she was looking at. The rules were very strict, their principal object being to dry up all the natural springs of affection in the human heart and imbue the nuns with an icy, stand-off manner towards their pupils. This was a great disadvantage for those same pupils, whose *guindées* style in later life, with all natural affection crushed out of them, were obnoxious to society and the world at large.

'It cannot be denied that the religious instruction at the Sacré Cœur in my time was simply perfect. I went there at twelve years old with my mind a complete blank as to the meaning of the Church Offices. The Mass was a myth to me. But Madame Cécile – bless her memory – who took me in hand, spared no pains to work me up for my First Communion, which I made on April 27th, 1828, together with Mademoiselles de Polignac, de Choiseul and de Châtelet.

'I met again at the S.C. some of my former companions of the Fossés, one or two of whom had been involved in *la Revolte de St. Cyr* – the usual case of officers and billets-doux – and had been transferred from one convent to the other. I well remember our dwarf colonel, Madame de Gramont, marching two of them into our class, one of whom was Blanche de Montaigu, a fine-grown, bold-looking girl with the fairest crop of hair parted at the side like a boy. In after days, when Marie Fox of Holland House was supposed to be a Montaigu, I thought that if so, then the real fair type of that family must have undergone a marvellous change. I met again, also, at the S.C., though they did not come as culprits, the two Perron girls, the sisters Gallifet, and my special friend, Thérèse de la Rochaquelin, as noble-hearted as of yore. We were all in the same class in that beautiful *salon doré* opening on to the lovely terrace.

'The Bourbons had always encouraged the Jesuits in their ambition to get the education of the young into their hands, and this policy was reflected at the S.C. in the way it went to work to increase the number of its pupils. Madame de Gramont, who was of good family, acted as a decoy duck to entice the girls of the Faubourg St. Germain, but they did not come in fast enough. More were wanted and more were soon found, but charity forbids me from revealing what sort of girls these actually were; suffice it to say that the convent became a school and a kind of reformatory in one. However great a mistake this was, it is fair to say that *la bande des méchantes* was very carefully supervised, while we were very closely guarded.

'The Duchesse de Berry, who was Thérèse de la Rochaquelin's godmother, used to send her a *parure* – of no great value – every *jour de l'an*. On such occasions Thérèse had to go to the Tuileries to return thanks, and wish her royal *marraine* a happy New Year, dressed up to look such a guy with a necklace on top of a high dress so as not to show a hairbreadth of her neck. Mademoiselle, her daughter, afterwards Duchess of Parma, came very often to the convent to play with us, accompanied by her *Dame d'honneur*. Madame de Gramont, our second-in-command, disliked the Duchess and would not refrain from going out of her way to annoy her. On one particular day Madame la Duchesse came to the

convent to see her godchild, and Thérèse, for some most
trivial fault, was declared to be *en penitence* and therefore
unavailable. The Duchess easily understood this action to
be intended as an insult, and never again visited the Sacré
Cœur.

'Whatever little games it pleased the amiable Duchess to
play, she was freely acknowledged as the most charming
member of the Bourbon family. She was always recognizable
from her lovely shaped foot. One day she boarded an
omnibus, her face hidden behind a thick, black veil. "*Ah!
le pied de Madame*," said the conductor as she put her foot
on the step and affected not to have heard the man's remark,
being on her way to a *rendez-vous*. At the christening of the
little Comte de Chambord, born seven months after the
assassination of his father, the pietists of the Faubourg St.
Germain were greatly scandalized because the populace
made fun of the name Dieudonné, which had been bestowed
on the royal infant in thankoffering for his timely birth,
though a dubious compliment to the deceased Duke. Braving
Jesuit disapproval – who held the Bourbons in the hollow of
their hand – one placard that was published read like this:
"*Baptême du Comte de Chambord – Le Roi le nomme Dieudonné mais le peuple en rit* (Henri)."

'One day the Duchesse d'Angoulème came to Benediction
at the Sacré Cœur, and afterwards into the garden where we
were all assembled, dressed in white frocks with white veils.
Her Royal Highness's delight was to make us run, all
bunched up together, down the middle walk *comme une
volée de colombes blanches*, as she said.

'H.R.H. was nearly as raddled as I and my brother
George once were when we tried to paint the garden gate,
and it struck many of us as odd, having been instructed
by Madame Cecile that rouging was disfiguring to the

image of God and a mortal sin, to see a royal lady so disfigured who had been held up to our admiration as of saintly
disposition.

'In the winter of 1828 we all left Versailles and took
another house in Paris, Rue de la Pepinière, from which my
sisters could plunge anew into the gay world. A Spanish
nobleman, the Duke d'Avicejès, who had been a friend of
Grandpapa Crathorne when both were *détenus* at Verdun,
was made welcome at our house *comme l'ami de la maison*.
He fell violently in love with my sister Fanny, then just
turned seventeen. His personal appearance was far from
objectionable, but he was far too old and far too poor, and
so was dismissed with all courtesy. In no ways disheartened
by dismissal, this noble of Spain bribed the French maid –
a thoroughly bad woman – to induce my sister to go off with
him, and arranged for a carriage to be ready in the small
hours at the corner of the street. Fanny, of course, firmly
rejected the proposal and the perfidious Abigail had to
convey her message of refusal. Our jailer-governess knew
nothing of this episode until some time later, but she took
to herself, and was accorded by my father, all the credit of
having frustrated the ducal design, being rewarded for her
circumspection with a doubled salary, a crimson silk dress,
and a pair of gold earrings. To do her justice, she consulted
her confessor before accepting these undeserved rewards,
but the priest quieted her conscience and advised her to take
the proffered gifts.

'In April, 1828, my family returned to Burghwallis,
leaving me alone in France at the convent, and I spent my
holidays at Versailles with the Brown Mostyns, who were
most kind to me.

'The year 1829 at the S.C. was almost a duplicate of my
previous year there; the same beautiful Church ceremonies

on Feast Days, the same exquisitely organized Processions in the grounds that feasted the eye if they did not touch the heart. My mother and sisters often wrote and kept me up-to-date with the goings-on at home. From them I heard that Jonathan Martin, a lunatic, had set York Minster on fire and had caused great damage, and how the Catholic Bishop Apostolic had preached a most beautiful, thrilling sermon on the occasion, exhorting his flock to come forward generously with money towards the repair and reminding them that the sacred edifice had been originally consecrated by Catholics, and might conceivably, on some future date, return to the True Faith. All the faithful, my letter told me, obeyed their Pastor to the letter. My sisters helped at Lady Fitzwilliam's stall at the bazaar in York held for the purpose, working many pretty things for it. Sir Edward Vavasour of Hazlewood gave the stone for the restoration, while the Stourtons, Langdales, Maxwells, and other prominent Catholic families gave liberally to the Bishop's fund.

'My sisters also wrote that Mr. and Mrs. Charlton of Hesleyside and their eldest son William, aged eighteen, my future husband, stayed a week at Burghwallis for the Doncaster races. They confessed it was not a very lively seven days, with Mrs. Charlton constantly bewailing her various forms of ill health, with Mr. Charlton wishing himself, instead, at Clintburn, one of his most distant moorland farms, and with their son William stretching himself at full length on a bench at a ball and going comfortably off to sleep. Poor fellow! It was his first ball and he only knew how to dance reels.

'My chilblains had been very seriously troublesome again, though not the smallest notice was ever taken of them by the nuns. But in the autumn of that year my father suddenly appeared and found my health in not at all a satisfactory condition. I had an idea at the time that Miss Mostyn, or some other friend of mine, had urged him to do so, and he, gladdened at the opportunity of visiting at Chantilly and once more enjoying the *battues*, very easily fell in with the suggestion. I was at once removed from the Sacré Cœur.

'Mrs. Stoner, the Superioress at the Fossés, on account of whose scruples about abstinence I was sent to the S.C., having become more and more mentally enfeebled, had been deposed, and a very sensible religious head, Mrs. Monica Finchet, put in her place. So it was decided that I should return to the Fossés, my earlier religious haunt.

'I found it much altered since the S.C. had succeeded in getting convent education into their more wily hands. When I went back to the Fossés there were only thirty-five pupils and no longer any French girls of good family. There was now only one class-room for all, the little ones being herded at one end of it. Where they used to do their lessons, and all that older part of the building, was closed as unsafe to live in.

'At the Fossés a professor from the Collège Ste. Barbe came to teach us thrice a week, and splendidly he taught. Abbé Fontange gave us religious instruction once a week, and the convent chaplain, Monsieur Dehenne, did the same on Sundays. The nuns taught us English literature and geography, but nothing else, and they still persisted in their unwise choice of secular mistresses. We had three bad specimens in nine months, one of whom, a Belgian, came to class one day so much the worse for liquor, and behaved so disgustingly, that she had to be turned out then and there. One reason for selecting such inferior types may have been that the Fossés was situated in the Quartier Mouffletard, which was of very bad repute and shunned by women of respectability. Even Sisters of Charity were insulted when on their errands of mercy, and had dirt thrown on their heads.

'Lent came and the terrible Black Lent was still in vogue. The nuns should never have allowed growing girls of whatever age to keep it; for we did not taste meat for forty days and were chiefly fed on salt fish and apple dumplings.

'It must have been in the second week of July, 1830, that I saw a lady walking in our garden talking to my pet nun, Sister Alicia Spiring, so highly spoken of in George Sand's *Histoire de ma Vie*. This lady actually was George Sand herself, or Madame Dudevant to give her married name, and she had come expressly for the purpose of telling the nuns that Paris was on the eve of revolution, and that the girls should be sent to their homes without delay. Very few days later Poulette informed me I would be sent back to England in charge of the housekeeper of Mr. Daly, the English banker, and that my father had arranged to meet me in London. No sooner had I arrived at Burghwallis than I heard all the news; of the flight of Charles X and his court, and of the brave behaviour of the Fossés nuns when the convent was broken into by unruly troops.

'The two chief heroines were Sister Mary Frances, a Miss Fairbairn of Carlisle, and Sister Teresa, a lay nun. The disorderly soldiers, bent on pillage, got in by the door of the lower garden which opened on to the Rue des Boulangers, and came straight to the upper garden leading to the cloisters. Sister Mary Frances went to meet them at the cloister entrance and greeted the noisy rabble with "*Bonjour, mes amis. Je vais faire vous dresser une table ici, et vous allez boire à notre santé.*" The corporal in charge, quite won over by the Sister's courage and *bonhomie*, ordered his men to halt and the table, set with wine and glasses, was soon in readiness. Sister Teresa and the other nuns acted as *cantoniéres*, pouring out and refilling the glasses for the men. "*Alors, ma Sœur, trinquez avec nous*," said the corporal invitingly to Sister Mary Frances. But she excused herself, saying it was against their rule to eat or drink between meals. "*Eh bien, ma bonne*," the corporal replied; "*donnez-nous un poignet de main*," and at that she readily shook hands with them all. The corporal, seeing some of his men straying in the direction of the cloisters, turned them back and said, "*Le premier qui entre dans les cloîtres, je le fusil.*" Thus was the old convent of the Rue des Fossés St. Victor saved from pillage by the action of a lion-hearted woman.

VIII

RENEWAL OF HOME LIFE

IT does not take the convent-bred young girl of fifteen summers long to get accustomed to her new-found freedom. She appears to take it in her stride, passing from the state of chrysalis to that of butterfly without apparent effort, without a vestige of that introspective agony which the novelists of the day depict, fluttering her wings in a variety of social atmospheres to most assured purpose.

The record of an eight-year period is now to be considered, from July, 1830, when the foreign pupils at Les Fossés are hurriedly dispersed to their homes with Paris on the eve of revolution, to January, 1839, when Barbara accepts the offer of his hand and heart from William Henry Charlton, eldest son and heir of the Squire of Hesleyside, herself at the time aged twenty-four, while he is twenty-nine.

Burghwallis does not prove altogether a happy home. The eccentricities of Mr. Tasburgh increase and weigh heavy on her. An air of gloom and depression pervades the house, gradually thickens, and culminates in parental discord, reaching such a height that her dearly beloved mother seeks, for years on end, the solitude of her chamber, declining all communication with her husband, but rejoicing in the society of her children.

But Barbara's heart is young, a glittering scene is beckoning from the world outside, and home cares can be lightly thrown aside. With a natural social inclination that befits the habit of the time, she joyfully puts out into the fashionable current and easefully progresses with its throng. There are visits of astonishing duration at various country houses. Private theatricals are very much the vogue, with usually an impromptu dance to follow, so that for the young people of the party dullness is unknown and, likewise, stiffness or formality. There are race-week balls, the annual excitement of York Festival, and for supreme enjoyment the London season with its round of dances, river parties, picnics and receptions.

Fanny, middle-born of the three beautiful Miss Tasburghs, is the first to marry and is followed, four years later, by the eldest, Mary; leaving Barbara, though not for long, a solitary pendant on the matrimonial bough. Meanwhile, her social circle is enlarged and cheerfully adorned. William IV departs this life and the young Victoria succeeds him as ruler of the land. There follow Coronation gaieties accompanied by public rejoicing on an unprecedented scale, while the great London hostesses vie with one another in the splendour and magnificence of their entertainment.

Amid the coming and going of her constant movement in society Barbara does not confess to suitors or admirers in the quantity one might expect from the way she gads about. She has not, it seems, an ardent disposition. A stray, devoted, gay and doubtless gallant Guardsman flits across the stage, turns up unexpectedly, and is obviously desirous of acceptance as a lover. Alas! he is a younger son and landless, and so ineligible from every point of view. Except for this one small amorous episode, Barbara escapes the toils of love until she is wooed and won by William Henry Charlton, the squirely heir to many acres and of rich estate.

'There was much company at Burghwallis the first winter of my return, for the militia had been called out to put down the riots against machinery and to prevent the rick-burning that was everywhere going on. Among others who used to

visit us was a certain Mr. Rigby, staying at Womesley with
Lord Hawke, who kept the Badsworth hounds. This Mr.
Rigby finally proposed to my sister Fanny and for a short
time they were engaged, but eventually for some reason it
was given up.

'Whether from the effects of that last Black Lent, or
because of the sudden change of climate after nine and a
half years abroad, I had not been feeling well, and in the
spring of 1831 I was seized with a most painful malady, few
cases of its sort being known in England then. It was tic
douloureux in the nape of the neck. The pain always began
in the finger-tips of my right hand and slowly crept up to
the neck, which was stiffened and immovable as if held in a
vice. The local doctor was nonplussed and could do nothing
for me. I regret to say that the utter lack of common sense
in my dear nuns was the cause of this attack, and for all my
cruel suffering on the many occasions of its return. I had
been terribly underfed on scanty and unwholesome food at
the Sacré Cœur. We had a sufficiency of wholesome English
fare at the Fossés, but the good of it was all undone by the
unheard of Black Lent folly. After weeks of agony I was
reduced to a shadow and my complexion became of a
transparent pallor. That summer a terrible epidemic of
Cholera Morbus broke out in the county and was especially
fatal at York.

'Here I will briefly record an incident that shows my
father, in spite of many foibles, to have been a practical man.
My sister Fanny was away from home on a long visit and
had taken with her Anne Firth, the maid she shared with
Mary. And then an invitation came from Mrs. Lumley of
Tickhill to Burghwallis for an archery meeting, an important social affair. Mary wanted very much to go, but she had
no smart day frock and Anne Firth, who could speedily

have made her one, was far away. That, however, was a matter of small account. Off she drives to Doncaster and buys some yards of lovely coloured muslin. She cuts out her dress and gets Nurse to run up the skirt, but no one touches the body except herself. All is ready in time and it fits beautifully. Then comes the question of her hair, for the old nurse is not clever that way with her hands. Again it is a matter of small account. Mary could dress her own hair just as well as a coiffeur. How came she to be so independent? In the spring of 1827, after baby Michael's death, my father insisted that a good style French dressmaker should come in twice a week to teach us how to cut out and make dresses. Myself I was only twelve at the time, and yet I sewed my own pink gingham frock, although Mary and Fanny cut it out, pieced it, and tried it on under Madame Cocher's eye. Hippolyte, the best coiffeur in Paris, also came to give hair-dressing lessons at ten francs each. My father said all young ladies should be taught such things as well as cooking, not only for self-help in emergency, but also to be able to direct others when in fault.

'That winter my tic douloureux came back, though the attack was neither so severe nor so prolonged as the first one.

'In September, 1832, instead of attending the Doncaster races, we all went to Syston Park, near Grantham, to spend a few weeks with Lady Thorold, a great friend of my parents and who, as Mrs. Dalton and a widow, had rented Skellow Grange near Burghwallis. Originally she was Marianne Cary of Tor Abbey, Co. Devon. I was not supposed to be out, but I did most things like my elders. In the autumn season Syston was an open house on an extensive scale. A stream of fashionable people came in quick succession, among whom were many M.Ps. We had much masquerading, dancing, and *tableaux vivants*. Lady Georgina

Cholmeley (Beauclerc), a dark beauty but very impassive, made an exquisite picture. Mary and Fanny were much more admired than any of the made-up London girls who came to Syston. The former had the advantage of good looks combined with well-formed features. She was medium in height on the tall side, but not too tall, and was especially graceful in her movements. The perfect oval of her face harmonized with her small, cameo-cut features. With all this, however, she lacked the sweet countenance and soft manners that attracted men, women and children at first sight to my dear Fanny. Of the two Mary had the stronger character and the stronger health, Fanny's disposition being naturally more pliant and amiable. The two were passionately devoted to each other through life.

'During that autumn George Fieschi Heneage, M.P., of Hainton Hall, Co. Lincoln, finally fixed his affections on my sister Fanny, while Henry Rich, Esq., afterwards Sir Henry Rich, Bart., who was a clever writer of political pamphlets in support of the Whigs, and who ultimately became an M.P. and the holder of a Court sinecure, fixed his on Mary. But whereas Fanny duly became Mrs. Heneage, Mary never became Lady Rich. Later Mr. Higgins, the Druid, of Skellow Grange proposed a marriage between his son Godfrey and Mary, but my father declined it for the reason that Charles Fairfax of Gilling Castle was supposed to be nibbling.

'As soon as it was fixed that the wedding of Fanny and George Heneage should take place about the middle of January, 1833, my father hied him off to Paris to order her trousseau, and because my enemy the tic was still active, it was thought that a few months spent in what might be called my native air would possibly arrest the evil. So he took me with him.

'I was put *en pension* with a Madame Liot from Martinique in the West Indies, who kept a small, but decidedly high-class, school with the aid of her two daughters. The elder had married a Baron Trigand de la Tour, first cousin to the Duc Décazes. She and her sister, Mademoiselle Liot, kept house and the old mother minded the girls, who were taught by professors and masters. Sight-singing was taught by a young person living in who could not have been more than eighteen years old. I was present sometimes during the sight-singing, although I was in no sense a pupil, having *le second* to myself together with the services of a beautifully featured old West Indian negress dressed in her Martiniquan bandanna head-dress.

'Fanny was married on January 17th, 1833, first in the Burghwallis chapel by Abbé le Roux, and afterwards in the Parish Church. It was a very pretty country wedding from all accounts. Mr. Heneage *père* was too ill to be present. Mary and Barbara Cholmeley were the bridesmaids.

'In the meantime I was very happy with Madame Liot in the Rue Pigale. On Sunday nights I usually went to Mrs. Callaghan's, the banker's wife, for dinner and an evening party, sleeping afterwards at her house, and there I often met Lady Tichborne, whom the Claimant called his mother, a very handsome woman. Old Mr. Berkeley of Spetchley would sometimes take me out driving in his carriage. On one occasion Mrs. Callaghan took me to her box at the opera to hear Grisi in the Cererentola. It was Grisi's *début* in Paris and she was greeted with furore. That particular opera suited me as I was then playing Herz's variations on its airs. Alas! I had a bout of tic douloureux. The 'native climate' cure had not succeeded and I returned to England at the end of June.

'Before going to Burghwallis I spent ten days in London

with my married sister and was taken to two balls, but I was too weak from tic to enjoy them. While I was there her father-in-law, old Mr. Heneage, died. His death was very painful inasmuch as he seemed to be in a panic of despair. In vain did his son-in-law, Mr. Howard, beseech him to call a priest and make his peace with God. "Howard, I never was a Catholic; no, I never was a Catholic," the poor, old dying renegade kept repeating. His son and Mr. Howard dutifully went in the carriage to fetch Mr. Wylde, the head priest of the church in Warwick Street, who drove back with them. But the dying man refused to see him and drew his last breath with the words "I never was a Catholic" on his lips.

'My other sister, Mary, enjoyed this London season to her heart's content, and was now acclaimed on all sides as a beauty. Young Mr. Towneley, eldest son and heir of old Mr. Towneley of Towneley Hall, Co. Lancs, had been paying her marked attention, never losing sight of her for long. At the end of the season, in wishing her goodbye, he added, "I hope, Miss Tasburgh, you will excuse me from following you to Scarborough until I see, and speak to, my father." Whereupon they parted with a half-understanding between them, but the flirtation was never renewed. Had it turned out otherwise, the Towneley family, in all probability, would still be flourishing.

'On January 29th, 1833, my mother succeeded to the Crathorne estate on the death of her Uncle Frank, the woman-hater, and at about the same time my brother George, who had been away for the last two years at Dresden University, came home. Neither of these events seemed to have elated my father, whose letters to his children were full of puerile complaints, and when I got home late in June father and son both had faces of funereal gloom. Glad indeed I was to get away from Burghwallis and go to Scarborough

F

with my mother. My piano was some consolation, for I had returned from Paris this time an effective performer and could brilliantly dash off pieces *à la* Herz, though without any real knowledge of the theory of music.

'As soon as Parliament was up, George Heneage and Fanny came to Scarborough, bringing Mary with them. They took a large house and had their carriage and horses, and it was altogether very pleasant. Alas! our merry family party soon came to an end, for my father and brother descended on us like two mutes at a funeral, and quickly dispelled all joy.

'In February Parliament met and the Heneages, George being an M.P., went up to London. It was arranged that my father should take me up to stay with them so that I could be under Dr. Warren, but when we arrived at Doncaster to stay the night with Miss Bacon Frank, I was seized with a very bad attack of my dreadful enemy. There I had perforce to remain. My mother came in haste from Burghwallis and for the first time in my life I was delirious from pain. Dr. Warren, when we got to London, thought badly of the case and gave me such violent remedies that my naturally pretty white rows of teeth were all but ruined. He said it was a matter of either kill or cure.

'In 1834 I went through my first London season, and, because Fanny was not well enough, Lady Thorold took me out. I enjoyed the season greatly. In those days London balls were far more enjoyable than nowadays; then a girl seldom missed a dance and invitations were not so difficult to procure as in these moon-eyed Tom and 'Arry times. The Catholics of that era were much handsomer and more distinguished than they are now; they have sadly dwindled down and uglified since then.

'I remember seeing Lady Shrewsbury with her two

daughters, afterwards Princesses Borghese and Doria, at a garden party, also the twin Miss Jerninghams, dark and stately, and these are only a few examples of distinguished-looking Catholics.

'Lord Fitzwilliam's balls were the great event of the season for everyone as well as me. They were smart and the exquisite, high-bred manners of his daughter, Lady Charlotte, made them still more enjoyable. They seldom gave a ball in London without the presence of royalty, but humbler guests were never overlooked. The last dance of all was danced at dawn with the candles extinguished and the shutters opened, a signal for all those ladies young or old, who indulged in dyes and paint to scuffle down the staircase and call loudly for their carriages.

'Sometimes on Sunday evenings Lady Thorold would take me to old Lady Salisbury's card parties, at which whist was the game. Lady Salisbury dressed *décolleté* and her poor old head shook with palsy. She used to wear a soft Indian muslin turban on her head, decorated with jewels, and her superb emerald and diamond necklace was fastened to the back of her dress with pack-thread, having become far too large for the bony, shrivelled neck. Not long after she was burnt to death owing to her turban catching fire. Her large room was never crowded but the whist players never failed to turn up, the salon being almost a Sunday card club. I used to sit in a retired spot with the two Lady Scotts whilst their mother, the Duchess of Buccleuch, sat at the card-table, and there were always a few young men who showed civility, and with whom I would ride in the Park during the week.

'It was in the summer of 1835 that a dark cloud settled over Burghwallis, never more to lift! I was alone and un-supported when the unfortunate rupture between my parents took place, and so had to bear the brunt of it. The case was as follows: When Francis Crathorne died in January, 1833, the Crathorne property descended to my mother, and was in her sole control. But Francis Crathorne, my mother's Uncle Frank, was not in a fit condition to manage his estate, and ever since his brother's death in 1825, that brother being my grandfather, George Crathorne, my father had seen to everything. My mother had no real idea of the testamentary effect of the will under which she inherited, and very probably had never even seen it. She knew that she had the power to settle it by division on her younger children, because her own father had told her so. But she was, it appears, in complete ignorance of the fact that the income from the property was hers to spend or save while she lived. Now my father's one aim was so to arrange matters that the Crathorne lands fell eventually to my brother George, and every ruse was practised to that end. To this my mother flatly refused consent, claiming very truly the Bodney property, which was also hers, had been settled on her son and that he was thus amply provided for, as of course he would have Burghwallis in addition. My father was frantic with disappointment at the failure of his plan and adopted an abusive and overbearing attitude.

'This unfortunate strife ended in a complete separation, with my mother living in the old part of the house and my father in the new. My own room, however, was opposite my dear mother's, so that she and I could be, and were, always together.'

An editorial comment on this extraordinary situation will be appropriate here. It cannot have escaped notice that Barbara accuses her father of, if not exactly sharp practice, at any rate of bringing undue influence to bear.

At the same time, it should be remembered, she was not

only warmly prejudiced in favour of her mother, to whom she bore a unique devotion, but also she most certainly derived her version of the case from her mother's lips; utterances, that is, from one who suffered from a burning indignation. It cannot, for instance, be imagined that Mr. Tasburgh, *grand seigneur* to his finger-tips and of distant manner, could condescend to justify himself before his youngest daughter. The prospect of consolidating the ownership of three large estates in the single person of a son and heir must, at the same time, have been pleasing to a landed proprietor whose own acres had descended to him in an unbroken succession for five centuries and more. That there was wrangling between husband and wife in regard to the Crathorne settlement is indisputable, though doubt may be said to exist as to whether it was sufficient in itself to cause the latter to immure herself within four walls. One story has it that Mrs. Tasburgh presented herself at the dining-table in a state of inebriation, and, being ordered by her husband to her room, chose to interpret his command in an absolutely literal sense.

As a self-captive, Mrs. Tasburgh's behaviour was not consistently meek and mild. Her husband was fond of gardening, and would hoe the flower borders set against the south front of Burghwallis. Whenever this operation took him near the bedroom of his wife, she would watch his movements closely from her window, and, given an opportunity, she would lean out and spit on his head.

Barbara concludes her account of the family rupture in words that show she is able to detach herself at will from the asperities of life. She writes as follows:

'In spite of the family wrangle, I had a pleasant enough summer with my music, drawing and books.'

IX

SOCIAL DEBUT AND ENGAGEMENT

'CAMPSALL, the Bacon Franks' place at which there had been a sale fifteen years back, was still to let, and about this time an extraordinary family called Wood came in as tenants. *Père et mère* were recluses and returned no calls. Mrs. Wood and her three daughters were never seen abroad and did not even walk out in their own park. They were strongly turned to education and carried out their bent in a peculiar and very expensive manner. Professors of French, German, Spanish, and a music-master besides, were housed in the village to the utter despair of all the neighbouring clergy, who saw havoc being made among the flowers of their congregations. These naughty foreigners earned money also round about by giving extra lessons. The son, Willoughby Wood, however, was by no means a recluse. He was a good deal at Burghwallis and he and I used to play duets together.

'There was a good deal of entertaining at home after my mother retired to her room, and, because my father thought I was a pretty *bouton de rose* for a *bout de table*, I had to take her place as hostess and do the honours.

'On the 5th September, 1835, the Princess Victoria and her mother, the Duchess of Kent, visited York for the Festival, held on the 8th, 9th, 10th and 11th of the month. I went with the Cliffords of Wykecliffe to the Bar Convent, just outside Micklegate, to see the royal party enter the city, which they did at four o'clock on a beautiful afternoon. It was a gay week. At the principal ball, a *bal costumé*, the Princess and her mother were present and the former went through a quadrille with Lord Morpeth, who danced like a shirt hanging in the wind to dry. Princess Victoria was very sweet to look at, dressed all in white with her hair *en bandeaux*. On their return journey the royal party stayed at Wentworth to see the St. Leger run on September 15th and my brother George, a Yorkshire Hussar, was on duty at the time.

'Most of that winter, and a large part of the summer of 1836, was spent with the Heneages at Hainton, where Mary, my eldest sister, and I were made most welcome. Fanny was not well, so there was no London season for either of us.

'George Heneage, who was a most generous and liberal-minded man, built and furnished a pretty Catholic chapel in his grounds, dedicated to St. Francis of Sales, and gave Mr. Simkiss, the priest appointed to it, a good house in the village.

'Mr. Howard, who had married George Heneage's sister, took Willingham, Mr. Boucherette's country seat near Hainton, and hardly a day passed on which some of us did not meet. I rode on horseback all about the countryside and did Fanny's shopping for her at Louth or Market Rasen.

'As summer advanced the party was increased by Aunt Anne, Miss Gage, her sister, and Francis and Mary Cholmeley, with Mr. and Mrs. Howard still constantly coming over and bringing with them Teddy and Charlie, their two little boys. Being the youngest of the party, it fell to me to amuse the children and play with them in the house's broad passages. Teddy, the eldest, was a pretty, graceful, greedy, spoilt little boy who developed into a Guardsman, and from that duly blossomed forth into the handsomest and, I have been told, the most learned cardinal in Rome.

'My sister Mary and I went as usual to the Doncaster races and the York balls, and in the autumn she became engaged to Charles Fairfax. At Burghwallis my father was as usual in a discontented frame of mind, making things so unpleasant with his incessant grumbling that Mary, very wisely, left her home to take up her abode at Hainton. In December, while all the preliminaries to her marriage, fixed for the end of January, 1837, were in full progress, my other sister, Fanny Heneage, gave birth to a daughter who was named Georgina Mary.

'Mary was duly married to Charles Fairfax from Hainton on January 28th, all of us being present except poor mother. Unfortunately, Mr. Simkiss, the priest, positively refused to marry a couple of different religion, although no canon law deterred him from doing so, his argument being that the Church of England ceremony was all that would be necessary. No other priest was available, so a hasty change of plan was contrived at the last minute. The Protestant ceremony, enjoined by law, was advanced to an early hour, and the bridal couple, after breakfast, posted with four horses to Burghwallis, a distance of forty miles, on a day of snow and bitter cold so that the roads were quite impassable in places, in order to be married according to the rites of Holy Church by our old French priest, Abbé le Roux, who was then in his eightieth year.

'The wedding couple did not reach the old priest's house till ten at night, and then they had to go for some distance on foot along a snowy path leading to his cottage. Of course, no one was up, but after loud knocking for some time the Abbé's maidservant appeared *en déshabille* and listened to their story with dismay. With difficulty, she roused her master, but it was still more difficult to get him to understand the intricacies of the situation, as he was not only deaf, but had a very imperfect knowledge of English. A fire was lit for the shivering twain and, after a long wait, the Abbé entered in a dirty old snuff-coloured dressing-gown and slippers, surmounted by a white night-cap sticking up a foot and a half above his head. The poor old man looked quite bewildered, not even then realizing what was expected of him. But when Mary explained the dilemma in beautiful Parisian French, he grasped the knotty point and sent at once for his Book and Holy Water. Alas! there was no *aspergés* with which to give a nuptial blessing. So the maid-servant took a lantern, went out into the garden, and cut a spray of old man, a plant that grew in every cottage garden then, and that was used; somewhat of a reproach, it may be, on Charles Fairfax, who was considerably older than his pretty bride.

'When the marriage ceremony was over the Abbé retreated to his bed, and the bridal couple drove on to Burghwallis, where they were welcomed at nigh midnight by my dear mother, who feared lest they had been lost in the snow. Mary's graphic account of the nocturnal ceremony was most comical; well worthy of a scene from a play by Molière.

'Abbé Louis le Roux came as chaplain to Burghwallis in 1828, having been formerly *Vicaire de Courbevoye* near Paris, and after that officiating priest to the nuns at Bodney. His English was all but unintelligible. Once, when giving religious instruction to a great big fellow, one of Lady Radcliffe's postilion boys, he admonished him in the words "Wash and you will be shaved," whereupon the youth put a hand to his chin and looked very puzzled. The Abbé died at Burghwallis in 1843, aged eighty-six, and is buried in the churchyard there.

'Soon after Mary's wedding I went to London, but it was

a short and dull season, on account of William IV's death. I was one of a huge Catholic party, not far short of a hundred altogether, that assembled at Richmond, going there by water, and we had a charming dance. The people at the Star and Garter vowed they had seldom seen so many handsome and distinguished men and women in an assembly before. It was truth they spoke! No Catholic party like that one could be got up in these days. The depression of the old Catholic type seems to have come on very rapidly; occasioned, it may be presumed, by an influx of converts and colonists.

'One evening in June I was playing the piano in my sister Fanny's drawing-room when the Great Bell tolled for the passing of the King, and Princess Victoria became Queen of England. Mr. Charlton of Hesleyside, my father-in-law to be, was High Sheriff of Northumberland that year and had to proclaim Her Majesty's accession. Lady Charlotte Copley, Fanny's great friend, was made a Lady in Waiting, and she often told us her experiences of Palace life.

'Doncaster race-week came round again and once more I was the guest of kind Miss Bacon Frank; although the festivities of race-week were already on the wane, I enjoyed myself very much. One event was old Lord Scarborough's cheery ball at Tickhill, at which Mrs. Lumley acted as mistress of the ceremonies, and there I made the acquaintance of Richard Monckton Miles, later Lord Houghton, the poet laureate of Yorkshire. Miss Seymour, Lady Tichborne's sister, was the belle of the ball, wearing the newest coiffure from Paris; the front hair parted in the middle, with each side frizzed and sticking out the breadth of a hand from her head. Englishmen as a rule dislike startling feminine fashions *qui sautent aux yeux*, and as my partner for the quadrille, Mr. Rich, was putting me in place he suddenly pulled me away, saying, "Don't let us stand opposite that horned bull; we shall be gored!" To compare a lovely girl, adorned with the latest Paris coiffure, to a dangerous animal was so comic as to make me laugh aloud; even Ovid could hardly have indulged in such a metamorphosis.

'In the spring of Coronation Year, 1838, Fanny came to Burghwallis on a visit, bringing with her Georgina and Adela, her two little girls, the latter of whom was only a few months old and unlikely, according to her looks, to live much longer. In fact, but for my mother's vigilance and care, she would undoubtedly have died. The matter was that Fanny wanted to have only Catholic servants about her and unfortunately engaged a most incompetent Irish Catholic nurse, who in spite of her shortcomings, came with an excellent character.

'With thoughts of the Coronation season in his head, my father, without taking any advice on the subject, sent off to Paris for three dresses for me, all three chosen by himself, at an average cost of about 500 francs. No. 1 was of very rich brocaded pink satin, elaborately trimmed with *blonde*; No. 2 was a rich white and blue flounced silk; No. 3 was of very thick white corded silk, with two deep flounces; and all three were utterly unsuitable for a girl of twenty-three who looked many years younger than her age. But my father, alas! had very little idea of the fitness of things.

'Early in May I went to London with the Heneages to stay with them at their house in Charles Street, and Mrs. Howard, George's sister, stayed there also while house-hunting. As might be expected, it was a first-rate season, and luckily Fanny was well enough to enjoy it. We had tickets in the Abbey for the crowning of the Queen, but George became alarmed on the very eve of the ceremony lest Fanny should overtire herself in consequence of the heat and crowd, and the long hours of waiting. We had been previously invited by Miss Burdett-Coutts to see the procession from the windows of her house in Stratton Street, overlooking Piccadilly, so the Abbey spectacle was abandoned and Fanny and I went there instead. It was a perfect day and I, for one, had a much pleasanter time than if I had been penned up for hours in Westminster Abbey; a very particular admirer of mine in the Life Guards was mounted just in front of the window at which I was stationed, and we exchanged a running current of blithesome smiles throughout the day.

'The pageantry of the royal procession to and from the Abbey was more compact and imposing than on the occasion of the Jubilee in 1887, which was all detached and ragged. But on this day it was splendid, the equipages of the foreign potentates were superb, and when the young Queen went by in her Coronation robes, and in majestic pomp, the deafening and joyous shouts of the people ran over London and were echoed from afar. We lunched at Miss Burdett-Coutts' and walked back to Charles Street for dinner, returning again in the evening for the illuminations and fireworks. Piccadilly was so chock-full of market carts, omnibuses, and country vehicles of all description, containing people up to see the fun, that we had to inch our way along. In the Abbey little Teddy Howard, the Cardinal to come, acted as page to the Duke of Norfolk, dressed in the most gorgeous attire, and I will vouch there was no prettier page than he to be seen that day. Among the many balls I went to that festive season Lord Fitzwilliam's was, as usual, easily the best. A great gathering of royalties was present, and all the distinguished guests, English and foreign, were ablaze with orders and decorations. To crown all, my Guardsman was on duty at it! So popular were the

Fitzwilliam balls that when they ceased the London house was called "Paradise Lost," Viscount Milton being one of the family's secondary titles.

'My sister Fanny's contribution to the Coronation gaieties was a magnificent drawing-room concert which she gave at 39 Charles Street, and at which the great singers of the Italian Opera, then in London, Grisi, Lablache, Rubini, Tamburini and Albertazzi, performed for her. Costa was the accompanist at the piano. Grisi in particular sang beautifully. Perhaps it was a bit of bravado on her part, being the day after her husband, Count de Melcy, had fought a duel with Lord Castlereagh. Fanny looked queen-like that evening, so dignified, so high-bred, and with such a beautiful presence. She was dressed in delicate green satin and Brussels lace, with a profusion of diamonds. As luck would have it, I was transfixed by my old enemy tic some days before the concert, and was in despair. As a last resort a general practitioner named Blackett, who lived just round the corner, was sent for who said he could put me right in a few hours if I did not mind my neck being slightly discoloured by the liquid he would apply to it. Willingly did I consent to have the nerves painted, and before the doctor had finished his task I was in a deep sleep, from which I awoke many hours later to a straight, painless neck, a flexible arm, and, what was of as much consequence to a young girl, a spotless skin on which no mark of the black tincture was visible. It was most pleasing, therefore, to be told on the night of the concert by Mr. Howard that he had never seen me look so pretty, and it became more than evident as the night progressed that my gallant Guardsman, who was present, corroborated this opinion. Dr. Blackett would not give away the secret of his magic phial.

'The expense of this grand musical entertainment to my

sister was not much over £100. Grisi and Lablache were paid £25 each, while the rest of the singers got £20 apiece, Costa at the piano getting only £10. The Italian Opera was then at its zenith and never again produced such a galaxy of super-excellent talent. The ballets were on the same footing of perfection, headed by such famous names as Taglioni, the Elssler sisters, Duvernay, Cherito, Perot, etc.

'Fanny had her opera box as usual, and I was with her on the night Victoria made her first appearance there as Queen. It was in July and she was in mourning. The shouting and hurrahing almost rent the roof and, time and time again, the young Queen came to the front of her box, not the royal box, to be gazed at by the multitude. She stood her ordeal manfully, but the Duchess of Kent, her mother, burst into floods of tears. After the curtain had dropped at the end of the last act it slowly was drawn up again to disclose the whole company in a group, with Grisi out a little way in front who led them in "God save the Queen"; a scene never to be forgotten.

'On presentation days everyone who had been at Court appeared as of due course at the opera in gala dress, befeathered and be-diamonded. And always there was a brilliant ballet to follow. Taglioni once told a friend of mine in confidence that the sparring in the green-room, up to the minute before going on with sweet smiles and sugar-candy expressions before the audience, between the two Elsslers, Duvernay and Cherito had to be seen and heard to be believed.

'Both my sisters were presented at the first Drawing-room after the Coronation, and I had made full preparation to be presented too, though not in one of the three Paris dresses, making me look like a dowager, that my father had bestowed on me, probably with this very occasion in his mind. Instead I would have worn a lovely tulle gown, for which my dear Fanny had provided the train. I was all keyed up and ready when, on the very eve of the Presentation there comes a letter from my father absolutely forbidding me to go. His letter gave no reason, for there was none to give; it was a mere passing fad! As usual, he regretted it when too late, and told my sister Mary that he had not expected I would have acted on his letter. Such excuse was sheer nonsense, for had I gone to Court after receiving the letter he would have done nothing but groan and sigh for weeks on end when I returned home, as if lamenting the disobedience of a daughter. It would have been just the cheerless atmosphere that, just then, I was particular to avoid, my mind being already fully occupied and over-weighted with regard to my young man in the Guards; whether he was quite the man for me to marry, being a second son? On the eventful day my two sisters, George Heneage and his sister, Mrs. Howard, drove off in all their grandeur to the Palace. Like Cinderella, I was left behind alone; but unlike Cinderella no Prince came to comfort me.

'William Henry Charlton, my future husband, called at Charles Street and was asked to dinner. He wrote home to his mother that I was quite the prettiest of the three sisters, and at first sight my peculiarly soft colouring might lead strangers to conclude so. But Mary it was who had the perfect features and a faultless figure, and walked with the French grace so uncommon in English ladies.

'Lady Essex lived opposite us in Charles Street and it was there, at her town house, that I first saw Mrs. Brinsley Sheridan, a Miss Colquhoun, who had just made a runaway marriage. She was plain, and yet it was astonishing how her three beautiful Sheridan sisters-in-law, by insisting she should adopt their fashion of wearing three long, thick curls, contrived somehow to make her partake of their charm.

'Some little time before this I went with Lady Thorold to some private theatricals at the Honourable Mrs. Leicester Stanhope's. Mr. and Mrs. Leicester Stanhope, I may mention, had the unenviable reputation of being the dirtiest couple in town. Not only themselves but everything about them was on the same scale of dirt; their carriage was dirty; the coachman and footman were dirty; sadder still, their child could never have had a tubbing. At these theatricals Mrs. Norton, George Meredith's *Diana of the Crossways*, second of the three Sheridan sisters, acted. She was then still living with her husband, who soon afterwards brought his abortive action against Lord Melbourne, and looked and acted very superior to the rest of the *corps dramatique*. Mrs. Leicester Stanhope, who had been a moneyed Miss Green, developed into the Countess of Harrington with two or three additional layers of dirt on her. The Sheridans gave constant garden parties at Holly Lodge, to which we were always invited. The sisters had the management of them and very smart and enjoyable they were.

'Lady Carnarvon gave a very smart evening party at Mivart's Hotel at which, among other distinguished guests, the Duchesses of Gloucester and Cambridge were present. It was quite the *soirée* of the season and exquisitely arranged. I went out so much that Coronation season that I wore my London frocks to shreds and was obliged to have recourse to my dowager costumes in the autumn.

'At the end of this wonderful season there was a migration of Heneages, Howards, Petres and Jerninghams to Brighton. London theatre companies came down, and I saw Kean act in *The Lady of Lyons*, the fashionable piece then. George Heneage and I left Brighton for the Doncaster races. We left all behind us well and merry, but no sooner had we got to Burghwallis than he received a letter of recall, saying that Fanny had been taken seriously ill. Mrs. Howard was on the spot and, in the circumstances, of much more use than George could be. Nevertheless, he posted back to Brighton with four horses that night.

'For the races that autumn my father, my sister Mary Fairfax, and I spent two nights with Miss Bacon Frank, and my young Life Guardsman was one of a rowdy bachelor party at a house some twenty miles from Doncaster. The race-week ball was all but over, with just one more dance to go, and my father had withdrawn his watchful gaze on my behaviour, when, to my great amazement, my gallant beau appeared on the scene. After a late dinner, and not-withstanding the quizzing of his friends, he had ordered horses and come post-haste to have at least one dance with me. Mary Fairfax, with great presence of mind, suddenly discovered she was hungry, so as to get my father out of the way and so prevent him, in the peculiar way he had, of in-sulting any of our admirers who did not have his approval. For a man to drive forty miles there and back for the chance of a single dance with the girl of his choice was a compliment that did not deserve being requited by an insult.

'Not long after the race-week Death was busy with our blithesome Brighton party. Fanny lost her baby girl, Adela, aged ten months, through the crass ignorance of the Irish nurse; and in October poor little Charlie Howard died from acute inflammation. I had so recently been taking him and his brother Teddy out for walks along the front, and paying too many visits with them, I fear, to confectioners, that it did not seem like truth. The poor father took his boy's death deeply to heart; he was beyond belief inconsolable and

G

became quite an altered man. Before the year was out a London doctor declared that Mr. Howard's lungs were in a most dangerous condition, and hurried him off to Madeira, where he died in the late autumn of 1839. Before leaving England he got Mr. Simkiss, the Hainton priest, to re-baptize his three little girls, wishing them to be brought up in the Catholic faith. But as he appointed four guardians, two Catholics and two Protestants, it fell out that they were instructed in their mother's religion. She, however, did eventually become a Catholic, though her conversion came too late for her to control her daughters' creed.

'That hunting season William Charlton came to Burgh-wallis from Hesleyside, bringing his hunters with him, and remained a month. At the close of the year, with the exception of my recluse mother, we all went to Hainton for Christmas, and William Charlton took his hunters on from Burghwallis. As usual my father did not stay away from Burghwallis long.

'The winter of 1838-9 was most severe; the outdoor amusement was sledging and indoors we had dancing and private theatricals. A lot of people were staying at the house, including Mary and Charles Fairfax, the Jerninghams, Claytons, Elwes, the Duke of St. Albans and Mr. Rich. We acted *The Day after the Wedding* and *Perfection*, with myself as Lady Elizabeth Freelove in the first and as Susan in the latter play.

'The first night was on January 18th and everything went off beautifully without the slightest hitch, and afterwards we had supper and a dance. On the second night, when the piece *Perfection* was just beginning and *The Day after the Wedding* had gone off with great success, Edward Heneage came in unobtrusively and whispered something to his elder brother George. Immediately the whole audience rose and hurried out. Mrs. Clayton's room was on fire! Her maid had left the candles burning too near the chintz curtains, they had caught alight, and the flames extended to the bed hangings before the fire was discovered. Luckily the fire buckets and the manual at Hainton were always kept in good order and, with a surplus of willing hands, a chain was quickly formed and the fire soon extinguished, though not before much damage had been done. Poor Mrs. Clayton lost many of her jewels, the jewel-case being on the dressing-table, but she saved her wardrobe owing to the large size of her bedroom. The Duke of St. Albans, silent and reserved in general society, showed himself as well up to the mark in the case of a house afire, organizing the bucket troop and personally assuring himself at the end that nothing was left smouldering.

'The gloom aroused by this untoward incident was soon dispersed, and George Heneage allowed us to have a third performance on the 21st to make amends for the one so tragically interrupted. A day or two later we had a grand servants' ball in the large dining-room and at the end of the week the bulk of the party went their several ways.

'My engagement to William Charlton was much approved of. . . .'

In such sententious style, without further preliminary and with no hint let fall that her inclination led that way, does Barbara announce her betrothal, which would appear to have come about divested of the customary courtship. As will soon be seen, difficulties must be overcome before she and her William actually become man and wife, and her staunchness to him, which is no less than his to her, amid these trials and tribulations are indeed sufficiently convincing that her heart had been affected ere she gave her hand. It seems obvious, at the same time, that she was never awhirl with love and that her feet unceasingly continued to touch the ground. A true conclusion, perhaps, would be that on the whole it was a matter of fact affair.

It must be remembered, as regards young ladies of good family in that age, that matrimony was their career, that to secure a husband was the be-all and the end-all of their purpose in society, and that the value of the prize they won, estimated according to a worldly standard of possession, was for them, and in the eyes of all, the criterion of success. In this sense Barbara had done pretty well. Without apparent effort, she had cast her line and caught a whopper, or at least an extremely well-conditioned fish.

At this crucial point in life, when she is about to change her state, what impression does she give? Self-admiring she plainly is, and also not at all averse to admiration, though neither to a very marked extent. Pleasure-loving too, but with much more of a butterfly propensity than with the fixed idea that enjoyment is the *summum bonum* of existence. That she possesses any superior powers of intellect may be at once denied. For instance, as far as she has gone, there is no mention of a book that struck her fancy or aroused her interest. It is the same with pictures. It is not quite the same with music, for she does possess a small piano talent and speaks with pleasure of her playing. Ability of the sort, however, was a female accomplishment normal to society in those days, while as for her not infrequent mention of attendance at the opera, it can safely be assumed that she was merely swimming in a fashionable stream.

Most certainly she did not possess an amatory disposition; except for her Life Guardsman, so prosaically turned away because the poor unfortunate was a second son and therefore would not do, and except for her William Henry, who happened to be a son and heir and therefore would, there is no mention of an affair that even verges on the romantic. Chaperons, it is true, were strict when Barbara was young, and doubtless her religious upbringing would have acted strongly in restraint of any love-sick tendency. She would have fitted ill into any of Jane Austen's books, even as a minor character, if called on to sustain a role of passion or to solve emotional perplexities. To revert to the analogy in former use: She may herself have caught a whopper, but her William, for his part, landed a pretty cool fish.

X

THE COURSE OF TRUE LOVE

B EFORE resuming the interrupted story of Barbara's engagement, it will not be inappropriate to say something of the family into which, in fulfilment of her destiny, she was soon to enter as a bride.

It was of an exceeding antiquity, being established in the North Tyne valley since before the Norman Conquest, and becoming in the centuries succeeding of principal importance in the district of its habitation. Those who bore the surname of Charlton were recognized in State Papers of the various periods as members of the most powerful 'grayne,' a word corresponding to the Scottish 'clan,' of the four by which the valley and its tributary dales were chiefly populated. From earliest days the Hesleyside branch of the family had assumed the 'hedesmanship,' or chieftancy, of the grayne of Charlton and Barbara's father-in-law to be, contemporary possessor by right of straight descent of the extensive lands and other heritable property, was the hedesman of his day.

When, in due course of time, the turbulence on the Border had to a large extent subsided, and the king's writ had at last begun to run, the Charltons of Hesleyside emerged from the long restless and unquiet period with enhanced importance as a family of notability in the Tynedale district and, in the more modern acceptation of the term, of high social standing. They had not only successfully retained their original holdings of land, but had added largely to them by purchase, by enclosure, and by judicious marriages.

No part of the Borderland was so lawless or so dangerously

agitated as the North Tyne valley and the boundless moorland tracts that lay on either side of it along the upper courses of the river. Until a peaceful state at length developed, a continuous predatory war persisted between the Lowland Scottish clans on one side of the Border and the graynes of North Tynedale on the other, with forcible seizure of sheep and cattle, not infrequently to the accompaniment of fatal blows. A relic is still preserved at Hesleyside typifying the kind of life that went on in those days, well known in local history as 'The Spur of the Charlton.'

This relic is an iron spur of the late Elizabethan age, with a long shank and a well-rowelled point, which was placed of old upon the board instead of meat, within a covered dish. Its appearance intimated that the larder was low, or that the young men were eager for a foray, or that a score needed to be wiped off; any plausible excuse, that is, for resort to boot and saddle, for an excursion over the Border, and for a homecoming laden with the spoils of war.

It was an achievement in itself to have held what was one's own amid such scenes of daily life, and to have managed as a family to survive. It was, at any rate, a full-time occupation, and when, in later days, a state of peace reigned on the Border the Hesleyside squires, as now they had become, found scope for their energies in district and estate improvement, in public duties of a local character, and in the active pursuance of a squirely way of life, restrained always on religious grounds from taking any part in national affairs.

For the rest, the later squires had always a peculiarly warm affection for their home surroundings and a pleasant popularity among the people of the valley, who held the name in deep respect for its antiquity and for its status in their eyes.

Barbara will now relate the history of her engagement and in what manner she was married. It is the beginning of 1839 and she has just announced the prior fact.

'My engagement to William Henry Charlton was much approved of, my father in especial being greatly pleased. No drawback appeared on the surface. We were of the same religion, of suitable ages, and there was nothing to choose between our families as regards their pedigrees. William was received with open hearts both by Father and Mother at Burghwallis, where he stopped on his way back from Hainton to Northumberland, and I got pleasant, congratulatory letters from them too. And then, one day soon after, what do I receive but a curt missive from my father in which he said I could do much better for myself, and the engagement must be broken off at once. No reason whatever was given for this freakish change, and we were all greatly astonished, not to say irate. But we were soon enlightened as to my father's sudden afterthought by the following letter from William, dated:

'Hesleyside – February 2 – 1839.

'My dearest Barbara, – You are indeed a good correspondent in every way of the word and I am not a little proud of the sense and spirit which animate your letters, as well as gratified by their kindness and affection. I have much to say to you, my dearest girl, and I know you will forgive me if I proceed at once to speak on business matters; but first let me beg of you to give my best regards to Mr. Heneage and tell him how grateful I feel for his good opinion of us both, and how much I appreciate his generosity. As a preliminary, howevei, it is quite necessary that he should be put in possession of all the facts that have taken place with regard to your father and mine. You will recollect, dearest, that in my last letter I said that Mr. Tasburgh had signified his refusal to contribute more to our maintenance than £2,000 down, stating his inability to do more. Upon hearing to this effect my father, assuming that the Crathorne property was in Mrs. Tasburgh's power and taking for granted that she had the inclination to do something for us, wrote to your mother requesting her assistance and, at the same time, to your father explaining the object of his letter. Two days since the letter to Mrs. Tasburgh was returned unopened, enclosed under the cover of one from Mr. Tasburgh to my father, upon the tone and manner of which I will forbear comment. Suffice it to say that in it my father was informed that his letter to your mother had been intercepted by Mr. Tasburgh, who would allow of no interference with his wife's affairs. I shall only conclude by observing that it was the very last sort of communication which my father, an old friend of both parties, a relation of your mother's, a trustee of her marriage settlements, had a right to expect, and that your father's conduct has precluded the possibility of any further correspondence with him, at present, on the part of mine. Such conduct, coupled with the obscurities and contradictions in your father's letter, made the situation perfectly unintelligible, though your own letter of yesterday has gone far towards unravelling the enigma even if by means of a disagreeable solution. It is certainly a strange business! However, my father has now come forward with a handsome allowance; but let Mr. Heneage, if your father will listen to him, and not persevere in his cruel conduct towards so kind and good a daughter as yourself, make any bargain possible. Nothing more astonished me than your father's precipitate announcement of the *break off*; it was so diametrically contrary to his express promise to me before I left Burghwallis. I have got a cold and between coughing and thinking of you, dearest, I fear my spirits are not so lively as heretofore. I did a bit of superstition the other night. I tied one of your long hairs round my wrist that I might dream of you, and I dreamt that I was with you in the flower garden at Hesleyside, gathering flowers – *A wreath around your youthful brow to twine.* Goodbye, my dearest Barbara,

'believe me ever most devotedly yours,

'WILLIAM.'

It is not an edifying spectacle this of the two male parents squabbling as to which should bear the major burden in respect of subsistence for the young couple.

Mr. Tasburgh does, however, advance openly to the attack and, like a good general, does not fail to secure his flank, realizing, doubtless, that there lies a weakness. Mr. Charlton, on the other hand, is skilfully, if somewhat lawlessly, rebuffed while endeavouring to steal a march preparatory to a surprise assault on his opponent's rear. Meanwhile, Barbara, as is only natural, views the situation from an angle of self-interest, quite hard-headed enough to appreciate the material side of the affair as it drags its dismal course.

'For nearly five months the contest continued between the two fathers, if, that is, a state of silent indignation on the part of one can be called contention; with Mr. Heneage in his kindness trying, though without success, to pour oil on the troubled waters. Mr. Charlton remained firm in his determination not to sanction the marriage until he had held communication with my mother, while my father was of equal resolution that no such communication should be held. The more my father tried, by hook or by crook, to break off our engagement the closer William and I stood side by side, writing daily to each other.

'With all this worry and disappointment the tic held me

in its grasp again. This was in April, and on my recovery I went to Leamington, to my sister Mary Fairfax who was staying there, in order to consult Dr. Jephson, who was a specialist in my complaint. Without his parents' knowledge, William came to see me there while *en route* from Hesleyside to London, whither they and his two sisters had gone for the season. When this came to Mr. Charlton's knowledge he was very displeased, and threatened to cut William off from the Cumberland estates, leaving him only the entailed property in Northumberland.

'On their way up to Town, the Charltons had broken their journey at York in order that Mr. George Meynell, the lawyer who had drawn the Crathorne will and a mutual friend of both parties, should be consulted. Mr. Meynell told Mr. Charlton that the property was completely and utterly at my mother's disposal to do with what she liked, and that my father had no rights of interference in any way, adding, moreover, that in his opinion Mr. Charlton had a perfect right in his turn to ask my mother to assist us. Mr. Charlton at once wrote off to my father, quoting Mr. Meynell's exact words, and my father writes back emphatically denying that he had been guilty of concealment with regard to my mother's power over her property, stigmatizing such conduct as highly dishonourable. So what was one to think? For three years my mother had never left Burghwallis, during which time she had led the life of a prisoner in two rooms and had hardly seen a five-pound note of her own money. She wrote to the tenants at election time at my father's behest enlisting their support for the Parliamentary candidate whom he wished to have returned; hence the appearance of *Currency* Cayley in Parliament in the Whig interest. And I was now to learn that my father, in order to put William off from wishing to marry me, had intimated that my mother had made a will in my sister Mary's favour, whereas he knew perfectly well it was in mine.

'About mid-May I left Leamington and, to everyone's surprise, not knowing of the plot that William and I were hatching, I offered to go back to Burghwallis, and home I went accordingly at the beginning of June. My father received me very coldly, taking up the attitude of being himself the injured party. But it did not matter, for I only saw him at meal-times, devoting myself all in all to my mother, who was most kind and sweet. For five months she had hardly spoken to a soul except her maid, who looked after her and brought her food.

'The following two letters from my dear sister Fanny, then staying with her husband at Aunt Anne's in York, shows how cautious William and I had to be. Fanny, George Heneage, and Aunt Anne, the widow of George Anne my father's elder brother, who died in 1802, were our chief supporters throughout this trying time. Mary, my other sister, possessed to a marked degree the faculty of running with the hare and hunting with the hounds.

'June 4th, 1839. York.

'My dearest Bab,—I have done nothing but think of you ever since we parted yesterday, and am longing for the post which does not come till seven at night. I told Aunt Anne the whole story and read over to her all the duplicates of your letters to Papa, even that one with which he found so much fault. Both she and her sister say they see nothing to complain of in it and maintain that all your other letters to him are beautiful. They both desire me to tell you, with their very best and kindest love, that if I had only said you were with me at Hainton they would certainly have found room for you here; but as I did not mention it they took for granted that you were at Burghwallis. Aunt Anne immediately wrote to Papa asking him your whereabouts, and got a letter in reply saying you were with him and that you were to be left there. Papa has not made any complaints to them about you, excepting that one letter, but they take your and William's part in everything; and they think Papa very greatly to blame; and they are highly indignant at Papa refusing to see George and I. When Papa was here last Aunt Anne told him she could not believe he would allow your engagement to be broken off, as it would be of the greatest possible disadvantage to you, and she also told him that everyone was most astonished at his conduct. But until George and I told them last night they did not know his reason for it, and now that they do know both Aunt Anne and Miss Gage wish most sincerely that Mama knew, as they feel convinced, in that case, she would help you. And they think you act most beautifully in doing nothing to injure Papa, who for that one reason is bound himself to help you, by fair means let us hope. Auntie and Miss Gage did not see the Charltons as they came through York as the latter did not call on them, but left word instead with the Goldies that they had deliberately avoided doing so as better not in consequence of what had passed between the two families. They not only contradicted the engagement themselves, but desired everyone to do the same, and it came to Aunt Anne's ears how highly indignant they were with Papa. Miss Cayley passed through York on Sunday on her way to Town; she knew the reason of the bother from the Charltons. Keep up your spirits, my dearest Bab. Both Aunt Anne and her sister think you quite right to stick to your engagement and all here send you their best love.

'Believe me, your truly affectionate sister,

'FANNY HENEAGE.'

'The following day I received another letter from Fanny, dated:

'York. 6th June, 1839.

'My DEAREST BAB,—I write so soon again because I had a letter from Mary last night, and I will now copy that part of it relating to you. She says: "I do not know where Barbara is, as I cannot believe she is so foolish as to thrust her head into such a den of uproar as she is likely to find at home. I wrote to Papa before I came up, saying that if I could do any good by telling Mama anything he might wish her to know (as in one of his latter letters he had seemed to express) I should be most happy when next at Burghwallis, where I thought we might find ourselves in ten days. To this I received for answer that he begged to decline seeing us for the present. So here Charles and I are, also banished! And now we shall not go to Yorkshire at all, the only idea when I consented being that I thought I might be some use at Burghwallis. As for what I said in my last letter to you about Bab and William, I may have expressed myself rather too severely; but it was with the hope of discouraging her as much as possible, for I am persuaded they never can marry, at least not under present circumstances; and how those can be changed without utter ruin to all I fail to see. My whole aim was from a pure motive of trying to enlighten Bab as to facts, so as to break to her the utter impossibility, and so make it fall lighter when the real truth comes out. I should advise her to go back to Hainton with you, where surely she is quiet and not every minute goaded and sighed into misery; for how well I can imagine it! Every one of us always so comfortably in the wrong too, excepting brother George, of course. I do think it very hard on Mama too, never to be cheered for one single instant by seeing any one of us; I am sure it is enough to drive her mad. In his letter to me Papa was furious about Barbara's going home. He said that notwithstanding all the fine talk she was turned out of Hainton at last!! Can you imagine such wilful perversion? As if he was not detected instantly! But pray do not repeat this, for otherwise I shall never be allowed to go back to Burghwallis. I only tell you to show how he can twist and twirl a thing for his own purpose. As for my going and speaking to old Charlton, what in the name of goodness would you have me say to him? I really cannot go begging for a husband for my sister; I think that would be rather beneath her dignity and ours, while as for all the rest, does not old Charlton know it as well as we do? Perhaps I may meet the Charltons at Lady Constable's concert tomorrow night. If so, and I am given an opening, I will speak as my reason shows me best. Do not say anything to hurt poor Barbara from me, as I am sure the last thing I wish is to add to her worries; but I did think that last letter for her good, as I fancied that you were too inclined to encourage the keeping on of the engagement." And now that I have told you what Mary says let me tell you, dearest child, something more agreeable, and which it gives me as much pleasure to tell you as it will give you to hear. Aunt Anne desires me to tell you that if you do marry *she* will help you, as far as she can, by allowing you something to enable you to live; that you must not expect any very great thing during her lifetime, but that you may depend on her doing as much as she can, and this you may tell William. I am so very, very happy at this, so cheer up, my dearest Bab. My George received your letter and all were much pleased. You may always depend on our taking your part and helping you whenever we can. Only think of Papa refusing to see Mary! What next will he do? I expect to hear from you to-night and shall not close this till after post time. I suppose you saw the letter I wrote to Mama; I thought it would please her. What did she say? Your

letter has just come, my dear Bab, and it has quite bewildered us so that we know not what to think. We are
all most anxious, and whatever you do *say not a word*, for
you will not repent afterwards having done it. It does
though appear hard at present, not being able to confide
in Mama. God bless you, with every kind wish and love
from all.

'Believe me, your sincerely affectionate sister,

'FANNY.'

'The last part of Fanny's letter referred to a determination
William and I had come to. We had turned over in our
heads every feasible plan for getting married privately,
naturally wishing to go through the Catholic ceremony first.
The Catholic chapel in Doncaster would have served our
purpose, but unfortunately it was not licensed for marriages.
At last, finding every scheme of the sort impracticable
owing to the strict surveillance under which I was kept at
home, William offered me, as our only possible means of
union, "a trip over the Border." He entreated me to manage
it from my end and, as will be seen from the following
letters, this I did, largely assisted by our village confidant,
Mrs. Firth, our bailiff's wife. William wrote from London
on June 13th as follows:

MY DEAR, DEAREST BARBARA, – Thanks, a thousand
thanks, for your most satisfactory letter. I rejoice to tell
you, my own dearest love, that your plan seems most
simple and feasible, and that I shall carry out my part
most implicitly. I will then, dearest, be punctual to the
day, the *place* and *hour* which you have decided upon, and
I have already secured my place in the mail. I am so
afraid of this letter being intercepted by your father that
I think it will scarcely be safe to repeat the letter of your
instructions; let me only assure you that I shall be at the
appointed place and hour. Soon, dearest, you will be

mine for ever! Oh! what joy will be ours! Rely, dearest, on me as upon yourself; indeed our minds and hearts seem to go so much in unison that I sometimes doubt if we are two distinct persons!!! I heard first of Mrs. Anne's kind offer from your sister Mary, whom I have seen several times of late, and yesterday, according to your desire, I wrote a grateful letter to the generous old lady which I hope will please her. I quite agree with you in thinking that *all* will soon be disclosed with regard to your mother's affairs; indeed, your present silence is most heroic and I do not wonder that you have gained praise by it. Let the Great Step be once taken and matters will settle down smoothly afterwards. I will not forget to secure the licence for London only. Remember, no human being can possibly hinder our marriage, so we may set all opposition at defiance. I can think of little or nothing but you, my dearest girl. Nobody here has any suspicion. I hope all will be equally safe with you. I was not in the least surprised at your father's letter to your mother; he evidently cannot bear the thought that she should assist us in any way. Depend upon it, dearest, that our good sense and tact will carry us triumphantly through. We must be careful to implicate no one, but take the blame entirely upon ourselves. I shall not forget the ring. And now, my own dearest love, I must conclude. How I long to meet you to press you to my heart, where your image always dwells. Pray for yourself, pray for me, and believe me heart and soul now and hereafter to remain,

'Your most devoted and affectionate,
'WILLIAM.'

'Before I give the other two letters from my sisters I will describe our runaway marriage, and my first introduction to my husband's people.

'I was worn out with anxiety and fatigue, and on the

H

afternoon of June 19th, I fell asleep in my mother's room, sleeping the sleep of the innocent, to her utter amazement, through a terrific storm. I had been short of sleep all during that time at home as all letters had to be taken to the post before my father was up. I had always been on friendly terms with the villagers and I put especial trust in Mrs. Firth, who found means to send my letters to London untampered with, and to whom letters for me were sent under cover in a feigned hand. In that way my father's cunning was completely outmanœuvred, while all the time he was flattering himself that he had gained his end. I was greatly grieved to leave my poor, long-suffering mother, who had been so unvariedly kind to me. I hardly know how I kept from breaking down. She always went to bed early, and after kissing her as usual on parting for the night I retired to my own room, locked myself in, and changed my light-coloured summer frock for one of a dark *cachemire*.

'As for the watch-dog that was kennelled under my bedroom window to keep guard over my slumbers, the good Mrs. Firth gave it some harmless drug which removed the danger from that direction. At half-past eleven I lit up my room, opened wide the window, and sat down to wait. At a quarter to midnight, on Wednesday the 19th June, William was under my window, having posted from Doncaster and left the chaise at the end of the lane so that the noise of wheels should not disturb the house. I threw my soft bundle of belongings out of the window, and then by means of torn-up sheets fastened to a heavy, old-fashioned sofa, I swung out and, wonderful to say, got down without a scratch. We ran for our lives to where the chaise was standing, the object of getting posters from Doncaster instead of from Robin Hood's Well (only a mile from Burghwallis) being to leave no clew behind for pursuit in the morning.

'We posted through the night, and all next day, until we reached the Blacksmith's house at Gretna Green at 6 p.m. on the evening of June 20th, when we became man and wife. The wily old blacksmith, recognizing the name of Charlton and well-knowing that William was heir to two Cumberland estates as well as that of Hesleyside in Northumberland, charged us £20 for his services, which for us runaways was a heavy charge enough, and drained our ready cash. Luckily, I had with me my jewels, very handsome and chiefly presents from my sister Fanny, and the next day I pawned them in Carlisle. The jeweller shrewdly guessed that the pledges would be likely very soon to be redeemed, and, without haggling over the price, gave us for them a very liberal sum. It was only later that we heard my brother George had set out after us on horseback, and had given up the chase at Barnside Bar.

'I wrote to Mama and Fanny from Carlisle, having previously left a note on my bedroom table before quitting Burghwallis. As fast as wheels and steam could convey us, we transplanted ourselves to London, where it was our intention to be remarried before William's father had been told of our union. We drove straight to the hotel which I had previously announced to my sister Fanny as the place of our stay, and there I received her letter of the 22nd June which I give in full. Her brother-in-law, Edward Heneage, who was also in the know, called there at 11 a.m. on the day of our arrival. But we had not been many hours in London when Mrs. Clayton came and whisked us off to her house in Portman Square. All necessary arrangements were quickly made for our remarriage the following day in the Protestant church close by, where the ceremony, funny to relate, was performed by a Rev. Mr. Charlton. I was attired in Mrs. Clayton's pink muslin dress (far too big for me), the witnesses being Mr. and Mrs. Clayton, Edward Heneage, and Mr. Rich, M.P., the same who at one time had fixed his attentions on my sister Mary.

'In the course of the morning William declared the case to his father, who was nothing wrathful; and as for his mother, whose whole married life had been passed in brooding over a particular grievance and who had not the capacity to entertain another as well, she was now so absorbed in the iniquity of her eldest daughter's recent engagement to a Welsh widower, of whom she highly disapproved, that she hardly gave a thought to our escapade.

'I looked with the utmost astonishment on my mother-in-law, whose face reflected long years of melancholy. Miss Cayley, *l'amie chérie* of all the Cholmeleys, Tasburghs, Fairfaxes, etc., told me that Mrs. Charlton, who had been a Miss Katherine Cholmeley of Brandsby, Yorks, was never pretty, but that when young she was a fine-looking person; and this I was forced to believe, as Miss Cayley always spoke the truth. Mrs. Charlton was now fifty years of age and had grown extremely coarse in every detail. Such an antependium I never saw before. But she did possess a very good nose, which sat in the middle of her face like a nymph surrounded by satyrs. After promising to dine with my new family, William and I returned to Portman Square.

'This is the letter from my dear Fanny, written from York on June 22nd:

'My dearest Child, – I have received your letter from Carlisle and long to fly to you, and I have sent it on to Mary, who is nearer, hoping that she may do so. I cannot here enter into any details of what my feelings were yesterday on hearing you had left Burghwallis, nor will I upbraid you with doubting for one minute our readiness to receive you both at Hainton; and now, by

George's desire, I write to request that you will come down to us immediately and remain till such time as you are comfortably ready to go abroad; it will be the only way in which you can repay what you call the kindness you have received from us. We shall now go straight home on Tuesday, and last night I wrote to Mama begging her to meet us at Doncaster for luncheon; and rest assured George will do all he can to serve you both with her; he has written to his brother Edward to call upon you immediately and entrusted him with a draft for £100 to give to William. And Aunt Anne is writing to you herself, and has given George directions to pay through Wright the banker £500 to your account. Aunt Anne and Miss Gage desire their kindest love, and are deeply interested in all that happens to you. I have been this morning to order my little present for you, and I think the plate chest will be very complete and just what you will require. When you have a moment to spare, just send me William's crest. And now, my dearest Barbara, let me again entreat you to make Hainton your home for the present; it is George's as well as my most earnest wish you should do so. I send this under cover to Edward begging he will deliver it immediately, for I shall be in such a state of excitement till I hear you have received it. Mrs. Bland was here to-day, and on being told of the event said, "I am very glad of it," a sentiment that appears indeed to represent the general feeling. She desired her very best and kindest wishes for both your happiness, and your healths were drunk in a bumper. George Meynell, who dined here, was in high force and said, "May they live a thousand years!" I must now say goodbye, my dearest child, and with our united kind love to William,

'Believe me, dearest sister,
'Yours most affectionately,
'Fanny Heneage.

'When we went to dinner with the Charltons in Montagu Street I found my mother-in-law ready dressed for an evening party and reception afterwards, but her two daughters quite unready and in great perplexity at their mother having sent the lady's maid off to the theatre without any consideration for them. "Never mind," I said, laughing. "I have learnt to do hair and I can help you as well as any maid." So after dinner I did so, while Mary told me all about her engagement to a widower of no wealth who had one child. She also confided to me that her mother was apt to have queer moods when she entirely forgot the very existence of her children, an example of which I had just been witness to. I own I was horrified at such a revelation of egotism on the part of both mistress and maid, the latter being an ill-conditioned Irishwoman who always took advantage of her mistress's shortcomings.

'We had the greatest difficulty in getting a priest to marry us in London; not on account of our escapade, but for the reason, if you please, that our great-grandmothers, Teresa and Isabel Swinburne, were sisters, and also, perhaps, a little on account of the Protestant ceremony having preceded the Catholic one. Mrs. Charlton and Mrs. Riddell threw themselves with zest into the good cause and at last, between them, unearthed a Jesuit, Mr. Lythgoe, the one solitary Jesuit then in London, who consented to perform the Catholic ceremony privately in his room. So we became linked together by three marriage ceremonies, one Scotch, one Protestant, and one Catholic.

'Here is my sister Mary's letter on my marriage, written from the Hotel Clarendon, Leamington:

'MY DEAREST BARBARA, – I have this moment read your letter from Carlisle to Fanny, which she sent me. So you *are* married, actually! My dearest Bab, may you be very, very happy, I am sure you will believe how earnestly I make this prayer, and I cannot say what pleasure it will give me to hear it from yourself, which I doubt not in the least I shall. Most unfortunately, I cannot meet you in London as Papa desired us to be at Burghwallis on Wednesday for dinner, and as I have written to say we should I *dare* not disappoint him – otherwise most happy would I have been to have gone to you in London. We leave Leamington to-morrow evening and go straight to Burghwallis. I send you what linen I can spare and hope it will help you a little. Fanny tells me that Aunt Anne has sent you a very handsome remittance. I must tell you what I have set my heart upon – which is that you should live close to, or in, York. I am convinced you could well do so quietly, and I think you would both like it better than going to Germany; and I am sure I should like you better in York than ever so far away. Mama tells me that Papa fainted away when told of your flight. However, don't be alarmed; he is better now, and both from his short note to Aunt Anne and our brother's to me, which would be but an echo, I do not feel you need fear any anger. But how I do dread going there. Oh! what sighs and moans! Pray write a line to me if you can find time. God bless you, my dearest sister, and your husband also, and that you may be very, very happy is the sincere wish of your ever affectionate sister,

'MARY B. FAIRFAX.

'On Thursday, June 27th, Fanny wrote from Hainton to say that Mama met them at Doncaster on the Tuesday as requested and was most kind, doing everything immediately suggested to her by George Heneage on our behalf in the most handsome and certain manner. It was left to George and his lawyers, Farrers & Co., to carry out her instructions, and the deeds were put in train that very day, in result of which the sum of £14,000, secured on the Crathorne estate, was to be settled at once on me, and subsequently a like amount on my two sisters. "I have got," said Fanny in the same letter, "Harriet Cholmeley's present for you here; a magnificent Missal, fit only for a bride!"

'My mother sent off all my goods and chattels to Hainton and set about getting me a trousseau of linen made. Rather a case of the day after the fair. On leaving our kind and more than hospitable friends at 14 Portman Square we went straight down to Hainton, remaining there until August 8th, on which date we commenced the journey by rail and sea to William's home in Northumberland. Mama, Aunt Anne and Miss Gage, the latter's sister, came down to Hainton to see us there before we left. My mother never returned to Burghwallis, but made Crathorne her future residence. She did not press my father for arrears or upbraid him in any way. She had far too generous a nature. But henceforth she received the rents herself in person, and remained at her old family home until her death in 1844. After this separation my father lived mostly on the Continent, returning ever and anon to England. He died eventually abroad. I can here affirm that I never heard my mother say one unkind or ungenerous word about my father after she parted from him. Like to her forefathers, she was large-hearted and generous-minded. When, in the summer of 1840, she came to Hesleyside to sign my deed of settlement, my mother-in-law stubbornly set to work to vilify my father in her estimation, instigating her, among other things, to claim from him seven years of arrears; but Mrs. Charlton completely failed in her endeavour. Poor Mrs. Charlton! Her dominant fault of jealousy added bitterness to her sad life.'

XI

ARRIVAL AT HESLEYSIDE

FROM Newcastle-on-Tyne the last stage of the bridal journey was necessarily performed by road, at least half of it alongside the Roman Wall as far as Chollerford, as it then was; Humshaugh now. After passing through the quiet little village of Wark, distant six miles from Barbara's new home, her husband could have told her that the fields and farms, and the heather-lands, extending far on either side of the rough, unmetalled way were a part of his inheritance, belonging to the Hesleyside estate, and that she was on ancestral property. Some little distance further on the cumbrous travelling carriage topped a rise, from which, had Barbara cared to call a halt, an unbroken, middle-distance view of the hall, its woods and its demesne might have been obtained. In truth, her eyes took in a very different landscape from that to which she was accusomed in the part of Yorkshire neighbouring on Burghwallis.

The North Tyne, which has a breadth of from 60 to 100 feet in the Hesleyside vicinity, has a shingly bed and a rippling flow, except where boulder-strewn and where occasional deeps serve to calm the surface of its waters. The valley through which it runs, North Tynedale in the language of the Border, has a fair width viewed in relation to the surrounding country and bottom lands of fair fertility. But soon, on either side, it begins to shelve upwards from the river-bed to be contained within bold sweeps of moorland, bare of all save heather, bent grass and stunted tree growth, down the slopes of which numerous fussy, spring-fed burns hasten to join their parent stream below. These moorland slopes have no great height or steepness and are only rarely marked by rocky outcrops or an abrupt cliff-face; but they have a massiveness instead, an assertion of eternity, as it were, and an appearance to the observing eye as of horizon on horizon endlessly extending in the self-same bulky and insistent way. They are bleak and unromatic; but they possess a placid beauty which is peculiarly their own.

Hesleyside itself, the lands of which to a large extent possess this scenery, stands a little back from the river on its right-hand side, sited on a haugh of semicircular shape which forms part of the demesne. The hall bursts on the view at close approach, and graciously presents itself to the beholder's eye; solid, three-storied and four-square; of freestone weathered to a mellow grey; backed by an extensive wood of tall trees, beech, oak, elm, lime, pine, planted on rising ground in the style of an amphitheatre; with a pebbly burn frothing along to mark the boundary between park and pleasure ground.

At rare intervals, on the valley slopes and on the heights above, stood sturdy, stone-built farmsteads with substantial barns and byres adjacent or adjoining, protected on the weather side by wind-belts of fir and pine. Two miles downstream from Hesleyside the small town of Bellingham, no more than an overgrown village in Barbara's day, stands in a rugged and homely fashion on a fine stretch of the Tyne. Facing the hall on the opposite bank of the river is Charlton, part of the Bellingham township, where the Hesleyside family was established in more ancient days. It is not a populous district, though signs are not wanting that it was more thickly inhabited before the coming of law and order.

'On the 8th August, 1839, we went to Hull by rail and thence by sea to Newcastle-on-Tyne *en route* for Hesleyside,

Hesleyside from the south today.

Hesleyside from the east in 1825. Drawn by J. P. Neale and engraved by
J. C. Varrell for *Views of Seats of Noblemen and Gentlemen* by J. P. Neale
(2nd Series, Vol II, 1825).

which we reached on the 11th, after sleeping the previous night at Newcastle. William's two brothers, Edward and Frank, met us in Newcastle and came on to Hesleyside separately on the 12th. The tenants and estate workmen were anxious to drag us in from the Bellingham turn to the hall, about a mile, but Mrs. Charlton put a damper on it by begging they would do no such thing. I arrived at my new home on a rainy afternoon; not an uncommon occurrence in that moist region.

'On our arrival the family came to the front entrance to meet and welcome us, consisting of Mr. and Mrs. Charlton, their two daughters Mary and Kate, the two younger boys, Tom and Henry, home from Ushaw for the holidays, and, last but not least, emerging from the library, an aristocratic-looking, octogenarian lady with a thin, straight, graceful figure and lovely features, who burst out crying when she greeted me, her pleasure was so great on welcoming my mother's daughter as a bride of Hesleyside. To my great astonishment, she spoke the broadest Northumbrian, this being the first occasion on which I had heard that peculiar, sing-song accent, and it seemed so strange hearing it for the first time from a lady looking like a duchess and speaking like a cook! But it was not long before I learnt to love that historical burr, immortalized by Shakespeare in Henry IV, Part 2, when he makes Lady Percy say of her brother Hotspur:

'And speaking thick, which nature made his blemish,
Became the accents of the valiant.

'With the mention of this remarkable and comely old lady, who was Miss Catherine Fenwick, then aged eighty-three, I must introduce into my recital an account of the important part played by her sister and herself, last remnants of the long line of Catholic Fenwicks, in the welfare of Hesleyside; for what with the penal laws, cockering up the Pretender, ancestral extravagance and, alas! the undying vice of drink, the estate was on the verge of ruin a generation or so back.

'In the year 1778 William Charlton, the then inebriate and hardly responsible Squire of Hesleyside, married Margaret, daughter of John Fenwick, M.D., of Morpeth, himself the youngest son of the Fenwick of Longframlington. Margaret had a sister Catherine, the old lady with the burr in her speech, and two brothers, both of whom followed in their father's footsteps and became doctors, and both of whom, I regret to say, apostasized from their religion.

'Many Catholics joined the medical profession. It should be remembered that, in order to break up the old Catholic families, the penal laws excluded them from the liberal professions, thus shutting them out from Parliament, the Magistracy, voting at elections, holding public office, keeping school and teaching in any way, so that they were driven to become farmers, merchants, or doctors.

'It became a usual proceeding to send the children of well-to-do Catholic families abroad, often under a feigned name, there to receive an education which at best was scanty and limited in scope. For many a long year Catholics were obliged to pay a double land tax, my own father being one of the first landowners to have this iniquity redressed, and besides that they had to keep their own priests and pay the parson too. Is it any wonder that they became impoverished while the penal laws were in force? In the risings of '15 and '45 most of the propertied Catholic families of the North deeded their estates to Protestant friends and relations, and right royally, when danger had gone by, did these redeem their trusts, for bad blood between neighbours of different religious belief in Northumberland during those dark days was hardly ever known – the case of Sir William Middleton of Belsay apart. A great many conformists were Jacobites themselves and extended a helping hand towards the prescribed Catholics, the new-made Protestant gentry, from those troublous times to the present day, ever holding the old Catholic families in great respect. But as regards Sir William Middleton, it was always said that he seized the then Mr. Charlton of Hesleyside's horses for a legal compensation of £5 a head, no matter what their real value, not from loyalty to the House of Hanover, but out of private ill will towards the owner.

'I was told by old Miss Catherine Fenwick, who was my husband's great-aunt, that when the Public Prosecutor visited Hesleyside in search of arms they used to conceal the guns and swords and other weapons in the curtains, which then rolled up like blinds instead of drawing aside. The octogenarian old lady had heard all the particulars of those stormy times at first hand from her sister's predecessor, that Teresa Swinburne, daughter of Sir John Swinburne of Capheaton, Co. Northumberland, who married Edward Charlton of Hesleyside, my husband's great-great-grandfather. More revealing still is the ample correspondence of this said Teresa with Sir Francis Delaval of Seaton Delaval, conducted from Hesleyside, which was brought to light at Ford Castle, once belonging to the Delavals, and eventually found its way by purchase into my husband's hands. Sir Francis although he sided with the House of Hanover, was none the less extremely devoted, in Teresa Charlton's time, to the house of Hesleyside, where his portrait still hangs, painted with a greyhound by his side, one of his own famous breed, for fox-hunting as a field sport was then in its infancy. All the letters between Teresa and Sir Francis were conveyed by private messenger on horseback to and from Hesleyside and Seaton Delaval, some thirty odd miles across a roadless country largely consisting of moor. Sometimes Sir Francis came himself to Hesleyside for a stay, on which occasions he would bring his friend, Samuel Foote, the dramatist and actor, who very likely had a professional engagement in Edinburgh.

'In those days no post was established in North Tyne and all the usual methods of communication were unsafe. At the time of the '15, the two Miss Swinburnes of Capheaton, who must have been Teresa's aunts, rode to and fro across the Border carrying rebel despatches, and so earned the nickname of "The Capheaton Gallopers." Even when I came to Hesleyside as late as 1839 the post only came twice a week, and that only as far as Bellingham. But my active and public-spirited husband soon put that matter right.

'In spite of no roads and an inebriate husband, Teresa Charlton seems to have carried on a fairly lively existence. She and her sister Isabel, my Crathorne great-grandmother, were by repute a particularly accomplished pair. They could strum a simple tune on a spinette, they were good at needlework, very cleverly made their own satin shoes, and were not without some small artistic talent; but best of all were they at horsemanship. They were both well favoured with good looks until Teresa caught the smallpox and lost all her beauty, in consequence of which, rumour had it, her husband made her wear a mask. An old woman cottager who lived at Hesleyside, and who knew Teresa both before and after her disfigurement, told me she was so badly marked as to be unrecognizable, and that she felt her misfortune most bitterly.

'For four generations, from father to son, a Dixon managed the affairs of the Hesleyside estate as agent, the first of

the name coming as under-agent in 1780 to live at Mantle
Hill, a little house halfway up a hill that overlooked the back
of the hall and was distant half a mile from it. Until then the
business side of the estate was overseen by Mr. Gibson, a
solicitor in Hexham. This first Dixon to become agent –
John was his name – was descended from that Thomas
Dixon who was the friend and tenant of Sir James Douglas,
and his grandmother, who died at Mantle Hill in her
ninetieth year, was a niece of Thomas Forster the rebel
general who led the Northumbrian Jacobites in the Old
Pretender's rising. Two of her brothers, John and Leonard
Hunter, suffered the extreme penalty at Preston after the
defeat of General Forster and his surrender to the King's
forces. The old lady had always been an enthusiastic
Jacobite and had sacrificed her beautiful hair to be made
into a wig for Charles Radclyffe, Earl of Derwentwater.

'Teresa, Mrs. Charlton, whose husband died in 1767,
was living as a widow with her only son at Mantle Hill,
when John Dixon was made agent, that small house having
become her temporary residence after a disastrous fire at
Hesleyside, the second of the sort that had occurred. An
old prophecy ran to the effect that Hesleyside would be
twice burnt and once sunk, and the last of the three fore-
tellings is not unlikely to be accomplished some day, considering it is built on a bog.

'Mr. MacDonald, who was under-agent before John
Dixon, lived at Goldisland, an outlying farm belonging to
the estate not far from Wark. He was a Roman Catholic,
and in his house, in the year 1778, William Charlton,
Teresa's only child, was married to Margaret Fenwick
according to the rites of the Old Faith, the couple having
previously undergone the marriage ceremony at Chollerton
Parish Church.

'Mrs. (Fenwick) Charlton was *une maitresse femme*, the only one that ever reigned at Hesleyside, a woman so clear-headed, and of such extraordinary ability and energy, that she grasped in a very short time the intricacies and the entanglement of the estate's affairs. Like the valiant woman she was, she thought no sacrifice too great to ensure, with the stout help of John Dixon who was a man stamped in the same character, a clear rent-roll at the coming of age of her only child William John Charlton, my father-in-law, who was born on May 6th, 1784. By sheer skill and intelligence she succeeded in so doing and was rightfully known as the saviour of Hesleyside. Not only was she hard-headed but, like most of her race, she was hard-natured as well. In feature she was particularly plain, but in 1831, when she came on a short visit to Burghwallis, her straight, slim, stately figure was still unbent by age. Both she and her spinster sister, Catherine, who greeted me on my arrival as a bride, threw their little all into a fund to help straighten out the affairs of the estate, and in return for this generosity the latter received a pension for her life and lived at Hesleyside as a member of the family. The hall in those days of non-development was in simple terms an oasis surrounded by moorland and swamp, roads, bridges, and all other means of facilitating communication being conspicuous by their absence.

'My father-in-law's early education was entirely under the superintendence of his masterful Mama, who was not only an extremely clever woman, but a tolerably well-educated one as well. At school age he was sent to Stonyhurst but did not stay there long. After two years he represented to his mother that there were certain rules laid down by the school authorities to which, as a gentleman's son and a boy of honour, he could not adhere. His mother instantly removed him and he never went to any other school, but had for tutor and travelling companion Henry Clifford, second son of the Honourable Thomas Clifford and his wife Barbara Aston, daughter of the last Lord Aston. This gentleman later earned the sobriquet of O.P. (Old Price) Clifford, having implicated himself in the riots which occurred at the opening of the New Covent Garden Theatre in 1809 over the question of the charge for seats. For nearly three months the case was contested between the managers and public, and was only terminated when the former gave way and returned to the old prices.

'In the late spring of 1803, when my father-in-law was nineteen years old and when, it may be presumed, the affairs of the estate were on a satisfactory footing, four travellers set out from London on a more extensive Continental tour than is usual nowadays in our luxurious times. They took their own travelling carriage and in it sat, with their faces to the horses, Mrs. (Fenwick) Charlton and her sister Catherine, both dressed in short riding habits and riding hats, unencumbered by the mountains of luggage which are necessary now; and, with their backs to the horses, sat the young squire and his much-loved tutor, Henry Clifford, the former close under his mother's eye. In this way they traversed a great deal of Europe and visited many capitals, including Berlin, Dresden, Vienna, Venice, Copenhagen and St. Petersburg, the whole tour taking more than two years of very rough going. I am still in possession of some exquisitely fine Moravian spun table-linen which Mrs. Charlton brought back with her. The young squire returned to England a first-class linguist. In after years he always spoke with the greatest reverence and affection of his tutor, describing him as a delightful companion and as brave as a lion. It undoubtedly required intelligence and bravery to

I

undertake the protection of two ladies, one of whom was exceedingly good-looking, on a tour of such extent, not to mention the anxious care for a youth who was an only son, during an unsettled period of history.

'Even in early days my father-in-law must have been a well-informed man and, before he grew to manhood, earned the nickname of "The Walking Encyclopedia of the North." But he certainly did not combine learning with respect for antiquity, and seemed to take pleasure in destroying the works of his forbears. As an instance, he did away with an ornamental fish-pond at Hesleyside, situated to the south-east of the big, harp-shaped lawn, and quite unnecessarily he knocked to pieces the statuary surrounding it. One he did spare for some reason, a female monkey nursing its young, which stood for a long time in a snug corner of the south front until my husband, as late as 1856, had it placed, with fragments of some others repaired as best could be, on the roof-parapet of the hall. This fish-pond was the creation of William Charlton, High Sheriff of Northumberland in 1722, whose taste ran to expensive innovations and alterations and who was better known as *Run-away Willie* because in very truth he outran the constable.

'While my father-in-law was still a boy the famous White Hall lawsuit was fought to a successful conclusion, John Dixon being the moving spirit in the matter. After much probing, John Dixon came to the conclusion that his youthful employer could lay rightful claim to the White Hall estate in Cumberland, a valuable and paying property for long in possession of the Salkeld family, but at the time without a direct heir. The Charlton claim rested on proof being given of a marriage between Edward Charlton of Hesleyside and Margaret, daughter of Sir Francis Salkeld of White Hall, in the year 1680, the opposing side stoutly

contesting the fact. At long last, after much journeying to
and fro, much sifting of evidence, and a great outpouring of
money, the claim was finally established at a cost to the
winning side of £20,000. Of this enormous sum £17,000
was raised by the sale to the Lonsdale interests of Blenner-
hasset Manor as far as concerned the mineral and manorial
rights, the manor being part of the property in dispute. It
was a very shortsighted policy and conducted by the
Carlisle solicitor in a haphazard manner, for rich deposits
were found under the land which, on development, brought
in something like £40,000 a year.

'My father-in-law, William John Charlton, was a
gentlemanly-looking, rather short man, with very plain
features relieved by the brilliancy of a pair of small eyes.
He had the features of his mother, a bad nose and a bad
mouth, the most sarcastic, disagreeable, sneering mouth I
ever saw. He had high shoulders and a round back, but an
undeniably good-shaped leg and foot. His teeth had decayed
when he was in his early teens, and he had a false set very
early in life. In 1809, at the age of twenty-five, he married
Katherine Henrietta Cholmeley, daughter of Francis
Cholmeley of Brandsby, Co. Yorks, and soon afterwards
lost all his former spirits, to sink gradually into a recluse
state, buried in his books.

'It was a sad story, the details of which I hold from my
mother, from Nancy Dixon, aunt to the Hesleyside agent
of my day, and above all from Miss Cayley, a cousin of Sir
George Cayley of Brompton, Yorks, who invented Cayley's
flying model in 1796.

'I have already written of Philadelphia Cayley as *l'amie
chérie* of the Cholmeleys, Tasburghs, Fairfaxes, and other
families tied together by religion and relationship. In spite
of the fact that she was a Unitarian, no less a person than

Doctor William Howley, Archbishop of Canterbury from 1828 to 1848, was anxious to marry Miss Cayley in her youth; but she lived and died single. Hers was a notable personality and, in spite of the many confidences she received, she never betrayed a trust or assisted to make bad blood among her countless friends. In all sickness, sorrow or turmoil it was always Philadelphia who was sent for to nurse, comfort and be asked for her advice. She was both intelligent and accomplished, and so scrupulously truthful that in the case of doubtful rumour or report people would say, "Oh! if Phil Cayley said so, then it must be true."

'Long before William and I met I had constantly heard my mother and Phil Cayley discussing his mother's unfortunate condition, and what they then said coincided exactly with what I heard from others later. Mrs. Charlton's mother was the beautiful Miss Englefield, sister to the very last baronet of that name, for Sir Henry never married and only left an illegitimate son behind him. Althought she was very highly educated and could make herself most agreeable to men, she was absolutely devoid of common sense, and had not sufficient intellect to accept advancing age as an inescapable fact nor the mental balance to suffer the decay of beauty, owing to smallpox, *en grande Dame*. A gentleman who had been an habitué of Brandsby in her reign told me it was painful to go and see her when she was a widow living in York, for all she did was to fall on his neck, cry bitterly, and bewail the loss of her beauty and position.

'As her daughter Katherine, who became my mother-in-law, was also wholly devoid of common sense I naturally concluded that she had inherited the deficiency from her mother. Phil Cayley told me that Mrs. Charlton, when a girl, was threatened with softening of the brain, one reason that her mother was so anxious to marry her off, and there was great jubilation at Brandsby when so valuable a prize as the young Squire of Hesleyside was caught. My father-in-law made no pretence of having fallen in love, his chief desire being, in response to the lesson so often inculcated by his mother, to procure a wife who was likely to produce children. At Brandsby, to quote his own words, there were four coarse, red-armed girls, sure to breed, and one of them he took.

'But there was a *revers de la medaille*! His mother, by whose sole effort the property was again on its feet, had in the most careful and anxious manner cautioned her son against marrying into certain Catholic families, and here it had happened that the one she had reason most to dread had entrapped him. It is not surprising that she wailed and gnashed her teeth. But in vain; things had gone too far for withdrawal; and only when it was too late did her son repent him of ungrateful behaviour towards so perfect a mother as his had been to him. Poor Katherine! It would have been better for her own happiness and for the welfare of many had she never entered a family the female head of which regarded her with loathing and contempt. During the first three or four years of her married life especially, she had most difficult cards to play, and a situation so hard to contend with that it would have broken down a brain healthier than hers. Her husband, for instance, promised his mother and aunt, old Katherine Fenwick, that they should live on at Hesleyside after his marriage, and rash was the promise that he made! He knew only of the hardy, self-sacrificing side of his mother's character, and had never experienced its cruel, agressive aspect. Home came the bride! But no word of welcome greeted her on arrival. She was shown to her room, for all the world as if Hesleyside were an hotel, and informed of the hours of the establishment in a dry, sententious manner. In addition, she came from a civilized part, where neighbours lived within the compass of a drive, and where the roads were tolerably well made. Now she found herself in an almost roadless district, entirely cut off from the social world.

'Almost up to the commencement of my time the roads in North Tyne were little more than tracks, following along the sides of fields with a gate at every boundary fence, with, ever and anon, a large stretch of common intervening which was nothing more than roadless heatherland, swampy in parts and treacherous underfoot, so that horses plunged through as best they could. The farmers, in their tenancy agreements, bound themselves to go twice yearly into New-castle, nearly forty miles, and carry out two horse loads, sixteen stone in each, of whatever was required at the hall. When the Hesleyside family went away by carriage, or returned home from a journey, the nearby farmers, up to the end of the last century, brought oxen to drag the heavy conveyance over Ealingham Rig, a boggy hill halfway between Wark and Bellingham. But every lady and gentleman was, of course, an expert rider and thought nothing of going long distances on horseback. Those ladies' maids accompanying their mistresses who were not equestrian sat perched on pillions, and saddle-bags accommodated an immense quantity of luggage.

'From Wark onwards, during her bridal journey, my mother-in-law had been greatly depressed by mile on mile of unreclaimed land, with only a rough cart track for the postilion's guidance, so that the chilling reception she received on arrival from the "Two Spirit-breaking Hags," by which name she designated her husband's mother and aunt, completely broke her down.

'It must be admitted that the spirit-breaking hags had themselves mostly to blame for the unfortunate alliance, seeing that they incessantly instilled into the young heir's mind that the inheritance hung on his life alone, and that he must not fail to marry a wife who had the appearance of a good breeder. In regard to this requisite, it must also be admitted, poor Katherine fulfilled every expectation, for she gave birth to twelve children, eight boys and four girls, of which number six, four boys and two girls, died either in infancy or at a very early age. It has been observed that the Charltons of the succeeding generation were conspicuous more for intellectuality than for amiability. If true, it is hardly to be wondered at, although poor Katherine herself was remarkably good-tempered. But who is there to disbelieve that the treatment she underwent, the harshness and cruelties of those two older women, supported on occasion by their brothers, and the patent, though galling, fact that her husband respected his mother's wishes more than those of his wife, had not a bad influence on the character of the poor creature's progeny?

'I had it all from her own mouth. Her new home was made wretched to her by constant insult and continual worry, her husband, all the time, not daring to raise his voice in protest for fear of incurring the displeasure of his mother. In spite of being so supremely miserable she was most anxious lest a rumour of her sad condition should reach the ear of her widowed mother, who was herself in fretful mood. There can be no doubt that Katherine Charlton, throughout her life, never completely recovered from the cruel humiliations that were heaped upon her.

'Should she sit reading in her own room for the sake of peace and quiet, then her mother-in-law would rout the poor woman out in double-quick time, impressing her destiny on her in words to this effect: "You will never breed if you mope over your books. My son, remember, only married you because you looked to be a good breeder." She was never allowed by her two elders to companion her husband, his own mother laying sole claim to that prerogative. In their walks it was the mother and son who always linked arms together, the wife being left to the other woman, who loathed the sight of her. And always was she forced to listen to the coarse-bred sentiment, asserted by the one and echoed by the other, that her business was to breed. One day she did retort, saying sharply, "I suppose I am tolerated by you two in this house only as a tame animal kept for breeding purposes?" And the answer, coming simultaneously from both, was "Just so!" And yet, what with those twelve children in the course of sixteen years, her natural tendency to increase and multiply should have conciliated the spirit-breakers. My husband's birth on October 22nd, 1809, a year almost to a day after Katherine Charlton's marriage, should have propitiated the *hags*, and at the same time comforted the poor mother. But my mother-in-law was never fond of children until they were old enough to be taught, and then her egoistic self came to the fore, and she applied herself to their instruction so as to gain reflected credit from their advancement.

'As proof of the thraldom of her existence, this incident, one of her many painful recollections, comes to mind. Her sister was staying at Hesleyside and, being in a cowed and timid state, she got her to ask her husband for leave to have a dressing-room of her own. "Yes," said he; "by all means if she can obtain consent." "But surely, Mr. Charlton," the sister said, unfortunately in the hearing of his mother, "your wife is mistress in her own house!" Whereupon the mother burst out, saying that they were all in a conspiracy to insult her, then and there insisting that her son should go down on his knees to beg her pardon.

'About two years after the marriage of my parents, which was in the same year, 1809, that my in-laws became man and wife, they went together for a long stay at Hesleyside, and I have the details from my mother, who was actually present, of as cruel and heartless a scene as can well be imagined. My future mother-in-law by that time was quite disturbed in mind, and when her brain was out of health she was apt to chatter nonsense, reminded all the time by the really regnant Mrs. Charlton that she was a born fool, quite daft, and had no business to proffer an opinion on any subject, all being beyond the scope of her intellect. One day, when all the ladies were grouped round the fire conversing, Katherine Charlton boldly asserted there was no such thing as bodily pain, but that all feeling of the sort emanated from, and was the creation of, the mind. "Indeed!" said the leading spirit-breaker and, taking hold of her daughter-in-law's hand, thrust it into the flame. At a convenient moment later my parents took it on themselves to remonstrate, representing the danger of such harshness towards a person in delicate health, and saying it might drive her mad. "Mad indeed!" spoke up Mrs. (Fenwick) Charlton. "Didn't they marry her to my son only to save her from suchlike?" An observation which, however soured, yet contained a morsel of truth.

'The pity of it was that Katherine Charlton was by nature a sweetly dispositioned and refined woman, with a genuine lady-like mentality. But ill usage removed these characteristic traces and in after years a malady, hurried on by the treatment she received, made her a prey to hallucinations and to a querulousness that completely wrecked the happiness of all who had to live with her. She was never coarse and seldom witty; just a woman of ordinary intellectual power with a craving to put more into her brain than it could carry. Instead of the usual musical accomplishment, she acquired Latin, a very good thing for a Catholic girl to do, and she was also extremely well up in English literature. Her education had been well contrived for a healthy person, but unfortunately she was not that. She was partially endowed, through her mother, with the wonderful Englefield memory, which she transmitted to my husband and, through him, to my second son and youngest daughter. As against her good qualities, she undoubtedly possessed an exceedingly jealous disposition and was sadly ridden by the demon of self-esteem. In general appearance she bore a coarse resemblance to the Bourbon family, having the same receding chin and forehead. The back part of her head, in a sense, was almost missing, and she never went without an indoor cap so as to hide this defect. Her daughter Mary used to say her mother was the image of a sheep, but to me she looked much more like a frightened hare.

'Soon after this horrible incident, Katherine Charlton's state became alarming; so depressed was she that Dr. Fenwick, her husband's uncle, advised that she be taken up to London to consult with Dr. Baillie, the mental specialist. This was accordingly done and Dr. Baillie's opinion was to this effect: Some brain trouble, he said, had been going on for long, and he could give small hope of a permanent recovery. Unless great care was taken attacks would recur, until eventually the case would end in a continuous mental malady. He thought that the brain had been overstrained when young. His recommendations were a cheerful home life with frequent change; and he stringently advised, in the case of further brain disturbance, that the patient should at once be separated from her family. His further advice was that Mr. Charlton should go back home alone and send his wife, accompanied by her sister, to Bath, there to stay until she herself felt an inclination to return to the north.

'Dr. Baillie, well-informed by Katherine Charlton's sister as to the true state of affairs at Hesleyside, probably indulged in some plain-speaking to the husband, for Mr. Charlton, on his solitary way back home, stopped off at Durham to consult his uncle, Dr. Fenwick, and to ask him to assist in resolving his perplexities. The result was that my father-in-law to be took the lease of a large house in Durham, had it repainted, repapered and thoroughly well furnished, and in every way made ready as the future residence of his mother and aunt, his filial, rather than his marital, affections no doubt causing his heart to palpitate in fear and sorrow at having to distress his mother with the announcement that, by doctor's orders, the joint Hesleyside establishment must be broken up ere his wife's return from Bath. To meet the expense of this rearrangement of domestic life it is probable that the beautiful old yew trees on the bank opposite the south-west corner of the hall were cut down for selling, and also the long row of stately Scotch firs facing the avenue of Spanish limes to the west. An old woodman, Milburn, still working on the estate, told me he was the executioner.

'To soften the immediate effect of these alterations and displacements, it was mutually agreed that Mr. Charlton should take his wife and children to spend two winter months in Durham with his mother, largely for the sake of society, which in that capital was the best in the North; and that, reciprocally, the two old ladies should come to Hesleyside during a part of the summer. The young wife readily accepted these suggestions, having recovered her health after a few months at Bath and returning thence, although still inclined to melancholy and absentmindedness, in a much less fretful state. So much was she improved that she undertook her entirely novel duties as chatelaine with as much verve as she was capable of. She took interest in the gardens and grounds and proposed improvements. She visited the cottages and the poor round about, bent on doing good. She went out sketching in the woods and on the river, for she had a decided talent for water-colour, although always a dirty colourist; and also she seldom finished her pictures and so had little to show. The scenery on North Tyne attracted artists on account of its rugged beauty, and some of the best masters of that day, such as Williams, Copley Fielding, Richardson and others, not to mention Cotman, who was at one time drawing-master at Hesleyside, made their headquarters at the hall, so giving my future mother-in-law advice and help in return for hospitality.

'Some years went quietly by in home duties, in bearing children at the rate of almost one a year, in the enjoyment of winter society at Durham, and in occasional visits to Brandsby and Burghwallis. Her children grew up apace and soon gave Mrs. Charlton plenty to do in teaching them the rudiments of knowledge, but so numerous were they that a governess appeared early on the scene. Nevertheless, Mrs. Charlton always helped in the teaching of her pet subject, the grammar of dead and foreign languages such as French, Italian and Latin. It was her habit to take some of the children for walking exercise after lunch, but she became very stout and unwieldy at an early age, so that a donkey carriage was necessary and in this she would drive up and down the rhododendron walk, made especially for her. This pretty path led to the large, walled kitchen gardens and ran along the edge of the park. But neither Mrs. (Fenwick) Charlton nor her sister, resentful of all innovation, would ever use it, preferring the longer, uphill and downhill high-way route when they visited the gardens. In exactly the same way, these two reacted to the first place of *general interest* that was placed inside the house soon after the advent of my mother-in-law, though it certainly was situated awkwardly just outside the library on the ground floor. Neither of them ever availed themselves of such a convenient appliance, alleging that *suchlike whims bred pestilence and fevers*. In all weathers they preferred to take their walks abroad, their aim and object being located in a shrubbery at the back. It had been there since time immemorial, and not until I had been married nearly twenty years was it effaced and the shrubbery uprooted.

'My mother always told me that in Mrs. (Fenwick) Charlton's reign the Hesleyside gardens were celebrated, especially for the growth of pineapples. But her daughter-in-law, when she came into her own, did away with the pineries and almost let the rest run wild. Even the hall became ill-kept and dirty, and the table, which had been admirably furnished till then, fell off sadly. So great was the falling off thereof that a gentleman once told me it could only be compared to a pig-trough. Katherine Charlton was a disgusting eater and was quite unable to teach her children nice ways at table. She was too much wrapt up in self, poor woman, to be either a good housewife or a capable organizer.

'It was probably Teresa (Swinburne) Mrs. Charlton who had the gardens removed from their former site not far from the north side of the hall to where they are to-day, within a high-walled enclosure of three and a half acres, about half-way between house and river in the direction of the ford to Charlton. The gardener's house, when the gardens were nearer the hall, was a cottage which I well remember just inside the Hesleyside wood near Mantle Hill, with a good well nearby; and Mrs. Humble, the housekeeper, told me that in her girlhood she could pick quite good gooseberries on very hoary bushes in the crow plantation by the old garden site.

'Such as it then was, the public highway at that time

followed the contour of the hill above the hall, and at the Mantle Hill bank-foot, within the Hesleyside wood, its course can still be traced nearly to Old-town Shiel, or Auld Man Shiel as it came to be called, now no more than a standing cottage amid stone ruins level with the ground, though at one time, to judge from existing road remains, a place of some importance with a good deal of traffic to and fro. Such roads used to run along the sides of hills because the valley ground was heavily wooded and swampy. It does not say much for the perspicaciousness of the Charlton ancestors that when they forsook their lands at Charlton, on safe, dry ground overlooking the left bank of the Tyne, they should have pitched their future abode under a hill on swampy soil. Old Dr. Fenwick, father of Mrs. (Fenwick) Charlton, told me that when he first knew Hesleyside the country all around was covered with a natural growth of trees, and that Charlton wood, on the opposite side of the river, is a remainder that was spared at the time of clearing. Tradition has it that at the time of the family's migration they removed to the same side of the river the historic mill, which for untold years has been a picturesque landmark on the Hesleyside bank and which was originally possessed, on its ancient site at the foot of Charlton burn, by Adam de Charlton, a progenitor who died in 1303. During my time I learnt much of the way the old roads and paths went in the vicinity of the hall. A hundred years ago the main highway from Wark ran past Dunterley Farm, a little less than a mile from the hall, and then bent left-handed below Woodhead, continuing west from there through Hesleyside wood and crossing the burn above the Ladies' Linn, where it came out on the bare hill and can still be traced to Auld Man Shiel and thence downhill to Carriteth, a farm corresponding as regards position to Dunterley on the other side. The road to Hesleyside itself left the main highway soon after Woodhead and ran sloping down to the Cragclose, joining when near the hall another coming from Charlton over the river via the ford, and the two routes after their union passed in front of the hall on the south. Three avenues of trees, east, north and west, radiated from the hall, and there might have been a fourth pointing south; but if so it was probably sacrificed to make space for Run-away Will's ornamental lake. Old Kitty Fenwick used to wax sentimental over this worthy Charlton forbear, and would tearfully insist that his sudden disappearance was to join James, the Old Pretender and not, as everyone declared, to evade his debts. When the first Dixon came as agent in 1780 the parkland, lying low between the hall and river, was generally under water, but his son and successor, John Dixon the second, had a sunk-fence made for drainage purposes and so as to divide the park into two large fields without their boundaries being an eyesore. Some fine old yew trees then stood over against the south-west corner of the hall, originally planted when the family migrated from across the river to provide bows, a very necessary weapon in early days on the Border.

'Poor Katherine Charlton! Sorrow seemed to dog her footsteps whichever way she turned. Her two young daughters, Teresa Ann and Harriet, aged six and two respectively, died in 1819 of diphtheria in its most virulent form. It was always understood that the first cases of this malignant type thus occurred at Hesleyside, many years before the ghastly disease became so widespread. Dr. Ramsay, Newcastle's first physician, posted with four horses to try and save the two children, but they were beyond his skill. Teresa was conscious to the last, but became both blind and speechless ere she died. There can be no doubt that the excessive damp and immoderate cold of Hesleyside caused these two deaths, as indeed they did four other of Katherine's children at an early age, and yet not even under this visitation of Providence was anything done for the improvement of conditions in the house. The poor mother was broken-hearted. Luckily, she had the power of venting grief by tears; otherwise her brain must surely have succumbed. After a short interval her husband escorted her to Ireland to stay with her sister Annie, wife of a Mr. Strickland, who was Lord Dillon's agent at Loch Linn.

'Mrs. Charlton had her last and twelfth child in 1826, a boy who died soon after christening, and this birth brought on a very long illness, during which she took an inveterate dislike to her husband and refused to see her children. It was a very serious attack of mental depression, so severe that it became dangerous to keep her at home, and so for two years on end she was separated from her family, living with a nurse at Porto Bello near Edinburgh, while a governess was installed at Hesleyside to take charge of the children.

'From this illness Mrs. Charlton duly recovered and stayed at Burghwallis for the Doncaster race-week of 1828, after my parents had returned from France, leaving me all alone at the convent. From Burghwallis she went on to her own old home at Brandsby. My sisters said that while at Burghwallis Mrs. Charlton was kind and amiable, but very sad, talking incessantly of her late illness and of the fear she felt of a recurrence.

'Mr. and Mrs. Charlton, as I have mentioned earlier, took with them their eldest son, William, my future husband, on this particular visit to Burghwallis for the race-week, although both he and his father would much have preferred to be at Clintburn instead, one of the Hesleyside moorland farms situated at the back of beyond. And it was at the race-week ball that William, just on eighteen at the time, ignorant of ballroom dancing and untaught, either at Ushaw or at home, as to the usual customs of society, stretched himself at full length on a bench and, to the vast amusement of the fashionable assembly, went fast asleep.

'Soon after this incident William was sent abroad for a few years to complete his education as a young man of position, but, most unwisely, his parents selected as companions for him on the tour a couple of Catholic young men, both from Stonyhurst and in each case lacking education and refinement, who failed to edify owing to their low drunken habits. William let them go their own ways and devoted himself to learning languages so that he got to know German well and could speak Italian fluently, and lionized to his heart's content in every notable place the party visited.

'William returned home in time for his coming of age and, young as he was, became a Justice of the Peace. Duties crowded on him, for his father had taken no interest in the welfare of the people of North Tyne, and it fell to my husband to make good the parental indolence and lack of enterprise, sparing neither time, trouble, nor money in bettering conditions in the district. It is fair to say that his mother did her utmost to encourage William in these laudable endeavours, but any sort of improvement in those early days, even so striking a necessity as roads and bridges, was difficult of accomplishment in that wild, distressful country.

'While her eldest son was abroad on his grand tour, lionizing and learning languages, Mrs. Charlton enjoyed a long spell of fairish health which came to an untimely end through fret and worry over a protégée of hers who had repaid the most loving care and kindness with ingratitude.

K

This protégée was some foreign waif, with a spinal complaint that kept her prostrate, whom Mrs. Charlton had encountered somehow and to whom she had taken a violent fancy, for which, it may be, her sick brain was in part responsible. My father-in-law, only too anxious to keep his wife amused and from incessant fretting, thought it well to encourage the unequal intimacy. So this waif, an accomplished person, very eccentric, and poor in circumstance as well as health, was housed at Hesleyside and remained there for two years, lying flat on her back for months at a time, attended to in every way, on a bed in Mr. Charlton's own study which had been converted for her use. If steady devotion and unrelenting care, in sickness as in health, could have touched the chord of gratitude in that waif's heart, then undying thankfulness was the due of Mrs. Charlton. But, as with most such cases of ill-advised kindness, low-bred oblivion of benefit received was her return, with the result that her feelings were so harried by their requital of all the affection she had lavished that she became unwell again. It was this that put a measure to the waif's protracted stay. She was civilly, though firmly, requested to vacate the study and return to wherever she belonged. She did so and, late in life, married an apothecary. The history of Mrs. Charlton's foreign waif so closely accords with that of an Irish stray who, some thirty years later, as will be seen, was similarly entertained by me, that I unhesitatingly affirm sorrow and lasting regret to be the sole reward for one who harbours any specimen of that limpet class.

'In the spring of 1833 Mrs. (Fenwick) Charlton died at Durham. She will forever stand on a high pedestal in the estimation of the Charlton family as an influential spirit that inspired fresh life into a worn-out line, and she ever deserves reverence and gratitude for the great and unselfish performance she achieved. Her inebriate and almost idiotic husband left her a widow after nineteen years of married life, and she herself outlived him a further thirty-six, so that she was untrammelled in the laying of her plans for the restoration of an old inheritance that had been nigh laid waste. Truly, she was a heroine of self-sacrifice. As truly, the son on whose behalf she laboured rewarded her with ingratitude as regards his choice of a wife. And, like a thunderbolt, almost instantaneous retribution fell on him changing him into a sad and smileless man through life and doubtlessly contributing to his comparatively early death at the age of sixty-two.

'After Mrs. (Fenwick) Charlton's death Hesleyside was shut up for two years, part of the family, consisting of the father and mother, their two daughters, Mary and Kate, and Frank, the third son, who was in delicate health, spending the first nine months in Paris. They stayed a week in London on their way abroad, and while there Mrs. Charlton took her daughters down to Strawberry Hill, between Twickenham and Hampton Court, to spend the day with her mother's old friends, the Misses Berry, whose friendship had been so dear to Horace Walpole. Mary Charlton, the elder daughter, was about fifteen at that time and very forward for her age. Her state of advancement was due largely to self education, and also to her wits having been sharpened by supplying the deficiencies of her mother during the latter's periods of ill health and haziness of mind. The Misses Berry were charmed with both intelligent sisters, and one of them very sensibly remarked to Mrs. Charlton that in one way it was a pity they had been so highly educated; for, being Catholic, they would seldom meet with intellectual equality in the society of their co-religionists. In this there was a large measure of truth, for both Mary and Kate

Charlton, who had moved more in Protestant than Catholic society in Northumberland, were simply nonplussed at the samples of Catholic witlessness and bad manners during their first London season in the year of my marriage. My husband described to me an *orthodox* party at which his sisters had been present, where a number of young ladies took possession of an ottoman in the middle of the room, making such a cackling and senseless noise that they could only be compared to a flock of geese on a pond.

'My father-in-law was pricked as High Sheriff for Northumberland in 1837, the extra expenses of the office, what with outriders, trumpeters and robes of state, coming to at least £800. The handsome stone bridge over the Tyne at Bellingham had been opened just before my arrival at Hesleyside as William's wife. The road from Wark to Bellingham, part of which I traversed on my bridal journey, was in a condition to take traffic, but its bed stones had not had proper time to bind. Already William had got the workhouse built at Bellingham. He was a magistrate, a Poor-law guardian, and the district's honorary road-surveyor. Everything that could conduce to the comfort and well-being of the inhabitants of North Tyne was actively furthered by my husband, who, until stopped by the hand of death, worked unremittingly for the good of his countryside. Of all the Charlton race he was the one to whom the people owed most, and he deserves to be held in memory by them and by their children's children as their benefactor. It is also fair to say that Sir John Swinburne, his cousin and neighbour of Capheaton, who died in his ninety-ninth year, gave freely in subscriptions for roads and bridges and, although not a Catholic himself, donated £50 towards the building of St. Oswald's Church at Bellingham, consecrated in the summer of 1839.'

XII

ACCOUNT OF THE HOME SCENE

IT is full time, after so lengthy a digression as in the preceding chapter, that Barbara should reoccupy the stage and, having already presented herself in various preliminary attitudes, should now narrate her experience in life as wife and mother. Perhaps it were advisable to jog the memory. She has just arrived at Hesleyside and is being greeted by her husband's family, suffering a warm, tearful embrace from that astonishing old lady, Miss Catherine Fenwick, who speaks in broad Northumbrian and has turned eighty-one years. So over-powering is the impression made on her by this reception that she forthwith puts aside the telling of her story, and embarks on a long recital of her mother-in-law's sad history when she, the older lady, exactly thirty years since, blushed bride-like on the threshold of the hall. For that deviation Barbara alone must bear the blame.

A word about Hesleyside, the house itself, now that Barbara has come to stay, will not be out of place. Originally, in keeping with the lawless times, it served the purpose of a stronghold, consisting of a peel, or square massive tower, with an agglomeration of dwellings at its foot, the inhabitants of which, when the Scotch were raiding over the Border, would seek protection inside the strong walls that towered overhead.

From this rough, practical beginning, typical of sixteenth-century life on both sides of the Border, a substantial

Jacobean mansion of dressed freestone was in course of time evolved, having a square ground plan, with an interior courtyard, and opposite arches for the ingress and egress of vehicles. It abutted on the east side of the tower and, during the same period, the woods were thrown back from the house, grounds were shaped, and a demesne was marked out. By the end of the seventeenth century this house, or hall, stood forth from its present surroundings, still backed by its ancient tower, as a gentleman's seat of attractive appearance and no mean importance.

And then, in part fulfilment of a prophecy, there occurred in quick succession two disastrous fires which necessitated a rebuilding in part, though the tower still survived and the whole of the south front escaped injury.

The core of the south front probably goes back to 1620, and there is in it a well-contrived priest's hiding-hole, formed by the unequal ceiling heights of two adjacent rooms. A sufficiency of fresh air was provided for the occupant through an opening in the outside wall, masked by an old stone carving affixed to the façade.

The tower, long in disuse, met a sad fate during the infancy of William John Charlton, Barbara's father-in-law. By order of the trustees, doubtlessly instigated thereto by Mrs. (Fenwick) Charlton, the *maitresse femme*, it was ruthlessly pulled down and the stone utilized for the erection of new stables and outhouses. It was a pity, even though it had to be, that a historic landmark should thus have been effaced, for in his *Survey of the Borders*, written in 1542, Sir Robert Bowes, one-time Ambassador to the Scottish Court, describes it as being the only tower of its kind in all Tynedale.

As regards the interior of the hall, it is spacious, high-ceilinged on the first two floors, and with double doors of

communication leading from room to room. At the period of
Barbara's arrival the main entrance gave on to a large, stone-
flagged hall, at the further end of which a graceful staircase,
branching right and left midway, ascended to the bedroom
story. It was a dignified and stately interior arrangement, to
which the furniture and decoration corresponded.

But alas! no sooner did Barbara feel the reins of power in
hand than she was seized with a fervour of innovation and
improvement. Influenced, no doubt, by her French upbringing she converted the stone hall into an Empire
drawing-room, with painted ceiling, elaborate upholstery
and polished flooring to match. She walled her creation off
from the staircase foot by a stucco partition, with sham
pilasters on the reverse side to relieve the deadness of the
surface. She sold the venerable fittings and appointments by
the cart-load on the village green, acquiring French abom-
inations in their place, and all this she honestly performed
in the name of beauty and embellishment. She, herself, will
tell about it as she goes along.

Back, then, to Barbara! – who in all innocence has placed
herself, it would appear, in a very trying situation; that,
namely, of starting newly married life under the same roof
as her in-laws, which also shelters their numerous family,
apart from William Henry, of six boys and girls varying in
age from fourteen to twenty-five. In some respects history
is beginning to repeat itself at Hesleyside.

'The day after I arrived as a bride at Hesleyside was the
12th August, and now, with the advent from Newcastle of
Edward and Frank, William's two brothers next to him in
years, the entire Charlton family, father, mother, five sons,
and two daughters, was assembled; all seven of the children,
thanks to the Fenwick alliance, far above the average in in-
ellect. But of all, Mary, elder of the two girls, was the

shining star that brightened up for each of us the gloom of our surroundings.

'Seldom did the sun come through in the late autumn months and all during winter, so that the house at such times was terribly cold and damp; a perfect temple of the winds, with every outer door left open. But in spite of all the discomfort a most lively imagination can portray Mary Charlton's bright face, with fun and laughter in her eyes, would appear like a sunbeam to chase dull care away. I have seen her placed in positions that would have broken most men down, always doing the right thing, never losing her presence of mind, and often cheering us all up with a flash of genuine wit. She had a light, elastic figure and rode like a bird, wading her pony through the Tyne and springing up the hills to carry help to some far-away cottagers, whose children were very likely down with typhoid. Mary's devoted love to her sister Kate, two years younger, was a most beautiful trait in her character. Kate was her idol, watched over and guarded by her in every way. Of the two Mary was by much the plainer. Kate was a fine-looking girl with good features and very soft eyes, and a pretty, sympathetic manner; but she rather inherited her mother's melancholy disposition, and also her coarse, red arms. It was entirely owing to Mary's devotion and good sense that Kate was drawn out of herself to become a charming, and even lively, companion. If there was a ball the burning question of what Kate was to wear, and what flowers would suit her best, was Mary's sole preoccupation, who quite forgot herself in her sisterly love. Mary was twenty-one, and Kate nineteen, when I first came to Hesleyside.

'On a September morning we all sallied forth to spend the day at Mounces, twelve miles up-river from Hesleyside where the Swinburne family were in temporary residence for

BARBARA AS A YOUNG MARRIED WOMAN

the shooting. Some rode, but it was my fate as usual to bear my mother-in-law company in the phaeton. Needless to say, in that valley of Nature's tears, it poured the whole day. Great was my astonishment at the first sight of my Swinburne relatives! Julia, who was then in her forties and lived to nearly a hundred, with her tight, straight skirt and prim appearance, gave me the idea that she had just come out of Noah's Ark, and never before or since had I heard a biped purr as she did; it was as if her mother had been frightened by a cat. Our clothes had to be dried and our appetites appeased, after which we returned under the same continuing deluge from above. I own that after my first visit to Mounces I never wished to see the place again, and, what is more, I never did.

'Soon after Lady Jane Swinburne, who had with her young Algernon Charles, then rising three, stopped at Hesleyside on her way to Mounces to pay her visit of congratulation to the bride. Master Algernon, a pretty-featured, carroty-haired, spoilt boy, paid his respects most unpoetically by pricking me with a large pin in a tender place. In the course of the autumn William and I, with four other of the Charlton family, went to stay at Capheaton, part of which is modern and part untouched Tudor work. The magnificent library and valuable collection of prints chased away all idea of dullness. To me, moreover, the house was of special interest, as I had heard so many stories relating to it from my mother. At the end of the sixteenth and the beginning of the seventeenth centuries no Catholic residence of any size was without its priest's hiding place, for it was death to say Mass. But at Capheaton, the seat in those days of the chief Northumbrian Catholic and Jacobite family, there were said to be no less than seven of these secret places. When the last Earl of Derwentwater gave up all hope of success after Preston he sent his family papers to be safely kept at Capheaton; and there, for thirty years after the Earl's execution, they stayed, until one day a mason, who was repairing the roof, came across some boxes with the Derwentwater coat-of-arms emblazoned on them and immediately informed Sir William Middleton of Belsay, the same who despoiled Hesleyside of its horses, who promptly laid his hands on them. By Act of Parliament the Derwentwater estates were sequestrated and a grant made of them to Greenwich Hospital.

'The Swinburne family, to which William and I, through our great-grandmothers, Teresa and Isabel Swinburne, were equally related, was always a prolific subject for a fireside talk at Hesleyside, and I well remember Mary Charlton, soon after my marriage, telling me of the discovery of the Derwentwater papers. She then also told me that most interesting story of "the lost heir of Capheaton", a narrative which she had from one of the family itself. I will try to tell it as she told it me, but hers was a much more graphic account that I can hope to imitate:

'In the time of the first Stuarts, when the religious troubles of the Northumbrian Catholics were at their height, the heir of the Swinburnes of Capheaton, a very young and only child, was confided to the care of a highly respectable and trustworthy old priest, for him to bestow his charge in some safe place of custody abroad until the rigour of persecution had abated.

'The good old man, travelling, both himself and child, under assumed names, faithfully discharged his trust and finally deposited the infant heir in some Belgian religious college. Deposited, and no more; for at the moment of arrival he was so overcome by fatigue that he was fain to seek a *pharmacien* and obtain a healing draught, murmuring to the superior that he would return anon and render full particulars. He never did return, for very shortly after he was seized with a fit and never spoke again. So here was the young heir of Capheaton left in strangers' hands, very much in the situation of a foundling. Of far too tender an age to give an account of himself, much less to establish his identity, he was adopted by the priests of the institution under a name bestowed by them and received among the ranks of the *élèves*. From both ends, as it were, he was lost to sight and sound; the priests of the college entirely in the dark about the boy's identity, and his parents, Sir William Swinburne and his Lady, equally ignorant as to the whereabouts of their son.

'Time rolled on and the good shepherds continued lovingly to tend the lamb entrusted to their care, convinced by the light of Faith that when the rage of bigotry and persecution had subsided all that it was necessary to know about the child would come to light. In the course of a few years the cruel laws against those who had adhered to the Faith of their fathers were to a certain extent subdued, and with the blessed relaxation an anxious search was put on foot for the missing Swinburne heir.

'Two English priests offered to go to Belgium and commence investigations there, for it was nearly always to that country, as being Catholic through and through, that our persecuted co-religionists sent their sons. The offer was gratefully accepted and the two divines set off on their errand of love, basing their first enquiries on the presumption that an unforeseen calamity had happened to the child's original custodian who had not been heard of from that day. The two charitable pilgrims, going from town to town, searched several educational institutions, but no child was produced to answer in the slightest degree the description of the one they looked for – pale, well-featured, red-haired, aged between eight and nine.

'The two seekers, thoroughly discouraged, were about to renounce all further search as useless when they suddenly bethought themselves of an unvisited college in a more distant part of Belgium, and thither, faint-heartedly, they journeyed. When they announced their embassy to the superior of the college, he raised their hopes on high by saying that a boy who might be the one of whom they were in search had been received by them at about the mentioned date. "The boys are now all at dinner in the refectory," added the superior, "and I will conduct you there as if showing you the house. We have only one boy who at all answers your description and he was *un enfant trouvé*, about whom, and everything connected with whom, we are still in utter darkness. Your attention will be riveted on him from the colour of his hair, and you must be careful not to stare him out of countenance, for he is a very sensitive boy – evidently a boy of breeding – and we here have often wondered what his origin could be. I must also beg you to make no remark about him in his hearing. When he first came he was much too young to give any information about himself; so young, indeed, that we had to engage an old woman to take charge of him. *Il était trop mignon même pour se débarbouiller!*"

'So conversing, the superior led his two visitors into the refectory, and on passing the red-haired boy one whispered to the other low, "Verily, it is he! A Swinburne in every feature. There can be not the least doubt." They were both agreed on the point, but this did not mean proof; nor was it anything but strong supposition on their part, though amounting, perhaps, to an instinctive feeling that their search was ended. It was finally agreed that the boy should return to England, and to Capheaton, with the two who came in search, to see if the sight of his home would arouse a dormant recollection of early childhood. The plan was duly carried out and, leaving their vehicle when near the ancient hall, they walked on with the boy ahead, entering in all humility by the back way. Somewhere inside the boy suddenly stood stock still, clapped a hand to his brow, assumed an expression of intense perplexity, and cried out "*La niche de Caesar! Mais qu'est devenu mon pauvre Caesar?*" and ere either of the priests accompanying him could make reply, or discover what had got into his head, he flew up to his nursery and to an old chest that stood within, flung open the lid and produced a china dog together with a china punch-bowl that had the figure of a cat upon it, excitedly repeating, "*Oh! Mon pauvre chien et chat.*" In this way the boy himself provided proof of his identity. Furthermore, the clothes in which he had originally travelled abroad, brought back with him from the Belgian college, were sworn to in every particular by his nurse. Thus was the lost heir of Capheaton, after having vanished from human ken for five or six years, restored to his rightful position and to those who sorrowed for him.

'As recently as 1891, not long before I started writing down my recollections, I mentioned the story to Sir John Swinburne, seventh Bart., who was at the time M.P. for Lichfield; but he told me he had never heard of it before. His assertion in no ways surprised me, as he was an alien to his family and to all his family records. I hardly think his grandfather, the renegade Sir John who died in 1860 just before numbering his ninety-ninth year, would have allowed the story to take root on North Tyne could he have contradicted it, as it asserted indubiously his own ignoble apostasy.

'Curious to relate, when I was in Brussels with William in 1842 we saw a dramatic version of the same story performed on the stage under the title: *César – le Chien et le Château.* It was a garbled version, though very well acted, the setting being that of French revolutionary days, and the religious interest entirely effaced.

'In the summer of 1840 we had Elliott Warburton at Hesleyside on a visit, soon to be distinguished as a traveller and novelist: and after that my mother came to stay a month or so, during which time the Crathorne deed of settlement was signed under which I was to receive £14,000. The Charlton family tactfully withdrew to Tynemouth, so that Mama was our sole guest. She gave a dance for the servants and country people nearby, with dancing in the dining-room and a most *recherché* supper consisting of beef, chickens, hams, etc. William arranged it all. She also ordered new ball dresses from London for Mary and Kate Charlton, to their intense delight, and in addition gave £6 towards the bell of St. Oswald's Church which was opened in June, 1839, while William and I were being remarried in London, by Bishop Briggs. Towards the total cost of £1,250, my father-in-law gave £200, the land, a small endowment, and an annual sum for upkeep of £50. Being alone like this at Hesleyside with my dear mother was the greatest relief to me; not but that Mrs. Charlton was always most kind and affectionate to me in every respect except one, – viz.: the incurable habit she had of running down, belittling more or less, all my relations, especially my dear sister Fanny, whom I loved above all others. Her brother at Brandsby, and the rest of them there, had thrown her completely off for having written to the effect that their father was living an immoral life, that his children ought to know of it, and that he ought to be induced to abandon evil ways. The consequence of Mrs. Charlton's imprudent letter was the complete separation of Mr. and Mrs. Cholmeley. Yorkshire people blamed Mrs. Charlton greatly for her unjustifiable conduct, but as for her, she conscientiously thought it was her mission in life to interfere in any family the members of which did not behave themselves; her muddle-headed argument being that she ought to put to use an intellect, the gift to her from Heaven, so far superior to that of others. It was her *idée fixe*, and good manners forbade me to correct her misconception. So I had to grin and bear it, often wishing that her husband or her daughters would relieve me as companion of her walks and drives. In time I recognized that my own husband, living always at home, had little by little imbibed his mother's habit of belittlement, and often, in answer to an ordinary question, he would let off intellectual fireworks, the rocket-sticks, as they came back to earth, never failing to light on somebody's unfortunate head to wound and scarify. It was a response to his mother's teaching.

'I was expecting my first child towards the end of August, 1840, and I was besought by Mrs. Charlton as a favour not to name it Harriet or Teresa if it were a girl, her contention being that those two names had always been unlucky in the families of Cholmeley and Charlton. On August 25th, our eldest son, William Francis, was born, alas! not to live a year, and then ensued a mighty tug-of-war. My sister Fanny, who was in a state of great anxiety over my welfare, wrote me a long letter of advice in case the nurse procured for me should not be good, and naturally, being in utter dependence on her, I showed it to my mother-in-law, who treated all the recommendations in it as coming from a weak-minded woman whose advice was of no account. A very third-rate woman was procured as a monthly nurse, whose practice lay among shopkeepers and such. She was no good whatever and only aggravated the evil of my condition. One of poor Fanny's strictest recommendations had been to remain in bed till the tenth day. But on the third day I was taken out of bed and dumped in chair, whereupon a most serious shivering fit came on suddenly, with much chattering of teeth, so that the wrong-headed creature, thoroughly alarmed, had me carried back to bed, so conquering the ill result of her folly.

'The fifth day came, and I was told by Mrs. Charlton that I would never be able to nurse my child if I did not get on to my feet. For the second time I was taken out of bed, and made to take steps up and down the room. I had not made many when I screamed with pain, and again I was hurriedly put back to bed, but this time I did not recover from the effects of my mother-in-law's egregious folly for almost the whole of two years. I had, it seemed, a weakly constitution and one very difficult to suit. Folly number three was then to feed me up on mutton chops and chicken until they brought on inflammation; whereupon even my useless monthly nurse had the sense to declare that Dr. Stokoe must be sent for at once from Hexham. He came, he bled me, and I overheard him whisper into Mrs. Charlton's ear, "You will kill her!" After his second visit I hoped I would be left to myself in peace, but my mother-in-law, poor woman, would not leave me alone for one moment. She sat by my bed hour on hour, ceaselessly discussing her own superiority to other women, the inferiority of her brother's offspring, and the shortcomings of my own two sisters, particularly Fanny. Dreadful headaches came on and twice I had to have leeches on my head; even so, my mother-in-law's jealous gabble never ceased.

'During my long period of recovery, for I was kept in bed for three weeks and was an invalid for another twelve, letters had been passing to and fro between Hesleyside and Hainton, and my sisters took alarm at the reports I gave of my condition. They wrote, unwisely perhaps, some stiff remonstrances, the upshot of which was that, weakened as I was, Mrs. Charlton came to me and requested that, from henceforth, all correspondence between my sisters and myself should cease, desiring at the same time my permission to write to them to that effect. So ill was I that I replied she could do anything she liked, and never can I forget her insane delight at having brought about the breach. It was a miserable winter for me that year. I knew my baby was not being properly nursed. Mama had gone to the trouble of getting me an excellent woman from Yorkshire, but Mrs. Charlton, with her demon jealousy in possession, gave her notice at the end of the second month, engaging in her place a most disreputable-looking, low Irishwoman who turned out very ill.

'The spring of 1841 came and the family, the Saints be praised, went to Leamington for February and March, leaving at Hesleyside William and I, and his old Aunt Fenwick. We paid a few visits roundabout – to Highwarden, Beaufront, Corby and one or two other places, the baby having to come along too. Unexpectedly, William's great-uncle, Dr. Fenwick, offered himself for a visit, and as his sister Kitty was living with us I thought it only natural. But his purpose, it appeared, was to warn William that his mother was on the eve of another serious breakdown, and to advise him to take me away before bad became worse. Old Aunt Kitty, who knew too well the symptoms, agreed with her brother in everything and further declared she had seen the illness coming on for months. William cheerfully announced that he had every intention of acting on such good advice, but he was so immersed in the Bellingham work-house project and road improvement that we did not get away till mid-June, and then only after great pressure had been put on him from without.

'In March, Henry Charlton, aged sixteen, the youngest

L

of the family, arrived from Ushaw, sent home by the school authorities on account of bad health. Before leaving Ushaw he had been stethoscoped by his older brother Edward, the one born next to William, who had adopted the medical profession, and his ailment pronounced to be nothing more than an idle attempt to exchange school for home: but in spite of Dr. Charlton's diagnosis Doctor Newsham, the President of Ushaw, very wisely had him sent away. Poor Henry languished at Hesleyside with us, and not until the family returned from Leamington was Dr. Stokoe sent for. He instantly pronounced the boy to be in a rapid decline; only too true a verdict, for he died early in May; a nice, clever lad. It was a most sad departure and gloom was everywhere reflected, but as usual Mary Charlton was the prop and stay of the mourning parents and of all alike.

'Mrs. Charlton seemed discontented with her stay at Leamington; she was more quiet, altered somewhat in face and even in figure. She meekly complained to me that Mary had been unkind to her, telling her before visitors that she was talking nonsense. I have been touched more than once to hear Mrs. Charlton say, while engaged in argumentative conversation, "Now, Mary, be sure not to let me talk nonsense!" Mary was the only person in the world who could at all control my mother-in-law, because she told her home truths irrespective of daughterly behaviour, and if only I had done the same I might have spared myself much misery. By now Mrs. Charlton had succeeded in embroiling me with nearly every member of the family excepting my dear mother, with whom, *Deo gratias*, I was spared a quarrel. Mrs. Allgood of Nunwick urged my husband to remove me from Hesleyside, while I, myself, made a solemn resolution never again, despite the claims of magistracy and work-house, to put my life in danger under my mother-in-law's nursing régime. After having brought me to the very edge of the grave, chiefly owing to her disdain of Fanny's sensible advice, Mrs. Charlton wrote about to say that, considering the extreme badness of my constitution, she had brought me through quite cleverly.

'In mid-June we at last left Hesleyside after a dreary and wearisome year and nine months there which would have been socially unendurable but for Mary and Kate Charlton, who had no jealousy in their composition and never belittled others for the sake of exalting themselves. We were bound for Schwalbach in Hesse-Nassau, where I was to take the waters, but when we had got as far *en route* as Brussels our poor baby, who had been so thoroughly mismanaged ever since his birth, was taken ill and so we were delayed. I fear we proceeded on our journey before the poor child was fit to travel, for we lost him at Liége. Our little William Francis, aged ten months, died at the hotel *l'Aigle Noire*, and was buried in the Liége cemetery. Mrs. Charlton wrote me two most sweet and loving letters of condolence, full of soft, motherly consolation, letters so perfect of their kind that they went far to efface all the sorrow she had caused. Those two kind, feeling letters—like the song of the swan while death approaches—were the last she ever wrote. Hardly had we arrived at Schwalbach when Mary wrote to say her mother's mind had become critically disordered once again, and that they were taking her to the Lakes for a change. While there she made some dauby sketches, but her melancholy so much increased that it was necessary to separate her from the family and place her with a nurse at Elswick, near Newcastle. There she remained about two years, constantly bewailing her mistakes in life, but with a mind too ill-balanced to confess herself at fault. Many were of opinion that if my mother-in-law had had more congenial society, and not been placed in such a direful and melancholy spot as Hesleyside then was, quite cut off from the world, her malady might have been in some measure mitigated, though never entirely remedied; for even when young she was not a cheerful person, and became a very heavy materfamilias. She always herself avowed that had she married a busy, professional man she would have been a different person altogether. Wives, she used to say, should not see too much of their husbands. I can truthfully assert that my father-in-law, never even when she was having hallucinations, took the smallest trouble about his wife. He breakfasted alone, and was alone all day, never offering to walk, drive or read with her, and he disliked extremely to be spoken to. In the early morning he pottered about on his pony and, otherwise, had his nose in a book from morning till night. Mary got her mother to put a little furniture in the stone-floored hall, and a lamp, so that we could sit there, for Mr. Charlton's taciturnity made the library too dreary for endurance. So trying was Mrs. Charlton in her constant droning on about being misprized by all and sundry, that even Mary was occasionally stirred to a comparison between the Fenwick and the Cholmeley strains in the Charlton blood, saying "How can it be otherwise? We owe all to the Fenwicks and certainly nothing to the Cholmeleys!" But she was forgetting that they owed their sweet, even temper and good principles to their mother, while their father was at least sober, honourable and moral.

'Wright's Bank broke about this time, whereby we lost £400 out of the £500 given to us by Aunt Anne on our marriage. William had been duly warned that the failure of Wright & Co. was at hand, but he took no heed of the advice. For thirty years he had dwelt in a North Tyne oasis, his mind wrapt up in the house of Charlton, unheeding of all save the details of his father's property, by which he measured all he saw, and latterly immersed in local business. Came the crash! and what then did his book-learning avail him in the common business of life? Worse than nothing! His shoe-maker or any servant would have had more *savoir faire* and have looked better to their interests after being warned.

'From Liége, both very sad at our loss, we journeyed to the Rhine, and on the boat we at once noticed two most distinguished-looking English fellow travellers, a lady and a gentleman. Shortly after, the lady came and sat by me and said, "You look so ill and in such distress – can I not help you in any way? My name is Beauclerc and I am making a summer tour with my brother." The ice was broken at once, for I knew so many of the Beauclerc family. I told her of our loss, and she was sweet and sympathetic. She said her sister, Diana Lady Vane, was at Schwalbach with husband and children, and she would write to her immediately about William and me. When we arrived the Vanes called on us at once, and it was difficult to decide which of the two sisters was the more stately and beautiful. Lady Vane introduced us to Madame Toutchskoff and her two daughters, Hélène and Marie. We all went for donkey rides, picnicking and spending the whole day from 8 a.m. to 10 p.m. in the open and in one another's company. The waters and baths soon recuperated my strength and, after a pleasant stay at the favourite health resort, we returned, at the end of August, 1841, to Brussels, there to take a tiny apartment and see how far an income of £600 a year would go.

'The winter of 1841–42 was a very brilliant season at Brussels, where there was a considerable English colony. Our minister, Sir Hamilton Seymour, waived all ceremony about my not having been presented at my own Court and chaffingly accepted the fact of my early presentation, at the age of eleven, to Charles X of France at Versailles, about which he had been fully informed by his sister, Mrs. Liddell, afterwards Lady Ravensworth. Balls and parties were profusely given and everybody was most kind to us, especially and extremely so Sir Patrick and Lady Bellew, the latter of whom was a perfect mother to me. Mr. and Mrs. Blount, who had been ruined by the failure of Wright's Bank, and their three daughters were wintering in Brussels for economy's sake. She was a charming, companiable old lady, full of amusing anecdotes without gall, and bearing her financial sorrows like *une grande dame Chretienne*. One afternoon in the spring of 1842 the French Ambassadress came to see me in my cupboard of a drawing-room, furnished very shabbily. She must have brought infection with her, or else I unknowingly had it on me at the time, for the next week she and I both sickened of measles, from which she died. I have often ruminated with amazement how different the English and foreign ideas of social dignity can be. When William and I arrived in Brussels we were completely unknown to the two great ladies there, the French Ambassadress and Madame de Vilain Quatorze. We were poor, unable to entertain, living in a *bouge*, as it were, and yet these and other first-class families did not think it unbecoming their position frequently to visit us and often bring me flowers. In London the whole dignity of a family seemed to be concentrated in the style and standard of the furniture. Any *nouveau riche*, any scalliwag of the present day who can produce, not quarterings, but yard on yard of smart upholstery is on a social footing with the aristocracy and, in a manner of speaking, give the latter their position in society. How came such an abuse? Merely because a widowed Queen, herself endowed with every virtue, resigned her hold on society into the hands of an ill-disciplined son, whose lovely and truly meritorious wife had not the sense to stop her royal spouse from gambling away the ancient rights of the British aristocracy, introducing into society the very dregs of the colonies and America, and selling for money down his invitations for private balls at Marlborough House. One woman from overseas, a certain Mrs. Mackay, is reported to have written out a cheque for £5,000 in favour of His Royal Highness, in 1890, for a single invitation. Money was wanted for baccarat!

'In April we took a good-sized house in the Place Verte, since done away with, and on the 18th June, 1842, a second little boy was born to us in the place of William Francis, whom we christened Edward Salkeld. Shortly after he was taken very ill, but we got him a good Belgian nurse and he rapidly grew better, while I myself suffered no evil effects from the mismanagement I had undergone when my first child was born. Mrs. Stewart, widow of the Archbishop of Armagh and the mother of Lady Ranfurly, with whom she had lived ever since her husband's death, was most anxious to see our new-born child and called one day for that purpose. When you g, and going out in London society, she had known Harry Crathorne, *l'enfant gâté des Dames*, and now she wished to see if she could trace any likeness to him in our baby boy. She told me it was quite sufficient for Harry Crathorne to take casual notice of a girl in a ball-room for her not to sleep at night.

'During our sojourn at Brussels the great French actress Rachel came from Paris with the Théâtre Français company and gave performances of *Thisbe, Adrienne Lecouvreur, Les Camilles* and *La Phèdre*. She had a perfect face and figure for tragedy and forbore to rant and scream as Sarah Bernhardt did. Rachel, in her most splendid scenes, was always quiet and solemn, and her wonderful, deep, sonorous voice well suited her majestic calm.

'We spent a quiet, though happy, summer at the house in the Place Verte, much of William's time occupied in sketching with water-colours under a master who never allowed his pupils to copy anything but Nature. My husband had a decided talent that way and would have become accomplished at it had he persevered; but the patience requisite for excellence was lacking.

'Time went on and it became a toss-up whether we should spend another winter in Brussels, which held so many advantages for us. William was straining at the leash, yearning for roads, workhouse, poor-law and paupers much as the Israelites craved after the flesh-pots of Egypt, while I was just as eager to stay on where we were with the many friends I had made. But an incident occurred that turned the scale in William's favour, and glad indeed was I afterwards that it did so. I heard one night – it was but a waking dream – a hearse rattle over the stones of the ill-paved Place Verte and stop before our house. The driver got down and knocked heavily at the door. The nurse went downstairs and opened it, and I heard her say distinctly, "*Vous vous trompez, monsieur; la morte n'est pas dans cette maison.*" I next distinctly saw the coachman drive away and I distinctly heard him say while doing so, "*La morte est dans cette famille, et je reviendrai bientôt la prendre.*" True, it was but a dream; but it made such an impression on me that at breakfast next morning I said to William, who was naturally delighted, that as he wished it we had better go home at once.'

XIII

BARBARA REIGNS SUPREME

IN the pages which immediately follow Barbara carries the reader forward for a further period of about six years, from September, 1842, to 1849, at the end of which she will have been staidly married for a complete decade and has, herself, reached the respectable maturity of thirty-four years. It will be agreed that she has very bravely surmounted the difficulty and inconvenience of encirclement by her husband's family during the first few years of her married life, a situation that was far from being ameliorated by her mother-in-law's unfortunate condition and peculiar habit of mind, the misanthropy of her father-in-law, and the raw discomforts of the house in which she lived.

But now inevitable time effects a change. By the death of the old squire, she and William are at last enabled to rule at Hesleyside with undisputed sway, and life's events, compounded equally of happiness and sorrow, begin to crowd. There are other deaths to be recorded, some of which assail her nearly. There are births as well, two daughters being born to her during this period of her recollection. Kate Charlton, younger of the sisters, goes abroad and marries 'foreign'.

Otherwise time flows on, though never placidly, yet with a not unquiet progress towards the fulfilment of the years. In the exercise of her unwonted freedom she bestirs herself to act her part as châtelaine and squire's wife, taking an active role in parochial affairs, assisting in the early education of her children, and setting aside a fair proportion of her time for the improvement of the lower orders.

The first person with whom she makes contact after her stay abroad is her beloved sister Fanny; a reunion, alas! that is all too short.

'Before leaving Brussels my dear sister Fanny wrote begging me not to over-fatigue myself, but to rest for a few days at her London house, 39 Charles Street; which, accordingly, we did, for I was far from strong at the time. Afterwards we went down to Aunt Anne at York, and from there to Brandsby, where my other sister, Mary Fairfax, and her husband were then living, Gilling Castle, their natural abode, being occupied by his mother and his two sisters, while old Fairfax dwelt with the priest at Leyburn. A regular family *décousue*! Harriet, the second Fairfax daughter, married Francis Cholmeley, who succeeded to Brandsby, bringing with her the Gilling Castle property, which was disposed of, in 1893, by young Hugh Cholmeley for £50,000. Lavinia, the elder Fairfax girl, an accomplished woman, married the Rector of Gilling. But when he went out of his mind she became a Catholic and inherited Gilling at her brother Charles' death, passing it on to Harriet on her own decease. Neither in youth nor age was Lavinia a safe person to ride the waters on. In her day she made terrible mischief, and almost up to the day of her death she went on working irreparable harm. R.I.P.

'My sister Fanny came with her little daughter Georgie to meet us at Brandsby late in September, her husband proceeding on to Hainton with the two boys. A little time before Fanny had caught a bad cold at Scarborough when visiting a poor, sick woman, and at Brandsby this turned to bronchitis, then to pneumonia, terminating fatally on the 13th November, 1842. Had it not been for my grim dream in Brussels I should not have been with her at her death! And so passed away one of the kindest, gentlest, justest and mostly sweetly amiable of women at the youthful age of thirty-one. Her marriage had been one of perfect happiness; her husband was attentive to her, kind and generous. The little girl Georgina was brought up by her aunt, my sister Mary, at Gilling as a Catholic, but the two boys were brought up Protestants, though in no bigoted sense, as their father retained the services of Mrs. Farrell, their Catholic nurse, and also those of Anne Firth from Burghwallis village, the Hainton housekeeper and also a Catholic. Of the two boys, the older Edward, first Baron Heneage, married the daughter of the Head of the Orange League and so became naturally indifferent about Catholicism.

'During poor Fanny's two months illness William and I had been to Hesleyside. My mother-in-law was still at Elswick under nurse's care; Mary and Kate Charlton were very low-spirited, though to me their usual charming selves; my father-in-law had aged much in a short time and was as taciturn as ever. We had decided on a house at Durham and made a stay with Dr. Fenwick, William's great-uncle, who lived there, for the purpose of buying furniture. We then returned to Brandsby, where we remained for some time after Fanny's death, and while there I paid a visit of a fortnight at Burghwallis, my sister Mary going with me, and was received by my father without much show of appreciation of my presence. It was a relief when the day for leaving came. While at Burghwallis, to add to the depression of the atmosphere, Lewins, who had been its valuable and honest butler for upwards of twelve years, had such a bad attack of delirium tremens that he had to go, my father at that time having a visit to France in contemplation. One Dunn came in place of Lewins, who married Crawley, the Irish housemaid; a miserable union that ended ill for both parties through the cursed drink.

'Eventually we settled down in Durham for three years, and while there mixed in the society of the prebends and their wives. Dean Waddington was most friendly to us. He seldom had a dinner party of any size without including us among the guests. Doctor Jenkins and his wife, the daughter of John Cam Hobhouse, were at the Residence; not a popular couple with their compeers. Mrs. Jenkins took umbrage at the Dean's partiality for William and me, seeing in us, no doubt, a dangerous influence; for High-Churchism was beginning to raise its head in Oxford, and such people as the Jenkins thought of every Catholic as *un chat qui dort*. That summer I was not well, and Mary Fairfax came up north to nurse me when the London season was over. In the autumn I was myself again and went to stay with Mamma at Seaton Carew and after that to Brandsby. I always regretted that I never went to Crathorne when my mother made it her home after shaking the dust of Burghwallis from her feet; in consequence of which I never set eyes on that old family home. Frank Charlton, William's third brother, who had adopted the profession of civil engineer, was working on a branch railway near Durham and nearly always spent the Sunday with us, his bedroom being constantly in readiness.

'Frank's was a beautiful character. It was impossible to know him and not love him, for he possessed all the qualities that command love and respect. A great wit, he was never known to use his talent in a sarcastic sense, nor to hurt feelings or to cast a slur. Of all the men I have known, he came nearest to an angelic being, and one could not hear the words, "Blessed is the man to whom the Lord hath not imputed sin and in whose spirit there is no guile", without the mind reverting to him. He was once the recipient of the greatest compliment that man can pay to man when, having to appear at Petty Sessions, and the clerk about to offer him the Bible, the judge said, "That ceremony will not be necessary. Mr. Francis Charlton's word is quite sufficient."

'In 1843 Mrs. Charlton returned to Hesleyside from Elswick a broken-down old woman. They had shaven her head and stuck on it a hideous black wig that was always awry. She was installed in the suite of rooms looking south on the ground floor. I thought her very meek and amenable to reason. She had a lady companion, a Mrs. Thelwell, who was not altogether a success. Some of us were usually with her in her room, and we used to get her to read to us; for she read well, in fact much better than she spoke, having a hesitation in her speech, like unto her sister, Mrs. Wright, which was more of a sob than a stutter. She could also play backgammon, and play it well. During our stay I used to drive out alone with her, and once or twice she raised her hand suddenly as if to strike, but never actually did so. As some of her pleasantest days had been spent in Durham, I could talk "Residence" to her, and of a few old fossil prebends, like Doctor Wellesley, whom she had known. She was slower of response, like to a child trying to remember a half-forgotten lesson, but when the answer came it made good sense, and her habit of running down others in order to exalt herself had disappeared. A most charming nurse was in attendance besides the lady companion, a young, comely widow, fair to look at; a right-down kind woman, never far away, never off duty, and sweet to my little Eddy, for she loved children. Subsequently she married Dr. Elliot who for upwards of thirty years was a most popular Bellingham practitioner, and who was succeeded by his son.

'On the 9th May, 1844, my dear, unselfish mother died at Crathorne, aged fifty-two, and was laid next to her father in the Crathorne vault, my father being in Paris at the time and only my brother George Anne at Burghwallis. We were sent for, but I was unable to go, and when William arrived she was insensible. I thus lost a last opportunity of seeing Crathorne, for the house and estate were sold to Mr. Dugdale. In July and August I was at Scarborough with Mary Fairfax, George Heneage and all the Heneage children. After that we went on to Brandsby for a short stay, and took part in private theatricals at Sutton Hall nearby. I acted Miss Hardcastle in *She Stoops to Conquer*. Back in Durham we invested in a little Victoria and two pretty ponies which William named Medora and Gulnare, out of Lord Byron's *Corsair*.

'The winter of 1844–45 was made lively by the strike of Durham pitmen. Mary and Kate Charlton came to stay with us, and we gave a dance for them and several dinner parties. I went to London for a month, staying at 39 Charles Street, and William joined me there later. One of the principal theatres was taken for a performance, half amateur, half professional, in aid of funds for the failure of the potato crop in Ireland, and George Heneage took a box. The Queen, Prince Albert, and the Duchess of Sutherland graced it with their presence, sitting in a middle side box so that they might be seen by as many as possible. Fanny Kemble acted in *The Provoked Husband*; I thought her a very vulgar actress. In the early summer we went to Schwalbach, taking Kate Charlton, who was out of health, in our train. It was a very wet season, with hardly a dry day, and the dullness of the society to be found there that year had no exhilarating effect.

'In September, 1845, we left Durham and took Brandsby for two years, the house being vacant owing to the death of old Mrs. Fairfax, which left her son Charles free to occupy Gilling Castle. Crace came from London to decorate the

gallery at Gilling and did it beautifully, not having as yet
developed his heavy, gloomy style of interior decoration. At
Brandsby we passed a very quiet winter with Kate Charlton
as our guest, her sister Mary wishing her to be removed
from the melancholy atmosphere of Hesleyside. My sister,
Mary Fairfax, constantly came over from Gilling to see us,
and I drove out daily with Medora and Gulnare. In the
evenings William read to me aloud, mostly Sir Walter Scott.
I paid one visit to Hesleyside and found the same dismal
routine going on. My father-in-law seemed much altered
and had grown fidgety. I thought there must be something
amiss with him when he caressed me in mistake for Kate.
He would wander aimlessly into his poor wife's room, but
without uttering a word, his silence very likely in remorse
for the past cruelty and heartlessness, in which he had
passively taken part, which had aggravated the condition
of an already weak brain, and caused his wife to take such
an intense dislike to him in the early years of her suffering. It
was indeed a sad Nemesis by which he had been overtaken.

'On 11th August, 1846, my eldest daughter Frances
Mary, which soon became Fanny, was born, William and
I going to York for the occasion.

'On October 5th of the same year Thomas Charlton, my
husband's fourth brother, who was studying for the priesthood and was then in minor orders, died at Florence aged
twenty-four. He had a high reputation in Rome for piety
and learning, and it was the general opinion in priestly
circles there, particularly with Doctor Wiseman, that the
Catholic Church had suffered a decided loss. There can be
no doubt that the seeds of consumption were sown during
his boyhood at Hesleyside. How could delicate children
thrive in that atmosphere of damp, cold and neglect; com-
fortless during their tenderest years? The father willing

enough as a paymaster, so to say, but given up to silence, moodiness and poring over his books by the fire. The mother wishful to help her children, but always in a dreamy and absent-minded state, wool-gathering when not asserting her superiority. The very cottagers' children roundabout were better tended, and had more care bestowed on them than my husband, his brothers, and his sisters during their growing years. They were left, literally, to battle with the elements. Coal and firewood they had in great abundance, it is true, but the long passages had no heat, the outside doors were never shut, the hall and corridors were paved with flagstones, while, to complete the resemblance of Hesleyside to a refrigerator, the grand staircase, also of stone, and the three large, old-fashioned full-length windows halfway up with their frames warped by the excessive damp, the pride of Mrs. (Fenwick) Charlton's heart, contrived to make the downstairs space a cave of icy blasts. Even in my early years at Hesleyside funguses grew on the passage woodwork. The dining-room, a corner room looking east with its northern windows ingeniously stopped up, did not have window curtains until some little time after my arrival in 1839. Without hangings of any sort, every noise re-echoed so that I could not hear what was being said distinctly; so Mrs. Charlton procured some cloth curtains and had them put up, short like kilts and quite unequal for keeping out the cold. In those days the food was execrable and coarsely served. I looked on with astonishment at Mrs. Charlton's disgusting way of eating, not to mention other nauseous table habits, and soon accustomed myself to eating my own rations with downcast eyes. How her mother, an Englefield who must have had a refined upbringing herself, could have allowed her children's lawlessness at table passes understanding. Of all my mother-in-law's generation that I knew her sister, Mrs. Wright, was the least offensive with a knife and fork in hand. Luckily, home-killed mutton of the very best saved my life; otherwise it would have been bad beef, unsound bread, mostly of the barley cake variety, salt butter, and diseased potatoes as the common fare. When in season, an undressed lettuce always occupied the middle of the table, at which each member of the family would dab in turn, tearing off a leaf, sprinkling salt on the dirty table-cloth, and so eating of it in that primitive fashion. Such a thing as a dressed salad was unknown in Mrs. Charlton's time. I begged to have dry biscuits to breakfast, as I could not stomach the unsound bread and over-salted butter. No wine was ever served at dinner, though this did not touch me, as at that time I drank nothing. Water, drunk out of black glass, was the family beverage. Nevertheless, the butler and his pantry cronies appeared to indulge freely in wine! In that way it was hardly possible to find a more drunken establishment; Hesleyside was simply a house of public refreshment for the neighbourhood and, I am sorry to say, remained so when William and I later had it to ourselves. Hauxwell, the butler, a sober enough man himself, gave drink out, he said, for the honour of the family! And my poor husband, who laboured latterly for the effervescent popularity of the lower orders, well knew that drink was a high road to their hearts. How mercilessly was his mistaken generosity taken advantage of! Most certainly Hesleyside in those days was a rum and disorderly establishment. When my mother-in-law was no longer fit to guide it, Mary Charlton did her best to fill the breach; and this again was a difficult undertaking, for the old nurse, Mrs. Hunt, who knew only Hesleyside ways and scorned innovation, and who had been with the family for upwards of thirty years, was promoted housekeeper.

M

'Ten days before Tom's death in Florence, my father-in-law, William John Charlton, died at Hesleyside, September 25th, 1846, aged sixty-two, of softening of the brain that had been coming on for some time. Poor Mrs. Charlton, whose room was next-door to her husband's death chamber, was perfectly docile and responsive to common-sense suggestion during his last illness; never expressing any wish to see him either then or after he had passed away, asking no questions, making no remarks, and what was passing through her mind no one could say. Once, however, she did flash out, when Mrs. Thelwell, the lady companion, tactlessly, though no doubt with the best intention, forbade that knives should come up at the meals they ate in common. Mrs. Charlton told her, rightly to my mind, that she should feel ashamed of her discreditable suspicions. Old Richardson the estate carpenter, made a simple, rough coffin, and the dead squire, as far as concerned his actual sepulture, was buried like a pauper.

'After her father's death, Mary Charlton's sole idea was to take her sister, whose lungs were now pronounced to be affected, out of England and into a warmer climate, although by then the mischief had gone too deep. When everything was all settled and they were ready to depart I came up from Brandsby to help them pack and leave things in order; for they had no maid, the Irishwoman who did for them having been sent hurriedly away after an attempt to cut her throat for love of Hauxwell, ugliest of butlers.

'Italy was their destination, and when they were fairly on their way the architect Bonomi, who designed St. Oswald's Church at Bellingham but was otherwise of no celebrity, came to Hesleyside to plan alterations in order to make the house warmer and more habitable for William and me. The large hall, hitherto paved with flags, was properly floored to help counteract the unbearable cold, and converted into a French drawing-room, beautifully decorated by Crace's foreman, Worthington. The carriage road was taken round the haugh and the main entrance made on the north side of the house. Lions rampant, the Charlton shield, were erected on either side of the inner driveway. A dressed-stone clock-tower was put up on the same side, and the old clock, fallen into disrepair, was made to go again. The hedge was uprooted round the haugh and iron railings substituted. There was no hall now for the front door to open on to, and the main entrance was unavoidably narrow and insignificant, but the alteration added greatly to the general comfort and, moreover, displayed to advantage the remnant of one of the avenues of olden days, that which radiated towards the river. While all this work was going on we remained at Brandsby, and as soon as it was quite convenient my poor mother-in-law, nothing loth to go, was removed to a good house with a splendid garden near Newcastle, where she remained until her death in 1849. Her sitting room and bedroom became our bedroom and my boudoir.

'The winter of 1846–47 was a gay one in Yorkshire, and we visited about a lot; at Hovingham where Lady Worsley gave a charming Christmas dance, at the Francis Cholmeleys at Spennithorne than which there was no one I liked better to go to see, and, for two nights, with Lord and Lady Prudhoe at Stanwick, where there was a large house-party and much discussion on the authorship of *Jane Eyre*, which had then been out two months.

'In the spring we became very anxious about our little Eddy, who had an ulcerated throat and a temperature. We had the best doctor from York to attend on him who, as we were given to suppose, effected a complete cure. So we hied us off to London for a short time. The ballets were danced that season by Viennese children, but it was promptly put a stop to on the score that they would come under immoral influences. We returned to Brandsby at the end of June for our final packing up before taking possession of Hesleyside, and in July we went to Redcar for a touch of sea air before heading north. There it was that our dear little Eddy caught the scarlet fever and died of it, at the age of exactly five years, July 27th, 1847. No language can express our grief. Merely to recall the memory of those sad days and months of sorrow, now as I write in my seventy-eighth year, causes me a sinking of the heart. Although so young, Eddy was a child of sweetest disposition and great promise, but God — who knows best — took the angel boy into His keeping. On the first of August, almost the eighth anniversary of my first arrival there, with heavy-laden hearts we went to Hesleyside, my poor William bearing up as best he could so as to help lighten my own burden. But men have their outdoor occupations, sport and business, to take their minds away from grief even if for the time being only; a mother's heart is naked and defenceless and she has to ward it off as best she can. Hesleyside was inexpressibly melancholy to me. I missed Mary above all others, and I also missed kind Kate, for they both loved our dear lost child. Rent in twain as was my heart, I did not recover for many months, and even now I feel a shudder when I recall that woeful time. As we drove up to the house, alighting at the back door as the new front entrance was not quite finished, George Dixon the agent and Hauxwell the butler met us with sorrow on their faces, for Eddy's sweet ways had endeared him to all who knew him. It had been a lovely season for growth and the foliage was super-luxuriant in the woods, but the dark, heavy green gave me the sensation of being enveloped in a shroud and nothing seemed to rouse me.

'Frank Charlton came to Hesleyside as often as he could get away from his railway-building operations, and on one of his visits he proposed to share with William the expense of setting up a school for Catholic children just behind St. Oswald's Church, whose priest should give religious instruction to the scholars. At that time there had been a small discovery of iron ore at Bellingham, and the place was full of dirty, ill-conditioned Irish labourers whose children sadly needed education and to be taught better ways than their parents. Odd to tell, the iron-works were begun before the Border Counties railway plan was set afoot, like putting the cart before the horse. However, it was a very thin deposit of ore and the enterprise came to an untimely end in a short time.

'A great annual event on North Tyne is the Bellingham Agricultural Show, held in September, which grew, always under the Presidency of the Squire of Hesleyside, from small local beginnings to a meeting of high repute, with special trains from Newcastle, a fair ground, and an ever increasing public attendance. It was inaugurated in this year, 1847, and its birth haphazardly occurred in the following manner: George Dixon, the Hesleyside agent, happened to be discussing with his brother-in-law, Mr. Coulson, North-country agricultural prospects in view of the high price time that was approaching; and in the course of the discussion Mr. Dixon, as if a happy thought had come to him, exclaimed, "We will have a Show at Bellingham. I'll get a pound out of the Squire and a few local subscriptions, and start it going." My husband took up the idea with enthusiasm and pulled the plan through to a finish, encouraged by the gentry and big farmers roundabout. Prizes were awarded, it would appear, on that first occasion more on a principle of consolation than of merit. Mr. Allgood of

Nunwick showed a hunter of high price; but Mr. Charlton of Hesleyside, who showed a hunter of low price, got the prize. Upon which, Mr. Allgood very naturally remonstrated, though to no avail. "Hout! Mr. Allgood," said George Dixon, looking down the prize-list. "Why, I see here ye have a prize for a pig; so of course the Squire must get a prize for his horse."

'On the 29th of February, 1848, the Feast of St. Mildred, my second daughter was born and christened Amy Mildred Mary, and once again, after many years of surcease, I had a recurrence of my painful tic.

'The old tower of Hesleyside, the only one of its kind on Tyne north of Chipchase, closely resembling the peels at Cockle Park, near Morpeth, and Halton, was probably constructed in the fourteenth century, and stood of old at the west end of the present house. This celebrated and picturesque relic of former days was ruthlessly destroyed during my father-in-law's minority by his two Gothic guardians, Mr. Salvin of Croxdale and Dr. Fenwick, elder of his two medical uncles, who pulled it down and used the stones for building on a tasteless east-front to the hall in decadent renaissance style. His mother must have been completely lacking in taste herself to have consented to such vandalism. Not only did they destroy the tower, but effaced the original beauty of the south-front, built about 1600 or even earlier. Hesleyside, before the hideous east-front was added, was a country seat somewhat on the lines of a smallish French *château*, standing at the meeting-point of four tree-lined avenues, of which the north, east and west are still existing or traceable. In that day, old Dr. Fenwick told me, the coachman drove his horses through the south-front archway, off-loaded in the courtyard beyond, and made an exit to the stables by a corresponding archway in the north-front. The arches are still as they were, though the courtyard is a billiard-room, but the ground level must have been considerably raised since then, for certainly no vehicle could drive beneath them now. The priest's hiding-place was known to exist somewhere behind the façade of the south-front, but it was not until 1868 that my husband had its situation definitely established, and opened up for the curious to come and see.

'In June of 1848 we went to London for a short visit. It was a season in which the Chartists held the foreground, and in the evenings long processions of them paraded the streets with banners, greatly to the disturbance of the public peace of mind. In August, back at Hesleyside, we gave a house-warming and entertained a great deal of company: Mr. and Mrs. Plowden, Marmion Ferrars, Mr. Scrope with his two daughters Florence and Adela, Edward, afterwards Cardinal, Howard, Edward Riddell of The Grange, Kate Strickland, Fanny Blackett, Sir Joseph and Lady Ratcliffe with son and two daughters, Francis Cholmeley, and Mr. and Mrs. Murray. Mr. Murray was at the Foreign Office, and was the man, much later on, who caused commotion by tearing up as so much waste paper King Thibaw's offer of marriage to Queen Victoria. In the evenings there was dancing, for with Adela Scrope and Edward Howard of the party it simply had to be. The future cardinal was then about twenty, and, although he talked about diplomacy, had not fixed on a career. He was a splendid linguist. Eventually he went into the Guards, and after a few years abandoned soldiering for the Church. A treasured family possession was then, and still is, a very beautiful Venetian glass goblet, probably of seventeenth-century workmanship and most richly ornamented, with the Charlton crest enamelled on it and inscribed "The Standard of Hesleyside." It held a bottle of claret, neither more nor less, and it was the custom and a challenge, originating in Jacobite days, to gulp the contents down without taking breath. On the occasion of our house-warming it was once brought out at supper, and the swallowing feat was duly performed by two daring youths, Edward Howard and a young clergyman, a Mr. Gibbs. As far as could be seen, neither was the worse for it, as they both danced steadily after supper. I always dreaded this calling for the Standard, for some boasters immediately succumbed to the gluttonous operation before they could reach their rooms, and such an exhibition before ladies was not quite in keeping with the refinement of the times. Many times I suggested that the convivial vessel should be put under a glass case and kept in the drawing-room; but I was always voted down, and in due course it suffered damage by the handling of a drunken butler. I have no doubt that the same inebriate exploits that went on in the dining-room were repeated in the butler's pantry, where the gardener, shepherd, woodman, and all the other rural employés daily met to assist in drinking dry their generous and too easy-going master's cellar. In our day Hesleyside was spoken of as a house in which the newest ideas were tried out. It was the first house in the county, for instance, where tub baths were to be found in every bedroom. But there was one old-fashioned custom my husband would never on any account give up; and that was sitting boozing after dinner until, sometimes, it was eleven o'clock and after before the servants could get in to take away the things.

'Came the news that Kate Charlton had married the Baron Rosario Cali de Fabio of Aci Reale, in Sicily on the east coast ten miles north of Catania. Furthermore, we were given to understand that the match had been engineered by no other than the unpleasant and ill-conditioned waif and stray who had imposed on my mother-in-law's kindness at Hesleyside, nearly twenty years ago, and who now, for a rental of £14 annually, was in occupation of a vast and empty Palazzo in Genoa.

'Rosario was in a position corresponding to a French *sous-préfet*—perhaps a little higher and possibly with more salary attached. But it was no great shakes, and Kate's consternation may be imagined, when making her bridal visit on her husband's family, at discovering the primitive, and poverty-stricken, state in which they lived; the mother and daughters no different in appearance and way of life than the peasant class. Kate told me herself that Mrs. Hunt, the Hesleyside housekeeper, was a lady compared to her Italian in-laws, despite their titles. They did all the house and kitchen work with cotton handkerchiefs on their heads and wearing print dresses and aprons in servant style; and the strange thing was that, bred to such ignoble labour, they had no wish for change. Besides this, they had no education and, to the eternal disgrace of the Sicilian priesthood, could neither read nor write. No wonder immorality in all shapes and forms reached such an unheard of pitch in Naples, Palermo, and all through Sicily, and was Italy's reproach, when women of every class in life were under the thraldom of an ignorant, superstitious, and often profligate priesthood. The home of the Cali family was diminutive and inconvenient, but Rosario was loving and attentive to his wife, and his people so kind, that Kate told me she felt supremely happy in spite of her motley and unconventional surroundings.

'Mary Charlton joined her sister at the beginning of 1849 and, during the spring of that year, wrote her clever and admirable account of the "War of Liberation" and the bombardment of the chief Sicilian cities, including Catania, which earned King Ferdinand the sobriquet of Bomba. In her letters back to William she also gives her brother a graphic account of her ascent of Mount Etna, where it is very probable she caught the low fever from which she never thoroughly recovered. Her letters were so brilliant that William had them printed for private circulation.

'In September, 1848, the Duke and Duchess of Northumberland paid Hesleyside a visit on their way down Tyne from Kielder Castle, the ducal shooting lodge built on an old site a few miles south of the border. The Duchess and I talked of schools, she of hers at Kielder and I of mine at Bellingham, in which I had begun to take great interest. A Mrs. Dury had succeeded to the first Irish mistress who had so hastily married; a widow of comely appearance with a nice little daughter. Mrs. Dury was a convert, a person of advanced education who knew her business, and would have been a great success had the priest in charge only been able to leave her to herself. But he became childish on her account and could not bear to have her out of sight, so eventually they both had to leave. Mrs. Dury came from over the Border and had a true Scotch sense of economy. She reckoned that she could reduce her living expenses if she and her daughter fed daily at the priest's house; but his housekeeper made a calculation of her own, coming to the conclusion that she was only paid for cooking and waiting on one person, not three, and a tense situation arose.

'In Mrs. Dury's time there were a few girls at the school who showed sufficient promise to blossom out in time as nursery-governesses; so I perched myself behind a table on a raised platform at one end of the school-room and sat for a couple of hours, twice a week, endeavouring to instil French into these more promising scholars. It was hard work indeed teaching these children to pronounce "u" as in "tu"; their tongues were too broad for such a subtlety. But I persevered in my laudable endeavours, worthy of a better cause, until one day Frank Charlton opened my eyes to the fact that the bookstall at Hexham station had a number of cheap, unsavoury, illustrated French novels on sale, hoping thereby to attract my class as purchasers. That was the end of language instruction for me; I dismissed the class for ever, following which the obnoxious publications promptly disappeared. Actuated by the example I had set, Eleanor, Duchess of Northumberland, had also secured the services of a teacher of French at Kielder, but the effort was no more successful in her case than in mine.

'I was then seeing a good deal of Mr. Surridge, the Greystead rector, and his wife, who lived about four miles upriver. Mary Charlton had asked me especially to show kindness to Mrs. Surridge, as the poor woman could not get accustomed to the *sauvagerie* of the district.

'I have already mentioned some way back that the sequestrated Derwentwater estates, which included the Church livings up and down North Tyne, were bestowed on Greenwich Hospital. Commissioners of only so-called honesty were sent expensively from London in chaises and four to parcel out these miserable benefices and, where necessary, to run up rectories and churches of tasteless design and regardless of the cost for a new set of incumbents. As was to be expected, retired Navy parsons took possession of these penurious livings, and a choice lot they must have been. Either at Wark, or at Simonburn another four miles downstream, Lord Sandwich had an edifying specimen installed who baptized a monkey and administered the sacrament to a dog. Others of similar kidney, but more out of sight in distant parishes, led sinful lives according to their individual predilections. These scandals were not of long

continuance, and in my time I was favoured with the society
of two very nice clerical families; the Surridges of Greystead
and the Powells of Bellingham, although it may be mentioned that there were some pretty curious articles as pastors
at the latter place before they came.

'When William and I took proper possession of Hesleyside in 1847 there stood in the very middle of the wood, with
quite a good road leading to it, a small but interesting looking cottage; sunless, dark, damp and gloomy, a worthy
setting for a gruesome story. In this lonely dwelling lived
the Adam Scotts, and son, until, two years later, on account
of a charge of defalcation against the latter, they were
obliged to leave the district; the cottage, much to my regret,
being then pulled down. I used often to go and see them
and, on one occasion, Adam told me how, in 1834, when
the Hesleyside family was travelling abroad, a great band
of poachers, lead-miners for the most part from Alston
Moor about twenty-five miles in a straight line south,
invaded William's game preserves. The then agent, John
Dixon the Second, had collected some estate workers,
gone out to meet the poaching band, met a separate
small party of them, and taken away their guns. Next morning John Dixon, with his beautiful wife and numerous
family, was at breakfast, the three captured weapons standing in a corner of the room, when suddenly the top of the
garden hedge of Mantle Hill bristled with heads. The main
band had arrived! John Dixon went out to interview them,
about thirty in number, keeping to his own side of the hedge,
and was abusively accosted by the leader, while a shirt-
sleeved aide-de-camp went busily about pouring whisky for
the rank and file from one of many bottles that he had on
him. The younger Dixon children huddled self-protectingly
in the rear, but his wife and eldest daughter stoutly stood

beside him in support. The head of the poaching gang declared that guns cost money and, unless the three that had been seized were given back, he would take his men to Gorcock Hill and take out thrice their value in game. This, as well John Dixon knew, would have spelt disaster to the Squire's sporting outlook, and so he compromised by offering the guns in exchange for an undertaking to leave Mr. Charlton's land at once. The promise was given and duly carried out. The whole band went across the Tyne at the Hesleyside mill and were captured shortly after while carousing in the shooting-box of Mr. Bell on Hareshaw Common. The landowners and big farmers then formed an association and engaged two mounted men to keep watch on the moors, after which there was no more poaching.'

XIV

HER FAMILY INCREASES

For the next few years, 1849–52, Barbara's life continues at an equable rate and on fairly ordered lines, lived for the most part at Hesleyside, but diversified by country-house visits, an occasional jaunt to London, an excursion to Paris, and a whole half-year at Leamington, selected for climatic reasons as a set-off to the wintry rigour of Northumberland. During this four-year period her family is increased by the birth of two male children, and now consists of a pair of either sex. She and her William approach the outpost years of early middle age confidingly and with a full sense of family responsibility; he, as ever, actively engaged in projects for the improvement of the countryside, and Barbara growingly awakened to the fact that motherhood brings care.

It was said in eulogy of William Charlton's part in the development of his native district that he found it without either roads or railways, and left it with both. It was no exaggeration, and in particular he mooted, activated, and carried through to completion a local railway plan by which, via the North Tyne valley and following the windings of the river all the way, the Newcastle-Carlisle line was linked, at Hexham, with the Lowland system to the north and thence to Edinburgh. It came into existence as *The Border Counties Railway* and to-day, a hundred years after, the London and North-Eastern trains of British Railways traverse the valley of the North Tyne over the way that was then constructed, the first sod of which, for the Bellingham-Falstone section, was ceremonially turned by Barbara on January 7th, 1858, trundling a highly decorated barrow and handling a most ladylike spade.

In this section of her memoirs the writer treats of the
once far-famed 'Papal Aggression' which so aroused
Protestant susceptibilities in the middle of the nineteenth
century. Barbara, however, is too discursive on the subject and takes too much for granted that her readers are
well posted on a happening of long ago. The plain matter
of the case was this: In mid-year, 1850, Pope Pius IX
created Doctor Nicholas Patrick Stephen Wiseman a
cardinal and, in furtherance of a papal plan for restoring a
diocesan hierarchy in England, issued simultaneously a
brief appointing him cardinal and Archbishop of Westminster. Soon after the issue of the papal brief Wiseman
wrote a pastoral to the faithful of his new English flock
and, of bombastic sound for Church of England ears, dated
it 'from out of the Flaminian Gate.' The contents also had
a bad sound, for Wiseman, with great want of tact, spoke of
the 'restoration of Catholic England to its orbit in the
ecclesiastical firmament,' an expression which could have
but one meaning for non-Catholics, namely: a rebirth of
Catholicism throughout the country. The pastoral letter and
the territorial distinction that had been assumed, together
aroused so fierce a popular indignation, and such a violence
of feeling, that when Wiseman, after a slow journey from
Rome to England via Vienna, finally arrived it was thought
that his life might be endangered by the unruliness of the
mob. He himself, however, remained calm and cool, and took
prompt steps, by publishing a thirty-page pamphlet and de-
livering a course of lectures at St. George's, Southwark, to allay
the storm his injudicious behaviour had provoked and still
the cries of 'Papal aggression' which were further stirring it.

The General Election in the autumn of 1852 which
Barbara mentions at the end of this chapter was an indirect
result of this tea-cup effervescence, so ruffling to the

religious susceptibility of that epoch. When the 'No Popery' agitation, aroused by Wiseman's pastoral, was at its height the then Prime Minister, Lord John Russell, promised in a letter to the Bishop of Durham to introduce an 'Ecclesiastical Titles Bill' forbidding the assumption of territorial distinctions by Roman Catholic priests and bishops. But the support this measure received in the House of Commons was so lukewarm that the Government, defeated also on another matter, took the opportunity to vacate office.

With the following final note on a different subject altogether, Barbara shall be allowed to resume her recollections. It concerns the marble Venus which was bought by William in the sale at Swinburne Castle. Until quite recent days this really handsome piece of statuary was a principal ornament in the library at Hesleyside, representing the goddess of love and beauty at her undraped best, with all her limbs seductively intact. It happened in some succeeding year that a young convent-bred girl was due to make a stay at Hesleyside, and a question of propriety arose in Barbara's mind, Was it seemly, so she put the matter to herself, that this pure-minded, youthful guest should be confronted, daily, hourly, by this pagan specimen of female nudity? Barbara negatived the bare idea and, with the best intention in the world, anxious only that modesty should not be shocked, changed a thing of beauty into an object of universal reprobation by enfolding poor Aphrodite in a suit of pink georgette.

'In January, 1849, we went to stay at Spennithorne with Francis Cholmeley, a perfect host and one of the cheeriest of good fellows, that house being a convenient centre for neighbouring festivities; such as a ball given by the Duchess of Leeds at Hornby Castle, a dance at Leyburn, and a smaller one at Brough. We finished up with a visit to Aunt Wright, my mother-in-law's sister, who was in her chronic state of nerves. In spite of her awkwardness of movement and coarse frame Mrs. Wright must have been not bad-looking before her right eye drooped. Her mouth was not disgusting like that of Mrs. Charlton, who always spoke of her, and no one else, as half daft. I never set eyes on Mrs. Strickland, the third sister, so cannot vouch for her appearance, excepting that I had always heard of her as being very good and very plain.

'When we got back home Caroline Strawbenzee, a quiet, amiable, ladylike young woman, came to stay and remained at Hesleyside three months. Arthur Weld also came to see the completion of his geometrical garden. Except those two, and of course Frank Charlton, who was constantly coming and going and who used to help me with Latin which I was learning to be of use to my children in the time to come, we saw no one at Hesleyside for upwards of a year. I had the chapel decorated and assisted in the good work by colouring with my own hands the Tabernacle, Crucifix and altar candleticks. I also had my bedroom papered. In the summer, acting on the thoughtless advice of Dr. Charlton, William's medical brother, I went to stay at Tynemouth; but finding it too rough underfoot I went on to Seton Carew, where at least I could walk about on smooth ground.

'The Border Counties Railway was then in contemplation, with my husband as principal promoter of the project and Algernon, Duke of Northumberland, as his zealous supporter. While I was at Seton William went to London to appear before the Parliamentary Committee. Odd to relate, Sir John Swinburne, who had so far been hand and glove with William in his improvement plans up Tyne, was a bitter opponent of this railway scheme. Sir Matthew White Ridley of Blagdon was another, and comical at that. He opposed the scheme tooth and nail, stating to the committee

N

that the only place he could get to now on wheels was his shooting-box on North Tyne, and that he did not feel like being deprived of that satisfaction. And apart from that, he added, why should that out-of-the-way part of the country be opened up by a railway? It would only disturb the game! Roars of laughter from the committee greeted this bit of specious pleading on Sir Matthew's part, and more still burst forth when he produced a sketch of the aforesaid shooting-box. Sir Matthew White Ridley was merely middle-aged, but Sir John Swinburne was eighty-seven. My husband, however, despite senility and self-interest, did not waver in his determination to get his scheme put through for the sake of the many who would benefit, and he fully succeeded in getting it accepted.

'Sir John Swinburne had evidently ceased to bear in mind the views he held as a young man in favour of changes and reforms in French revolutionary days; how the country-folk were much amused, and the old Jacobites greatly scandalized, to see him, old Dr. Fenwick, both renegades, and Lord Grey riding about with one spur on and calling themselves Citizen Swinburne, Citizen Fenwick and Citizen Grey; and how Lady Swinburne, unmindful of her London butler and two 6-foot, powdered footmen, lisped out "All for equality!" as her carriage and four greys drove up to the Capheaton door. No wonder their eldest son Edward, father to the remarkably austere baronet of to-day (June 11th, 1892) imbibed his sire's principles in downright earnest and strictly adhered throughout life to his well-taught lesson, wearing neither shoes, nor stockings, nor even a coat when not absolutely necessary, at his Windermere home.

'Poor Mrs. Charlton died on July 30th, 1849, aged sixty. Before her death occurred the brain derangement that had so often offuscated her intellect at intervals since a very early age completely disappeared. After nearly seven years of seclusion she awoke one morning with a clear mind and talked most sensibly of her past life and of all the mistakes she had made. She confessed, and received Holy Communion for the first time in many years. Soon after she was taken with a fit, and all was over. Mary Charlton had wished to have her mother's head examined after death, for the good of others; but Dr. Edward Charlton willed it otherwise.

'I do not know if Hesleyside was better or worse than other houses of its sort as regards drink and morals, but whereas I had good reason to know all about the former evil, I remained in ignorance all the time I was in residence of immoral goings-on. It was not in fact till the winter of 1893, when I went down to Brighton on the sad occasion of my eldest son's last illness, that I really got to know the truth. For he talked much of the olden days at Hesleyside when he was but a boy, as in a wandering way sick persons do, and of the scandals in the laundry which, according to him, was nothing but a brothel until a new entrance was built and gates put up to keep intruders out. He gave the names of some of the upper servants as among the most licentious, women of whom I had no suspicion, believing them to lead blameless lives. It horrified me, so long ago as that, to hear about the scenes of profligacy he himself had witnessed as he passed the laundry to and fro at odd times of the day; and I had no doubt, although he did not say so, that he was similarly *au fait* at the indoor servants' amours in the pantry. My boys must have been well aware of all the wrongdoings inside and outside the house, but some distorted sense of fair play kept them from ever telling of it. How many years had it been, I wondered, and how many young girls had been ruined, before the simple expedient William and I adopted for making the laundry precincts private put a stop to these malpractices.

'My son told me on that same sad occasion of something else that happened when he was a growing lad, showing how thoroughly tricky and untrustworthy those of our retainers were who gathered nightly in the saddle-room for the concoction of evil deeds. There was a still in the garden-shed for the distillation of mint, as was the custom in old-fashioned gardens, and which, as far as we knew, was used for no other purpose. But in Hodgson's time as gardener this was not the case. It was in the days of home-brewing, and the brewing refuse was always thrown to the pigs. Hodgson, however, begged it from his unsuspecting master for the raising of carrots, which did not thrive in the Hesley-side garden soil, and had to be bought. Some fine carrots were duly produced as evidence of what a manufactured soil could do, although in reality they had been introduced from outside. For Hodgson was using the refuse for the distillation of something a good deal more potent than peppermint, and the inmates of the saddle-room were in the secret with him.

'The pigs were also supposed to get the potatoes not fit for our table, and here again Hodgson played a wily and dishonest game. He begged to have them for his own use, and after that no crop ever seemed to thrive, so that in spite of keeping a gardener to grow potatoes for us we had to buy as well from others. Mrs. Hunt used often to say to me with marked significance, "Hodgson is a very greedy man!" but I did not ever ask her what she meant; while she, having afforded me my chance of knowledge, thought her duty done. For servants, like children, have that same strange, distorted sense of fair play, and a marvellous faculty of secretiveness. They know of all the wrongful things that go on in a household but, otherwise than on rare occasions vaguely hinting, speak they will not.

'On the 7th January, 1850, I had the inexpressible joy of giving birth to a son, my fifth child, but so far the only boy to survive. He was christened William Oswald by Mr. Brown, the priest, in our newly decorated chapel for which Eliza, Dr. Edward Charlton's wife, had provided a beautiful stained-glass window, shortly after smashed to atoms, while in his cups, by Henderson, the estate carpenter. In its place Eliza sent an oak-carved St. Barbara, my patron saint, complete with tower, sword and crown, too massive for any drunkard to break. Eliza came to Hesleyside from Newcastle with her husband to stand sponsor to the new-born infant. She remained on for some time, and I then first learned to appreciate her many inestimable qualities. It was a most bitterly cold winter. William had lately become a member of the Catholic School Board, and went up to London now and then to attend the periodic meetings.

'It was in the spring of 1850 that the Cookson sale at Swinburne Castle took place, at which we bought the marble Venus, a picture by Caracci, another of a game of quoits, and sundry other articles. The Tom Cooksons had always been extremely kind to Mary and Kate Charlton in their trials and distresses, and we thought these purchases were the least we could do in recognition.

'We remained quietly at Hesleyside till May, and I busied myself with my children's education, Fanny the elder of my two girls, now nearly four, being remarkably clever and forward; there was also the music lessons I gave twice a week to the two little Surridge girls at Greystead Rectory. In May we went to London and put up at the Pulteney Hotel, our stay there being longer than was intended owing to the hard mouth of a hired hack, which became restive in the Park one day and sprained my right arm in the effort to pull it in. Both arm and hand swelled up and gave me great pain. We had been invited to Alnwick Castle for the great Agricultural Meeting of August 5th, and now the Duchess came to see me at the hotel to say she would be entertaining a very large house-party. So I got busy with my diamonds for the occasion and had them mounted by Tessier in tiara shape, a setting that has been universally admired both in England and abroad. By permission of the Duchess, I took old Cholmeley, who, because of his kindness to me when I was young, always occupied a soft corner of my heart, and Mary Douglas, who stood apart from her race as a woman of perfection, without worldliness or selfishness, to Sion House at Isleworth, the Middlesex seat of the Percys since 1600, built originally by Inigo Jones on the former site of a convent for Bridgetine nuns, and therefore an interesting house to Catholics.

'In June we went to Paris for a short time. William had been given a letter of introduction to Montalembert, famous as a favourer of liberal Catholicism, but it only went as far as an exchange of cards.

'On August 5th we duly went to Alnwick for the great Show. Forty guests sat down to dinner and, in every particular, it was a ducal entertainment, with an orchestra concert on the first night. Besides all the principal county families, the guests invited for the Show included Lord and Lady Tankerville, the latter looking lovely as a bride, Lord and Lady Lovaine, Lord Northampton, William Prescot the American historian, young Mr. Wentworth Beaumon who became our Member of Parliament two years later, and was the first Baron Allendale, Sir Edward Blackett and his daughter Louisa, Sir Matthew White Ridley, Sir Charles and Lady Mary Monck, Mr. and Mrs. Monck, Mr. Orc and, last but not least, Mr. Abbott Laurence, the U.S Minister, and his wife.

'The two latter personages took a great fancy to William and myself, wanting us to go over to America with them in the autumn and see, among all else, the falls of Niagara; but our three young children stood in the way of acceptance. They had a pretty daughter with them, Kitty by name, who was *éprise* with Sir Walter Riddell of Hepple, near Morpeth, at that time a very good-looking man of forty. The Abbott Laurences were treated *en princes* at Alnwick, with a whole suite of beautiful apartments to themselves and a carriage at command. They usually invited William and me to drive out with them. The Great Day was on August 6th, and we all drove to the Show ground in carriages and four. The day was very warm and so the *toilettes* chosen were in keeping with it.

'One laughable recollection of our visit was Sir Charles Monck's state of fume and fret at a leading article in *The Times* which described him as eccentric and, in no flattering terms, commented on his consequential behaviour at the Newcastle Assizes a little while ago. It was an important criminal trial, and the two judges had retired to their separate rooms during a short adjournment, leaving the prisoner standing at the bar of justice. It was then that Sir Charles, an old man of seventy-one who ought to have known better, locked the judges in, an action which he maintained through thick and thin to be strictly according to his rights as a court functionary. Unfortunately, one of the judges had occasion to consult his brother in the adjoining room, but was unable to leave his own to do so. Without more ado, the door was beaten in, and His Honour, in passing through, gave Sir Charles a piece of his mind in rasping terms.

'Sir Charles Miles Lambert Monck, be it said, was the son and heir of Sir William Middleton of Belsay, and descended from that scourge of the north-country Catholics and Jacobites alike who had carried out a thievish perquisition at Hesleyside and taken away the Squire's horses for a payment of £5 each. He changed his paternal surname for that of Monck, his mother's maiden name, owing to a strict clause in the will of his maternal grandfather.

'The great ball at the Alnwick assembly rooms was on the night of Show Day, at which, for the second time, I wore my diamond tiara. I had worn it at the Assize ball in Newcastle the week before, where it had caused a sensation.

'On the afternoon of next day all the schoolchildren of Alnwick town passed, two and two, in procession before the ducal couple standing at the Castle door, the girls in white and all saluting as they passed. When the ceremony was over the whole lot sat down to a well-provided table and were feasted. Mrs. Abbott was greatly moved at the display of youth and shed copious tears of emotion. William and I were asked by the Duchess to stay on over two more days until Saturday, which we were very glad to do, and when it came to saying goodbye to Mrs. Abbott Laurence she burst into tears, making us promise to look her up in London. We invited her and her husband, and Mr. Prescott, to Hesleyside, but their engagements caused them reluctantly to decline. Mr. Prescott came to William one day during the visit, and said to him, "What a very peculiar man that Sir Charles Monck is! I think *The Times* just about hit him off He has been catechizing me on the subject of education in my country, and when I mentioned that our curriculum was much the same as in English schools he said he was very glad indeed to hear it. 'It will civilize you! Civilize you all!' he added." William explained that Sir Charles was an *original* and no one paid much attention to anything he said

'It had been a busy and arduous week for the Duke, who retired to Kielder when all was over to nurse a bad fit of

gout brought on by the pressure he had undergone, and we
went to see them while they were there.

'Towards the end of August we gave a dance at Hesleyside which was well-attended and successful, but not so
merry as the impromptu effort of 1848. We had the house
full putting people up, among others being Colonel and
Mrs. Blake from the Newcastle garrison, Sir Edward
Blackett with his daughter Louisa, and a decidedly merry
widow, Mrs. W. Ord (*née* Loraine). Some of our guests,
such as those officers of Colonel Blake's regiment who had
been invited, were obliged to sleep in Bellingham, and the
military got a day's sport next morning on the moors before
returning to duty. As usual, William called for a reel to
finish up the dancing, and in the middle of it Mrs. W. Ord
slipped on a carnation that had been let fall, sprained her
tendon of Achilles, and retired disabled. With some
difficulty, for she was a big woman, we got her upstairs, and
Dr. Elliot came early in the morning to bandage up her
ankle. In the afternoon she was sufficiently recovered to come
downstairs and recline on the sofa in the drawing-room, for
it was in her mind to run the forty-five-year-old bart to
ground, knowing of certain dispositions that had been made.
For Louisa Blackett had expressed a great desire to visit
Sir Matthew White Ridley's shooting-box up Tyne, the
one he had displayed a picture of to the Railway Committee
in London, and I offered to drive her there myself. I was
using the Blakes' carriage and pair, which they had put at
my disposal for the day, and it was wonderful to see the
prancing and dancing that the well-groomed, city-exercised
horses indulged in under the influence of the moorland air.
On the way back we passed, at or near Greystead, a picnick
party of clergy and their ladies, at sight of which Louisa
Blackett became almost as excited as the horses. Arrived

home, I hurried in to tell Mrs. W. Ord all about our pleasant drive, Louisa being hard at heel, when, lo and behold!, there was Sir Edward Blackett on his knees before the widow, herself in tears. Hastily I withdrew, bundling Louisa out before me, not knowing whether what I saw had, or had not, been seen by her. It was a proposal without mistake about it, and the marriage duly came off in just over a year. Let it be said to the credit of Lady Blackett No. 2 that she devoted herself to marrying her step-daughters, and succeeded with all except Frances Julia, who was not matrimonially inclined.

'Early in October we stayed with the Cooke Widdringtons at Swaland for the Alnwick Sessions ball, which was largely spoiled for us by the inane cackle of elderly addlepates about a so-called popish conspiracy, and their mysterious asides among themselves on the restoration of the Catholic Hierarchy in England by Pope Pius IX. And all because His Holiness, at a Consistory holden in Rome on September 30th, 1850, had bestowed a red hat on Doctor Wiseman and raised him to the dignity of Cardinal-Archbishop of Westminster. This it was that sent the cry of "No Popery!" throughout the length and breadth of the land, turning the nation into a pack of ravening wolves, while "No Popery" meetings took place in every town and district. One county alone was free from the wild uproar, due entirely to the good sense and feeling of the noble Algernon, Duke of Northumberland, who would not sanction or in any way give countenance to what would cause pain to the numerous Catholics of his acquaintance, whom he held in high esteem. Nevertheless, when he was in Rome the winter following, and gave a grand reception to all the high Church dignitaries there, Cardinal Wiseman, whose want of tact and bombast had produced the rumpus, was not included in the invitation list.

'1851 was the year of the Great Exhibition, and in April we came to London for it, taking a large house in Eaton Place West. William had all the tenants up, at huge expense, to see the Exhibition. Of course it was the first of its kind and most successful, but, although beautifully and artistically arranged, it was a pigmy compared to the subsequent similar displays in Paris. I was much struck, myself, with the effect produced by the Hyde Park elm which was left quite undisturbed to be enclosed, as it were, in glass, as also by the Hancock collection of rare stuffed birds, both lit up by a bright June sun.

'I have not mentioned in its place that Mary Charlton followed her sister Kate's example in June of the previous year, and also married an Italian, the Marquis Guiseppe Pasqualino of Palermo, and in June, together with Dr. Edward Charlton and his wife Eliza, they came from Sicily to stay with us at the house in Eaton Place. Previous to this slight influx we had given several quite large dinner-parties, one to Cardinal Wiseman at which we had professional singers to entertain the company. On that occasion I got Gunter to make me a cake in the shape of a cardinal's hat, which amused the great man much. The three exiled Princes of Palermo, Prince Scordia, Prince Guiseppe and Prince Torremuzza, who had been at the head of the deputation to Charles Albert, King of Sardinia, at the time of the War of Liberation, were in London and bore letters of introduction to us, and we gave them dinners and two evening parties. At one of these was Henry Matthews, then a rising young man, who became Home Secretary in Lord Salisbury's administration from 1886–1892. Florence and Adela Scrope were almost daily at the house and helped to entertain the foreigners. Florence was the most distinguished-looking girl in London, but of the two sisters I always liked

Adela the better. Adela was a universal favourite and, certainly for upwards of twenty years, a chronic *coqueluche des messieurs*. Both sisters were far superior in appearance and education to all other Catholic girls.

'We were inexpressibly shocked at the alteration that had taken place in Mary, the clinging result of her Mount Etna fever. She was excitable, irritable, easily upset and plainly *souffrante*, although always her sweet self to me. She had come to speak Italian fluently, and with a much purer accent than her good-tempered husband. Every morning, after breakfast, she would take up *The Times* and, without a stutter or a hesitation, proceed to translate the leading article for her husband's benefit, who could neither read nor speak a word of English. Poor dear Mary, how fretful she was! And it was no wonder, for she was suffering bodily pain continuously, but with that indomitable spirit inherited from Fenwick blood she would allow no complaint to pass her mouth. Four months later she had a tumour high up by her left temple lanced, which unbeknownst to us had been forming all the time in London and which was also another ill effect of her Etna fever. She bore the painful operation with surpassing courage. In Palermo, where society is notoriously corrupt, Mary was considered a veritable dragon of virtue. She had in fact become over-precise to the point of being strait-laced, adversely criticizing the leading part played by young girls in English society, and especially captious at Prince Torremuzza's most gentlemanly and innocent flirtation with Florence Scrope.

'While the Scropes (at that time written Scroop) were in London, we made up parties to Kew, Richmond and Vauxhall, we had suppers after the opera, and all manner of amusement for young people. William and I went to a grand soirée at the house of our Alnwick friends, the Abbott

Laurences, at which the Dukes of Wellington and Cambridge were present; and we went also to a beautiful garden party outside London to find them there as well. We had our riding horses, as well as carriage horses, down to town, and altogether the season passed most pleasantly in spite of dear Mary's disapproval of the freedom of society in England and the frivolous attitude of men towards female youth and beauty. She and Prince Torremuzza simply could not hit it off and were always sparring. In especial he used to get furious when she attacked the virtue of the women of his country. Poor Peppino Pasqualino used to sit on thorns, and once at a Richmond dinner there was very nearly a row. Mary was quite right in her assessment of Palermitan morality, but wrong in naming names and attacking individual reputations.

'Peppino was a quiet, easy-going, good-tempered kind of man; uneducated, though with a clear head for business; brought up by the Jesuits; a thoroughly just man in all his dealings. In position and worldly circumstance he was superior to Kate's husband, Baron Cali, his brother-in-law and fellow Sicilian. Peppino did not belong to *crème de la crème* of Italian aristocracy, although, during Mary's short time as his wife, he moved among them as an accepted equal. But he soon lost his place in society, after Mary's death in 1854, when he married his little daughter Marietta's nursery-governess. Peppino had a good house in Palermo, and a nice little country-house at Passo di Rigano, four miles out. He had so good a head for business that he was always foremost in the city councils and very much respected by his associates. Like all Italians, he was extremely fond of money. His features were good, but by no means refined, and he had a tall, thick-set, slouching, awkward, unwieldy figure. On the whole, a good fellow! And capable of bearing with Christian resignation an undue quantity of baiting. He spoke indifferent French and would repeatedly exclaim, when speaking of Florence Scrope, "*O! Che beaux épaules!*" And with me he would go on like this: "*Ma chère Barbara, quand j'étois garçon les dames de Palerme m'épouvantoient! Je ne pouvois pas trouver une seule femme vertueuse! Alors, je me suis dit: Peppino, il faut que tu épouses une Anglaise.*" He certainly kept to his resolve, for he ended by marrying three.

'The Pasqualinos came back with us for a good long stay at Hesleyside when the season was over, and so also did Florence and Adela Scrope. We also had at different times Mrs. Ogle and the two Miss Ogles, Annie and Sophia, Mr. G. Manby, Mr. Charles Langdale, Mr. Silvertop, then a bachelor, Mr. and Miss Selby, Simon Scrope, and others the names of whom escape me. It was August and grouse shooting was in full swing, a time of year after William's heart. We females had a cart lined with mattresses, featherbeds and cushions, and, reposing in luxury on this kind of Eastern couch, used to take out luncheon to the guns, who were sometimes several miles away. Poor Peppino was made to carry a gun, and the fatigue of riding a rough shooting-pony from place to place over well-grown heather, and of walking about all day in between with a considerable weight on his shoulder, did not suit by any manner of means his lazy Sicilian ways of life. "*Ma chère Barbara,*" he would say to me, "*quel plaisir terrible cette chasse!*"

'We took the Pasqualinos with us on a visit to Minster-acres, the home of the Silvertops five miles south of Corbridge, a house with Italian gardens and a foreign expression set down amid a typical north-country landscape. There we met a right-down Orthodox party consisting of Mr. and Mrs. Marmaduke Salvin, neither of them agreeable, Mr. and Miss Selby, Constantia and Francisca Clifford, and

George Manley. I took along with me the new race-game, but it did not go with *éclat* as at Hesleyside. There was much noise and a vast deal of horse-play, so that Mary was driven wild with what she called Catholic childishness.

'The Pasqualinos left us at the end of October and went back to Naples, where Kate and Rosario Cali had arranged to meet them. While stepping ashore from the boat, Mary fell into the water, by which accident her daughter, Marietta, born in February, 1852, was rather hurried into the world. Anyhow, the old Etna fever, the consequences thereof, and now this ducking in the sea no doubt contributed to the formation of tubercles in Marietta's brain, from which she died at the age of twenty-one while giving birth to her second child. The child survived to be an idiot and a cripple, and it seemed an irony of Fate that the Cholmeley heritage of brain-disorder should, by some tragic freak of nature, have been transmitted by the brilliant Mary Charlton, cleverest, most sparkling and most agreeable woman of my whole acquaintance, to clutch in its relentless grip her grandson. But who can account for family defects? I once knew an albino girl, white-haired and with red eyes forever rolling, whose parents were perfect in form and feature, and well-gifted in every other sense.

'As the winter of 1851 approached we wended south to Leamington for the next six months, taking all three children with us. My eldest daughter Fanny had turned out delicate and a warmer climate than that provided by the Hesleyside vicinity was thought advisable for her. I went on ahead to choose a house and settled on No. 3 Waterloo Place, a really sunny spot. We saw much of Mr. and Mrs. Charles Petre, who had a large house in which they entertained considerably and were quite the fashion. The Petres had their hunters there, and so had William. At first I went out a good deal in the evenings, to the Granvilles, Petres, Bradshaws and so on, but little by little I withdrew from Leamington society and, more and more, devoted myself to my children. A Miss Molteni called to offer her services as day governess, but my five-year-old Fanny convinced her that she had little useful knowledge to impart by reading fluently to the astonished woman from her primers in English, French, German, and a little Latin for good measure. Even little Amy, not yet four, my second child, helped to convince Miss Molteni that her instruction for the present would be redundant. In mid-winter Fanny developed an inflammation of the lungs, which caused us some alarm, and was attended by Dr. Babington. Little Oswald, aged two, had a frightful eruption on his face from being fed daily on oatmeal porridge. In a climate like that of Hesleyside daily meals of porridge were harmless and produced no ill-effects but it was far different in the relaxing atmosphere of Leamington. William and I went over once or twice to Bilton Grange, and we both thought that Lady Gwendoline Talbot, who was just out, was a very pretty girl. Hamilton the opera singer, always referred to as Hamilton Aïda, was staying at Leamington with his mother and used to act and sing at Mrs. Bradshaw's parties, he and Mrs. Petre being the principal performers. But Mr. Bradshaw also acted on occasion and dropped his "h's" *ad libitum*, much to the amusement of his audience.

'While yet we were at Leamington, though not long before the end of May, 1852, when we would have left in any case, Kate and Rosario arrived in England and travelled on to Hesleyside without breaking their journey. William went up north at once to welcome them and I followed soon after. Kate was looking prettier and even more graceful than in her maiden days. She was much more cheerful and only fretted because she had no children. I found Rosario a good-looking fellow in a bourgeois way; affected, it is true, and full of conceit, somewhat like an actor, but he made Kate supremely happy, which was the principal thing after all, and she worshipped him. Rosario was better educated than Peppino and endured *le plaisir terrible* with greater equanimity. He ended by really liking to shoot, though he seldom brought down anything when he fired.

'When we got back from Leamington it was to find that Mr. Brown and Mrs. Dury, whose infatuations were a subject of gossip, had both left, and that Mr. Hothersall, a priest from Lisbon, had been appointed to St. Oswald's in the former's place.

'August was the month of the celebrated dual storm in the valley of North Tyne, to which no other before or after could be compared. A little after ten o'clock in the morning the sky darkened suddenly and echoing in the distance loud rolling peals of thunder could be heard, while all around the blackness above was rent by continuous blinding flashes of forked lightning; rain in torrents, and heavy hail, fell, and ever louder rolled the thunder. By midday the storm reached a terrific height, but that was not the worst! Another similar storm, approaching from an opposite direction in obedience to some natural law of attraction, met the first one overhead with an appalling crash. Even Rosario, used to such convulsions in his native country, had never seen the like and could only compare it to the bombardment of Catania by King Bomba. About three o'clock the combined storms simultaneously abated, causing the rushing roar of water in the Hesleyside linn to fall with deafening loudness on the ear, carrying with it sticks, stones and general rubbish enough to fill the sunk fence in front of the hall, so that cows and sheep grazing in the park walked quietly over and

o

stood looking at us through the drawing-room windows. The carts were at work a full week clearing away the refuse. In the early evening William and Rosario rode through Bellingham to Hareshaw linn just beyond, a fine waterfall at any time, but now a magnificent cascade vieing with Lodore. Lives of men and cattle were lost in the resulting flood when the Tyne came down as big as a Severn bore, and there was great injury to crops.

'Soon after the General Election took place, and because of the part Sir George Grey, Member for North Northumberland and in the Government as Home Secretary, had played as regards the passing of the Ecclesiastical Titles Bill the Catholic interest in the county caused him to be unseated. Mr. Wentworth Beaumont and Harry Liddell were the opposing candidates in our part and William voted for the former, telling his tenants to vote whichever way they liked. The two Ridleys, father and son, of Park End, a mile or so the other side of Wark, canvassed the Hesleyside tenants without having the courtesy to call first and ask permission, a step that was considered unpardonable at that date. Old Ridley did his canvassing in a rough and bullying fashion and, not having met with much success, spread a report to the effect that the Squire of Hesleyside had been putting the thumbscrew on. Such an unscrupulous falsehood hurt William very much, and his agent, George Dixon, found means to have the rumour amply contradicted. Mr. Beaumont, the Liberal candidate, was elected.

'On the 17th September, 1852, my second surviving son was born and christened Ernest Lambert Swinburne. Kate and Rosario were due to return to Sicily, and as soon as I was strong enough to travel I accompanied them as far as Paris, remaining there with them for about ten days on account of Kate being unwell. Mrs. Butler, who had lately made a stay at Hesleyside, was most kind in coming to see her and bringing strong soups and jellies. We had rooms in the Hotel Choiseul, Rue St. Honoré, a very second-rate establishment, but suited to Rosario's pocket. The Calis had been at Hesleyside with us for the last six months, living quite free of expense, and yet here was Rosario counting his pennies with the utmost care. I knew that the poor man was next-door to a pauper, and now I clearly saw that Kate, in her weak state, was not receiving proper nourishment. So I paid their hotel expenses myself, gave him £10 to carry them well on their journey south, and to Kate I gave my fur cloak, knowing William well enough to feel that he would have wished me to extend such help. And to think it was poor, dead Mrs. Charlton's former waif and stray, who had heaped such ingratitude on the head of her benefactress and in other ways behaved so ill, who had added to her wrongdoings by making Kate's beggarly marriage!

'After saying goodbye to the Calis I went to stay with Mrs. Butler at her house in the Champs Elysées, her husband and Miss Emma Cator having left for England to attend the Duke of Wellington's funeral. From Mrs. Butler's house I obtained a first-rate view of Napoleon III's entry into Paris as Emperor of the French.

'In my absence William went to a sort of thanksgiving election party, given by Lord Ravensworth at Eslington Hall, which he spoke of as a highly agreeable occasion. Lady Mandeville was one of the guests, she who married *en second noces* the eighth Duke of Devonshire. William described her as beautiful and a perfect Juno of a bride. He had also had his play *The Son of the Wilderness*, translated from the German, staged at Newcastle, and had taken the upper servants in to see it.

XV

LAKES, HIGHLANDS AND ISLE OF MAN

IN this section Barbara carries her story forward a further seven years, 1853–60, a septennium at the end of which she, herself, is forty-five and William fifty. In 1855 she presents her husband with another boy, and in 1860, at an advanced age for child-bearing, she is delivered of a girl. There are now six children altogether, three of either sex, with two daughters at the head of the line and a third at its far end.

These seven years are curiously composed, though on the whole they roll smoothly by. Her father dies abroad in voluntary exile. William loses his two sisters, Mary and Kate. Butlers come and go at Hesleyside in unsatisfactory procession; ditto nurses. World events, such as the Crimean War, the Indian Mutiny, the taking of the Taku Forts, the marriage of the Princess Royal, find mention, it is true, but are touched so lightly that, as far as Barbara is concerned, they hardly seem to happen.

She becomes more and more domestic in her habits and educational towards her children, lamenting that the school summer holidays must necessarily conflict with her duties as a hostess at the opening of the shooting season. She and William appear to have survived twenty years of married life with affection unimpaired, although, peeping from her pages, there are implications that she finds him easy-going to a fault, rather readily imposed upon, too fond of having irons in the fire, and, this of very vague expression, lacking in discretion on occasion when the wifely apron-strings do not act as a restraint.

There is a good deal of travelling and gadding about in

this portion of the record; a holiday in the Lake District, a tour of the Highlands, a pilgrimage to Haworth Rectory. But Barbara's *forte* is not descriptive writing and she treats of such sight-seeing journeys with characteristic lightness of touch.

Four successive winters are spent at Clifton, which at that time was, for various reasons, the resort of numerous converts to Rome. The town had been, for instance, until the re-establishment of the Catholic hierarchy by Pius IX, the headquarters of the Western Vicariate and the residence of the Vicar Apostolic under whose charge it was. Barbara expresses herself in plain terms on the subject of the airs put on by those *received*, and thence drifts into a somewhat loosely-worded account of the Church quarrel between Doctor Errington, on the one side, and Manning on the other. It is an old, forgotten story now, but a short word on the subject may not come amiss.

Briefly then: Manning was a recent and most energetic convert, and Errington a warm representative of the old Catholics of England who had been appointed by Cardinal-Archbishop Wiseman as his coadjutor in, and successor to, the See of Westminster. As a result of the Oxford Movement, which aimed at a revival of Catholic doctrine and observance in the Church of England, a large new body of distinguished converts had been received into the Roman Church, at whose head, with Wiseman approving strongly in the background, Manning promptly installed himself with the self-appointed mission of increasing the Italian spirit in the English Catholic community. But Errington resisted this Romanizing tendency with all his might and a seven-year period of conflict ensued, terminated finally in Manning's favour by a papal decree which *liberated* his opponent from his coadjutorship and deprived him thenceforth of all clerical importance. Once Errington had been removed from the path of his ambition, Manning turned his guns on Newman, the one remaining dignitary capable of challenging his supremacy. Through his instrumentality, Newman was despatched to Ireland on a fruitless mission, on the failure of which he was allowed to rust at the Oratory, Hagley Road, Edgbaston, of which community he was the head.

Finally, the Volunteer Movement: Napoleon III, whose entry into Paris as Emperor of France Barbara had witnessed from Mrs. Butler's house in the Champs Elysées, was showing signs of stepping over the ropes which had been set up at the Congress of Vienna. By his annexation of Nice and Savoy, he stirred the House of Commons to stern remonstrance, on which occasion Palmerston used language to the French Ambassador in London that threatened war. Great uneasiness was felt throughout the country, a state of feeling that became bellicose when it was learnt that the Emperor was strengthening his fleet and hastily completing the naval defences of Cherbourg. One of the most remarkable movements in English history resulted. Able-bodied men came forward in their tens of thousands to enrol as volunteers for the defence of the realm, the Government supplying nothing but arms and military instruction, until a small grant of money in aid was grudgingly allowed. In the opinion of the Radical politician, Richard Cobden, the foundation and organization of a Volunteer Force was the most fruitful consequence of the panic aroused by the activities of the French colonels in 1859.

And now let Barbara again take up her pen:

'Till the end of June, 1853, I remained at home, chiefly occupied with the teaching of my children. William made frequent trips to London on Border Counties Railway business, generally in company with Tom John Taylor, brother to Hugh Taylor, Esq., of Chipchase Castle, his willing colleague in carrying out the project. Some alterations and additions were also made to the house and grounds. For instance, we had the terrace on the east side balustered, and flower vases in carved stone-work erected, fourteen in number, at equal intervals. The vases were sculptured by an itinerant workman who went by the name of Ned o' the West, and similar ones were set up on pedestals by the same hand at the radial points of the geometrical garden on the south front, making a very good show when filled with scarlet geraniums. But they were poor specimens of native art and better could have been bought with less money. William was always anxious to support local talent, and never inquired sufficiently into the character of his various protégés. In my experience, the Charltons are not a suspicious race, and my husband was certainly of a single-minded, generous, unsuspecting nature, never giving a thought to the possibility of being overreached by those to whom he did good turns. The heavy, uncouth balustrade itself was designed by Frank Charlton, somewhat on engineering lines.

'During the winter of that year an attempt was made to rob the house with the collusion of someone inside, but a fresh fall of snow effaced the would-be robber's footsteps. Anne Vaughan, the housemaid, found the drawing-room window fastenings tampered with when she came down early in the morning, and gave the alarm. The butler, Hauxwell, who had been many years in the family and was beyond suspicion, had been lately confined to bed by illness, the work falling on our Catholic footman, Percival, who was well known to have been stealing from the cellar while his superior lay abed. But he had gone home that night to his wife, and, in any case, knew how to get to the silver in the pantry without fear of detection. Suspicion fell on Ned o' the West, and George Dixon urged William to get him work out of the district. It was also considered best to get rid of Percival, who was placed with a Mr. Dunn of Newcastle, where he did not mend his thievish ways. He pawned valuables belonging to his master, was discovered, and committed for trial. William went up to speak in his favour when the case was called, which, considering the man's dishonesty when in our service, was too great a stretch of good nature. However, it was of no avail, for he was sent to prison for two years.

'Mr. Hothersall, the priest who had succeeded Mr. Brown, helped me most kindly with my Latin, and I read through the first two books of the *Aeneid* with him. I also took up Greek and went through the *Frogs* of Aristophanes with Mr. Hothersall.

'My father died abroad on July 10th, 1853, aged seventy-five, and, as far as concerned my interest in the Burghwallis property, I found myself cut off with a shilling. By the marriage settlement of my father and mother £12,000 was charged against the estate to be divided among the younger children, with a clause, however, allowing them to divide it as they thought proper. My dear mother, being dead, could not see that justice was done, and I have every reason to believe that my share remained incorporate with the estate and fell to my brother George Anne, to whom it came. But as he never married and left Burghwallis to my second son, it became a case of robbing Peter to pay Paul, for the £4,000 which I ought to have got went ultimately to him instead of to his father. Perhaps it was just as well, for otherwise that money, like so many other thousands unaccounted for, would probably also have fallen through the sieve. Nevertheless, I was deprived of my rights!

'In January, 1854, England and France declared war

against the Czar Nicholas. In May, Eliza Charlton came to stay with us at Hesleyside, and for the first few days of her visit we walked and talked together, with the children running on before, in the most natural way possible. I remember her remarking how happy we all were, and that these years would be for me and them the most joyful in our lives. But by degrees, unaccountably and for no apparent cause, she fell off, at last taking to her bed and becoming seriously ill. I loved her so dearly I was only too happy to nurse her day and night. Her husband pronounced her ailment to be scarlet fever, but that complaint was Dr. Charlton's *specialité médicale* and the more imaginary cases of it he cured the higher did his reputation mount. It was a low fever she was ill of, a type so prevalent at Hesleyside, and so near was she to death that Dr. Humble actually said at the Infirmary, on his return to Newcastle, that she was almost certain to have died since he had left her that very morning. Mr. Hothersall had administered the Last Sacraments and was most attentive in giving her Communion nearly every morning. Her brothers came to say goodbye to their sister, and her mother, Mrs. Kirsopp of the Spital, Hexham, a most high-bred person, daughter of Sir Thomas and Lady Janet Livingstone, herself a Cranstown, likewise came to stay, remaining on to nurse her daughter when the worst was over.

'We left Mrs. Kirsopp at Hesleyside during dear Eliza's convalescence and went off with all the children to the Lakes. Our lodgings at Ambleside were close to The Knoll, where Harriet Martineau dwelt in a lovely house she had built herself in equally lovely grounds. We got to know Miss Martineau very well, who took a fancy to little Oswald, then four years old, and encouraged him to speak to her through her ear-trumpet. I went to one of her great tea-parties at The Knoll and was introduced to her friend and adviser, Mr. Atkinson, a zealous exponent of mesmerism. She asked me whether I did not consider Mr. H. G. Atkinson the perfect image of Christ and I was mightily puzzled for a suitable reply. She told me all about her travels in Egypt, Palestine and Syria, and other places which I little thought at the time I would one day see for myself.

'I had not then seen Switzerland and was simply enchanted with the beauty of the Lakes. We had brought Lily and Mosstrooper with us from Hesleyside, the former of which was quiet enough for me to ride about alone on, for William, as usual, was much away on railway affairs. It was during our stay at Ambleside that the Bill went through, and now the only requirement was money to commence the work of construction and carry it to a finish. Whether on horseback or on wheels, at which times we always took the children, we scoured the district throughout its length and breadth. Two kind old Miss Gills, who, like Miss Martineau, took a fancy to the children, escorted us one day to Mount Rydal to introduce us to the long-suffering widow of the verbose and cantankerous poet, Wordsworth. Every spot we visited was startlingly beautiful with always some interesting legend attached. With a guide, for safety's sake, William and I conquered Fairfield, Helvellyn, and the Langdales both Great and Little.

'Edward Swinburne, eldest son and heir of Sir John Swinburne of Capheaton, was living at Callgarth Park on Lake Windermere with his second wife and five out of the six children by his first, the eldest about fifteen. His second wife had been his children's governess. Edward Swinburne was born in 1788 at the time when his father, fervently an admirer of the French Revolution, was riding about "with one spur on," in company with Lord Grey and Dr. Fenwick, dubbing each other *citizen*. Certainly the lessons in democracy he then learnt at his father's knee made an ineffaceable impression, for even now, at this late date, he was leading the life of a day labourer, wearing workman's clothes, with seldom a hat on his head, and altogether as odd an object to set eyes on as could well be seen. He had all clocks put on an hour to ensure that the household was really up at four, even though they thought it five. Like to himself, his children wore neither shoes nor stockings, and he also hardened them by taking them out on the lake in a boat, chucking them into the water one by one, and leaving them to swim to shore. He and his wife were very kind to us and our children much enjoyed the company of their young cousins.

'We got back to Hesleyside at the beginning of August, timed of course so as not to miss the opening of the shooting season. Susette left us to be married and I got a Frenchwoman in her place, elderly and yet exceedingly fond of her toilette. She had at one time been housekeeper to the Abbé Lamennais, and had many curious anecdotes to tell of that rebellious priest, who, by his own direction, was buried at Père-Lachaise without funeral rites, refusing to be reconciled to the Church.

'Hauxwell left us after many years of faithful service and a succession of inefficients came in his place. The first was an uncouth type of man who had lived in Australia, and who was honest but incompetent. Then came Patterson who, with the willing help of Hodgson, Wilkinson and the other saddle-room boozers, got through a half-year's supply of home-brewed ale in three months, giving as excuse that it was the German bandsmen, who came our way from time to time and played in front of the house, who had drunk it. He was soon dispatched! At last in despair we got a statelylooking, idle, Catholic butler, a regular Orthodox do-little, by the name of Bartlett; on the whole a well-conducted man whose wife kept the Bellingham bridge and had a small barley-sugar shop. Those of our visitors who had seen how the silver was kept in Hauxwell's time could not refrain from remarking on its dullness now. Bartlett was pompous, slow and indolent, and trying beyond all measure.

'Alas! 1854 was a sad year for us. In March dear, amiable Kate Cali died at Nice of consumption, that *ver rongeur* of a neglected childhood. Although Kate's sister, Mary Pasqualino, had only recently been confined of a boy, she hurried off to Nice from Palermo when Rosario's first tardy word arrived; but, alas! too late. Not only was I greatly grieved at Kate's death, but I felt most deeply for poor Mary, who had loved her sister with a heart-whole affection and had devoted to her without stint the best days of her youth. Four months after this sad blow Mary wrote to say that the cholera was expected in Palermo, and that, what with the complete absence of sanitation and the dirty habits of the populace, it was likely to prove a serious visitation. She added in a postscript these words: "With our shattered family constitutions I should stand no chance if I got it; but Peppino is syndic and I cannot leave him." Little did Mary think when writing her misgivings that she would be one of the first victims! She was struck down in the evening of August 11th, and succumbed to the fatal disease at 4 a.m. the next day. It was a case of *cholera foudroyant*.

'Thus passed away, within the space of a few months, two of the most interesting sisters of the North. If ever two sisters deserved high places in Heaven, then Mary and Kate Charlton did. Adversity had tried them in their youth and they had not been found wanting in courage and resignation. They were generous, prudent and provident, always avoiding to run their father into useless expenditure, and constantly aware that their mother's illnesses were serious. Mary's baby died very shortly after its mother.

'In February, 1855, we went to Clifton, which was the resort at that time of the converts to the Holy Roman Church, until the flow of those *received* had fallen off in consequence of the Pope's restoration of the Hierarchy, so woefully mismanaged by Wiseman owing to a combination of ill health and natural lack of tact. We took a nice sunny house on the Terrace, a few doors down from Mr. Scrope and Adela, which gave her the opportunity of being a great deal with me.

'Doctor Errington left shortly after we went to Clifton; he and Wiseman were at loggerheads. The Cardinal, responding to the influence of Manning, was cockering up the converts to such a puerile degree that these newly baptized misbelievers began to treat the old Catholics as the neophytes and themselves as ancient in the Faith, while in reality their peculiar antics and far-fetched ideas were making a caricature of Catholic religion. But perhaps, after all, it is better to believe too much than too little! Doctor Errington was no sort of man to act to any gallery and could not play the sycophant. He said with truth that those worthy of being held up for respect and esteem should first of all be the Catholics whose ancestors had abided with the Faith in the days of bitter persecution, and NOT newcomers, quite unried; more especially considering the converts very often gained in worldly consequence with their change of faith.

'Doctor Errington invited William to visit the Russian prisoners-of-war with him. From all I have seen and heard of Errington he had the right head-piece and organizing brain to suit a great prelate of the Roman Catholic Church, but he also had uncouth Ushaw manners and lacked social training. And then, a few years later, came the final rupture between the two foremost ecclesiastics of the Catholic Church, by which Archbishop Errington was put *hors concours* for any further distinction. Then came Newman's turn! The converts ruled the Cardinal, but even he put his foot into it with them, firstly by sending Newman, his superior in intellect, to Ireland, where he had no chance with the ignorant and unworthy priesthood there, and secondly by putting him on the shelf in Hagley Road. It was quite evident that Wiseman was of the same opinion as Shakespeare: "Two stars keep not their motion in one sphere."

'In June Peppino came to Clifton to look out for a nurse for his little daughter, Marietta. I could do little myself to be of help, but a certain, not over-wise, Dr. Gillow selected a proper person, as he called her, from among his patients, able not only as a nurse but a governess as well. In this manner Peppino took into his employ Mrs. Fry, daughter of John Frost, the Chartist leader who led the attack on New-port, Monmouthshire, in 1839, was found guilty of high treason, condemned to death, transported to Van Diemen's Land instead, and now, a pardoned man, was living in his native land again. In two years' time Peppino married Mrs. Fry, who, although now a marchioness, remained none the less his servant. Peppino, with his thirst for saving, had calculated it was a cheap way of keeping two in one. Although his wife, the Marchioness Pasqualino still washed and dressed Marietta, made the child's clothes and her own, ironed Peppino's shirts and, a good bargainer at a counter, exercised on his behalf every form of economy. Naturally she had no place in society, and he himself lost the good social position in Palermo Mary had made for him. In default of better, he took his servant-wife to tradesmen's balls, and on one of these occasions little Marietta, between three and four years old, seeing her *nurse* all dressed-up in her mother's lace flounces and jewels, kicked her shins in a transport of rage. It was a curious, if not an extraordinary, coincidence that poor dear Mary, who always suffered martyrdom from the cold of Hesleyside, used to say at the first approach of winter, when the trial of the Chartists was in everybody's mouth, "Oh! John Frost is here again to cause me torment." Poor Mary! Little did she know that all her money would eventually go to the real John Frost's granddaughter; for Peppino had a daughter by his second wife who married and had healthy children. Marietta, Mary's child, married at a youthful age the Marchese Amorosi, a thoroughly bad man and known as such to Peppino. But the Marchese happened to be rich and Peppino's five senses were all wrapped up in money. Mrs. Fry, that was, died in 1864 of consumption after about six years of matrimonial service. Shortly before death Mrs. Glover, an English dressmaker in Palermo, went to see her and found her bathed in tears. On being asked why she was so dejected, the dying woman cried anew, saying she had no money to send her daughter Fry to buy mourning for her; she had tried to sell her silkworms, the only assets she possessed, but could not find a purchaser. This affecting situation was conveyed to Princess Rancabili, who thought the dying woman's appeal so piteous that she promptly took the silkworms for herself at the price of 250 francs.

'On June 28th, 1855, I gave birth to a boy, who was christened Ulric Edmund Emmanuel by the Abbé Miot, Isabella Riddell and Edmund Bastard standing sponsors. Just as we were about to leave Clifton, my new baby was taken ill with bronchitis, and, determined that the poor little dot's life should not be endangered on account of the open season for grouse, I elected to stay behind with the monthly nurse; otherwise he would have surely died at Derby. As it was he was well nursed and recovered in less than a week. No sooner was all ready for the departure home of the rest of the family than a telegram from George Dixon informed us that the scarlet fever had broken out in the vicinity of Hesleyside, a piece of news that necessitated an instant change of plan. We therefore forgathered instead, William and I, five children and four nurses, at Seton Carew and took rooms in the hotel there.

'We duly returned to Hesleyside when the fever scare was over and had a peaceful winter with the usual Christmas excitements. The house became almost an educational institution, for while the children went to school to me, I went to school, prosecuting my own classical studies, to Mr. Hothersall.

'A little later in the spring William, at my suggestion, instituted the best improvement of his time by dismantling and removing Ante Richardson's workshop and slaughter-house from the entrance of the west avenue to the sawmill among trees and well out of sight behind the house. It had always been to me an unmitigated eyesore, to whom it seemed most disgusting to have a slaughter-house actually in the grounds and so *en évidence*. One spring afternoon while walking in the grounds I planned in my mind the removal of the obnoxious sight and, at the same time, the proper opening up of the west avenue. William was highly approving and said, "The very thing! And quite an easy thing to do. Why did I never think of it before?" Not only William, but Ante himself and everyone concerned were delighted at the idea, and it was amusing to watch them heart and soul at work to get the last stone out of sight. It might have been the Bastille for the joy shown at the work of destruction. How Catherine, Mrs. (Fenwick) Charlton who had made a small garden on that very side of the house, with a greenhouse up against the back wall of the stable, could endure the proximity of reeking sheepskins and flayed carcasses will always be a marvel.

'To celebrate the passing of the Border Counties Railway Bill, and to commemorate the winning of a courageously conducted and fairly fought contest, we decided to have a week of theatricals at Hesleyside, sending the younger children to Roker so as to be out of the way. The big barn by the sawmill was cleaned out, scoured, and lined with calico in white and pink stripes. The stage was well boarded and the benches arranged in tiers with a passage-way in between. All the arrangements were perfection. The cart-horse stable nearby was cleaned and made in every way convenient as a ladies green-room. Davis, manager of the New-castle theatre, brought his men with lighting, drop-scenes, and everything else necessary for the performances to be *en règle*. He also coached the actors. William composed an epilogue with a railway twist to it and spoke it beautifully. I give it here:

> 'A hundred years, 'tis said, are past away,
> Since Hesleyside was witness to a Play:
> So, deeming it high time, we've now made bold
> Once more this aloe-blossom to unfold:
> But say, an aloe-blossom shall it be
> That blooms and withers — once a century?
> No! for we trust to see it bloom again
> When the loud whistle of the flying train,
> That speeds along our *Border Counties* line,
> Shall wake the mountain echoes of North Tyne.
> Then shall we hope, once more, with joy to greet
> Your well-known faces on each rising seat;
> Beauty and talent, mingled, shall once more
> Court your applause upon this self-same floor.

P

Give then your aid, like honest hearts and true,
Hard-worked *Directors* with approval view;
Our word is *Forward*! now – we mean to have it through!
Let this our promise in remembrance dwell,
Till then, my friends and neighbours, fare-ye-well!
(*August* 19, 1856.)

'On the first night we gave the popular *Away with Melancholy*, with *Perfection or The Lady of Munster* as an afterpiece. A prologue, written by Tom Stonor, was spoken by Minna Biddulph dressed as "The Tyne" in white silk covered with water-lilies. After the fall of the last curtain the farming tenants and their wives, etc., ate of a supper laid out in the servants' hall, while we, the quality, fed in the big dining-room and danced till the small hours. On the second night a comedy of the late seventeenth century, called *Faint Heart never won Fair Lady*, was given, which was undeniably dull, quite unfit for the audience we played to, and not at all a success. Among stiff-backed county ladies, chaperones, and fossilized country squires it is preferable for amateur actresses to keep to their own style of dress for fear of shocking the proprieties. *Twice Killed* was the afterpiece on the second night, followed as before by suppers and dancing. The company rested then for two or three days, after which the whole programme was repeated.

'Soon after the theatricals we went to Roker to enjoy sea air and give the servants a much needed rest, and at the end of a short stay we sent the children back home and went on ourselves to Manchester to see the Exhibition which was beautiful and interesting beyond all measure.

'William had always expressed immense admiration for Charlotte Brontë and was, moreover, very interested in the fact that she had been governess in the White family who now owned the old Charlton lands across the river. So we came back home from Manchester in pilgrimage fashion, stopping off at Haworth. We walked up the steep hill and knocked at the Rectory door, which was opened to us by the Reverend Patrick Brontë in a high, white choker, giving us an impression that he was wearing it for effect. He discoursed overflowingly on his own merits, which he seemed to prize highly, and also on the injustice done him by Mrs. Gaskell in her life of Charlotte, who had then been in her grave about a year and a half. To William and me the old man, then in his eightieth year, appeared pompous, uncomely, and a full-blown balloon of vanity. According to him, his gifted daughters, Charlotte in especial, owed everything to their father, and in particular he had, he boasted, taught them to write in the purest Anglo-Saxon instead of in the tedious, latinized style of Sir Walter Scott. He showed us Charlotte's room and desk, but all the time he was so imbued with his *idée fixe* that he was the pivotal centre round which his offspring's talents revolved that I was thoroughly disgusted with the self-conceit of the cruel, old parson, who sat before us, a mass of self-satisfaction, although he had contributed by his crabbed, morose, peevish nature to the untimely deaths of his delicate wife and daughters. Afterwards we walked on the moor nearby which Charlotte so well described in *Jane Eyre*, a softer, smoother, more refined and polished moor than ours about Hesleyside. We went to the little church to see Charlotte's tomb, and then to the inn, a mere public-house, where Bramwell Brontë, either for love or on account of despair, drank himself into his grave. We each took a glass of wine to his memory and in excuse of our curiosity. The gloomy little town of Haworth, situated on a hill slope, certainly fulfilled for us the impression insinuated by *Currer Bell* that the local roughs were wont to heave bricks at one another.

'On the 3rd November we went again to Clifton for our second winter there, taking Arlington House for seven months. On our way south my youngest, Ulric, a year and five months old, showed a touch of temperature, so I remained behind at York with him and Hannah Jameson and there saw the Piedmontese contingent that had been quartered in the city throughout the Crimean War march out. William had his hunters down as usual and, otherwise, he was constantly at Bath with Mr. and Mrs. Stone, Kathleen Biddulph before her marriage and a most beautiful young woman. At Christmas I gave several children's parties, and we stayed with the Stones for the Great Fancy Ball at Bath at which Mrs. Stone was the belle. Miss Rankin, cousin to Miss Martineau, became very fond of the children and exerted herself to give them pleasure and amusement.

'That winter of 1856–57 I went out more into society, dining at various houses and giving a few dinner parties in my turn. I also went much among the poor of Mother Margaret Hallahan, the Foundress of Stone Convent; all Irish, all dirty, and helpless, sackless and unworthy objects. I never knew to what degree of perfection Irish filth could be raised until I visited the Hibernian colony in Bristol, and duplicity went hand in hand with dirt. A gloom was cast over the town in the spring when diphtheria broke out rather badly, and some friends of ours, Mr. and Mrs. Ford, lost two of their children by it, a young girl and boy. Doctor Clifford, appointed Bishop of Clifton, was consecrated and installed under peculiarly trying circumstances. In May the Indian Mutiny broke out, and on June 1st we went back to Hesleyside.

'Mrs. Hunt, who always went south with us, was ever the most delighted to regain her happy hunting ground at Hesleyside, where we now remained quietly until the end of August. Mr. and Mrs. Stone, and the latter's sister Minna (afterwards Mrs. Charles Ratcliffe), spent September with us, and Mr. King came following after, bent on courtship. No marriage resulted. For some unexplained reason Mr. King backed out of it in time to leave no wound, behaving, indeed, very like a gentleman.

'September, on the whole, was wearisome, and at the end of it we made up a party for a tour of the Highlands, viz.: ourselves, Fanny, Amy, Johanna to look after them, Mr. and Mrs. Stone, her maid Herrn, and Mr. Stone's jockey, Harrison, who joined us at Edinburgh and went on with us from there. From Edinburgh we travelled to Linlithgow, Stirling, Loch Lomond, and from the latter place we took the coach. The date was 30th September and it was the last run of the coaching season on that route. The horses were played out and one of the poor, exhausted animals fell down dead about one and a half miles short of the King's House Inn. It was raining heavily and we all had to walk the distance over Bannock Moor to reach that shelter. We were passed by a gentleman and his wife, travelling privately, who promised there would be a roaring fire and lots of good cheer at the inn when we arrived, including hot toddy. Luckily, Johanna, who did not usually show such sense, had taken dry shoes and stockings for Fanny and Amy in a bag. It was my first taste of toddy, and never since have I so enjoyed it as on that memorable afternoon at the King's House Inn. A little later our coach came in with the aid of a veteran white horse which had been grazing peacably on the moor until our driver pressed it into service to replace the one that had dropped down dead. We had now fallen well behind our timetable, but the rain had ceased, and with a good relay of horses we proceeded on our way to Ballachulish and thence to Glencoe. It was dark when we drove through the dismal

Pass; night had closed in, but the vivid play of sheet-lightning seemed to impart a greater ghastliness to the ill-omened place of unholy massacre. We slept at Fort William on Loch Linnhe and woke in the morning to find the huge head, and most of the body, of Ben Nevis enveloped in a misty shroud. We went up the Caledonian Canal to Inverness; we visited the field of Culloden; we made a circuit by Forres and Glamis, and down to Blair Athole through the Pass of Killiecrankie. The spot where fell Claverhouse at the famous fight was marked by a rude memorial in granite, which Mrs. Stone fell on her knees to kiss out of sentiment for Bonnie Dundee. It struck me as most difficult ground for fighting a battle.

'On January 7th, 1858, I cut the first sod of the Bellingham-Falstone section of the Border Counties Railway. The richly ornamented wheelbarrow which I used for the purpose was emblazoned by poor Mr. Hothersall, and it, together with the silver trowel with which I cut the sod, have been preserved at Hesleyside. I made a short, congratulatory, complimentary, encouraging speech, which was received with loud hurrahing. Soon after that we went to London; William and I, with all the children except little Ulric, and two nurses, Johanna the German and *Venus* Adelaide from Paris. We took lodgings in Green Street. On January 25th the Princess Royal was married to Frederic, future Emperor of Germany, and the illuminations were very fine. All the excitement of rejoicing, and the throng and bustle of the streets, delighted the Parisian Adelaide, but Johanna took it very stolidly. The children, varying in age from twelve to six, were old enough to enjoy the shows and we took them to as many as we could.

'Twelve days before the royal marriage there was a wedding in the family when, on January 13th, my niece

Georgina Mary, poor Fanny's only daughter, was taken to
the altar by Colonel the Honourable Alexander Edward
Fraser, second son of Lord Lovat. It was a poor enough
marriage for her to make, and it turned out not a happy one.

'I went to Clifton to look for a house, William and I
having agreed to spend the rest of the winter there, and I
took Arlington Villas. One or two days passed, and I went
with Amy down to St. Leonards, to the convent there which
I had in mind as a place of education for both my daughters
in the autumn, when it would be time they made their First
Communions. We arrived in the midst of holidays and
plays, and I was much pleased with what I saw of Mrs.
Conolly and the nuns, who seemed not to have thrown off
all common sense with their worldly raiment.

'In the early spring William and I, taking Oswald with
us, travelled to Malvern and Torquay, prospecting those
two places for a future winter stay instead of Clifton. We
also took an opportunity to visit Longleat, near Warmin-
ster, and Lord Charles Thynne, uncle of the then Marquess
of Bath, gave us a personal note to the butler directing that
important functionary to show little Ozzy all the secret
passages in the huge house and, in particular, the bloody
waistcoat of King Charles I. We also took in Berkeley Castle
in company with Swinburne Berkeley, nephew to the then
sixth Earl. We lunched in the housekeeper's room, as the
old lord and his elderly lady-love were in residence. After
lunch we watched the pair of them get into their carriage
and drive away, leaving us free to go all over the historical
old house. The room in which Edward II was murdered,
than which a more barbarous and detestable act of cruelty
never happened, was not better than a servant's room at the
time of our visit.

'A large house-party assembled at Hesleyside on August

11th, 1858, for grouse shooting. There were Mr. and Lady Emma Anderton, Sir James and Lady Fitzgerald, Count Zamoiski, Charlie Searle, Adela Scrope and others; luckily they did not stay long, as the burden of entertainment was heavy for me to bear. Fanny and Amy, in spite of their tender ages, dined in French fashion with the general company. This was perhaps a mistake, but the great trial and disadvantage of that time of year was that the school holidays and shooting parties always clashed.

'In September, also, I took Fanny and Amy to the convent at St. Leonard's, as it was now time for them to make their First Communion and I wished them to be prepared for it in the best possible manner. Poor little Amy, aged ten, was dreadfully distressed at this her first real parting from me, but Fanny, two years older, found the companionship of school-mates quite congenial to her spirit and seemed from the first quite reconciled to school life.

'On my way back home I stayed at Danby, family seat of the Scropes, where William joined me for a few days. Only Adela was at home, her father and her sister Florence being off together somewhere. Mrs. Biddulph and her two daughters then had a house at Middleham, not very far away, and her third daughter Kathleen (Mrs. Stone) was staying with them. One afternoon at Danby when we were at tea we heard the sound of sweet singing, and on looking out saw three women singing to a guitar. They were dark of complexion and had raven black hair, but twilight had begun to fall so that their features were indistinguishable. William produced half a crown from his pocket, and was on the point of giving it to the tallest of the three, when he stopped dead in sudden recognition of our good friend, Kathleen Stone. The three sisters, it appeared, had walked over from Middleham and, pressing Adela into the secret, had under-

The Spur in the Dish by William Bell Scott (see pp. 103 and 233). Detail from a painting at Wallington. William Henry is the model for the chief of the Charltons. On his left is the 'Standard of Hesleyside' (see pp. 183-4).

gone their transformation in her room. Just thirty-four years ago to-day! And, writing entirely from memory, I remember that and many other incidents as if they had occurred but yesterday in spite of my seventy-seven years.

'Poor, dear Kathleen! She was my kind friend to the last and much sorrow did I feel on hearing of her sad death in July back (1892). She was eccentric in her ways, for the same blood that occasioned the offensive oddities and flights of lunacy in the Wrights of Keleden, and in the Ls. and Bs., ran in Kathleen's veins, her Biddulph parent being himself a ci-devant Wright; as a family uninteresting and commonplace. In Kathleen the noble, chivalrous blood of the Scropes raised her mind, her talents, and even her eccentricities far above those of her father's kindred; so that she was like unto an eagle soaring high over a flock of crows. And when misfortune came upon her she knew how to bear it like a *grande dame* and a Christian. Peace be to her memory!

'As soon as I returned to Hesleyside from Danby I began to feel very unwell, and was laid up for several weeks. As I showed very few signs of improvement, William took me up to London in an invalid carriage so as to be under a specialist, and I occupied lodgings in Brompton for three weeks.

'On account of this arrangement, William and the children spent Christmas at home without me, and, from what I gathered on my return, there were some pretty strange goings-on, with the Dodd family seeming fairly to have the run of the place. The artist, William Bell Scott, who was also master of the government school of design at Newcastle, had been painting the picture of *The Spur in the Dish* on commission from Sir Walter Trevelyan of Wallington, who desired to have his dining-room walls decorated with representative scenes of Northumbrian life and history. My husband himself sat for the life-sized figure of his sixteenth-century ancestor, William Charlton of Hesleyside, and Mary Jane Dodd, a strikingly handsome young woman of yeoman family, who lived with her parents nearby, sat, or rather stood, for the female figure, lady of the house, who presents the dish with nothing but the spur on it to males of the family, hungry for their meat. There was a Christmas dance for the servants of Hesleyside that year and, probably in recognition of Mary Jane's services as model, all the Dodd family were invited by William to take up their quarters for the night.

'In 1859 there was some changes in the Hesleyside household. Bartlett, the do-nothing Catholic butler, had to be parted with as Walker, the footman who had now been with us some years, declared he would no longer work under so idle a man. In his place came Peacock, whom we procured from Highwarden, a most peculiar-looking man, perfectly inefficient for the situation and only lasting a few months. Finally, and most unfortunately, William took over from Mr. Cookson a butler called Inkley, whose late employer frankly admitted him to be, although a first-class butler, yet a very immoral man, for which reason he had parted with him. Woe betide the day that Inkley came!

'The summer of that year passed very happily at Hesleyside, and, in July, Fanny and Amy returned from their convent at St. Leonard's for the holidays. Fanny was loaded down with four prizes, one each for Latin, French, Italian and Christian Doctrine. Owing to my not being strong, we had no company or shooting-party in August, but picnicks and various home enjoyments instead. In the ensuing years it was a great disadvantage to the boys, and a certain source of detriment to my own health and happiness, that the summer school holidays always had to happen at the only time of the year – the grouse season, that is – when William insisted on entertaining a large company. I used to loathe

the very sight of visitors, and I always think it was that annual ordeal that gave me ever after almost a morbid repugnance to society.

'Christmas was always celebrated in great style at Hesleyside when the children were young and growing up. The chapel had been recently redecorated and for eight consecutive years Midnight Mass was said in it on Christmas Eve, first by Mr. Hothersall and, when he left in 1859, by Mr. Flint, who, as I write, is still going strong. When in Paris in 1852 I procured white and red artificial camelias to twist on to Hodgson's flowerless plants, so exquisitely manufactured that no one, however near, could imagine they were not natural. On these occasions the altar was ablaze with wax lights, and the three older children assisted at the ceremony as a special treat. We always had a Christmas tree and a small *crèche* in the schoolroom, now the library.

'The Volunteer Movement was well under way during the latter half of 1859, and William, who was ever foremost in furthering those undertakings which were for the good of his country, threw himself heart and soul into the Government's enrolment plan. The general idea amongst the general public was that Napoleon III, after having behaved so well in regard to the Crimean War, the Indian Mutiny, and the War with China, had no other means of keeping his restless nation quiet than by a threat of war against England. The Bellingham volunteer company was raised by William in April, 1860. He had to go to London to see about it, and while he was away my third daughter and last child was born at Hesleyside, May 6th, and christened Geneviève Mabel Mary by Mr. Flint.

'Dear Oswald went to the Oratory School, Hagley Road, Edgbaston, on the 10th January, 1860, at exactly the age of ten.'

XVI

SICKNESS AND DEATH ABROAD

IN this section we are advanced a further two years to the Christmas of 1862, a period which presents a lively picture of domestic happenings, foreign travel, parochial events and visiting abroad. The two eldest children, as daughters will, rapidly approach the adult stage of life and lay on Barbara the anxious responsibility of preparing them, in manner and deportment, for the outside world. There is bad butler trouble at Hesleyside.

The scene is on the whole domestic, with the children ill and well again, a change of governess, bazaars and subscription dances in aid of the Volunteer Fund, a broken arm, a football injury and so on.

In the great world the Duchess of Kent and the Prince Consort die in the same year, but Barbara, beyond a curious death-bed story in the former case, is typically brief with regard to these royal bereavements. Similarly, she hears at first hand from inside sources the true story of the unfortunate Lady Flora Hastings; but she carelessly, or carefully, refrains from passing on that knowledge to her readers. Truly may it be said of Barbara that, although anecdotal and full of reminiscence where her own circle in society is concerned, she is not of a gossipy nature otherwise.

Of the 'Stone *versus* Llanover' case which begins this chapter and which must have shaken contemporary society to the core she writes abstrusely, though with every evidence of sincere regret. It would take profound study in *Debrett* and *Burke* to unravel the relationships of the various families concerned; suffice it to say that those she mentions are, either distinctly or closely, connected by intermarriage, cousinship and long years of social and religious intercourse. Little purpose would be served by raking over the cold embers of the scandal now. No more is necessary than to mention that Mr. Stone, with whom and with whose wife William and Barbara were intimate in friendship's way, was a race-horse owner, and that Harrison, who joined the touring party in the Highlands, was his private jockey. The rest we will leave to Barbara:

'The Stone and Harrison episode burst forth towards the end of 1859 to leave a sad impression on the families of Scrope and Herbert. Some there were who firmly insisted that it was Lady Llanover, jealous of Kathleen Stone because her beauty was so superior to that of her daughter, Mrs. Herbert of Llanarth, who blew into flame the dark smouldering embers of hitherto undreamt of evil, and in so doing roused her lord to attack the character of Mr. Stone. Unfortunately the Stones had rented Llangattock House, in Llandover country so to say, for the autumn of that year, and Kathleen duly put in an appearance, arrayed in all her beauty, at the races, garden-parties and various seasonal festivities of that countryside. This proved too much altogether for Lady Llandover's high-strung disposition, descended from Plantagenets, as she was, and with royal Welsh blood flowing in her veins; and the beautiful Mrs. Stone – at least so said the world – must be suppressed at any cost! Lord Llandover's defamatory attack on Mr. Stone's character was of such a nature that the latter had no option other than to bring an action for slander against his lordship. In the course of the proceedings Lord Llandover relentlessly besmeared Mr. Stone's good name – and then withdrew his allegations! The court was therefore never called on for a ruling, but a lasting stigma rested on Mr. Stone and he was requested to take his name off his clubs. In a most ill-advised manner, Mr. Stone published the court proceedings, as far as they had gone, and distributed copies to his friends, although, alas! these were few indeed by then. Throughout it all Kathleen stood with unswerving firmness by her husband's side, and we, William and I, stood sympathizing friends in need to her whose bearing was so deserving of admiration. Adela Scrope came to Hesleyside in the spring of 1860, havoc-stricken and suffering from the ineffaceable scars which the heat, and the division of opinion, of this celebrated family contest had caused. In July William went down to Bath to see the Stones, to find that they had sold all their goods and chattels and were on the eve of their departure for Italy. In Italy they attached themselves to the losing cause of the Neapolitan royal family, against whom Garibaldi was advancing. In the year 1864 Kathleen separated from her husband and henceforth lived alone in Rome, embracing this time the cause of Pope Pius IX against the Garibaldian bands which were threatening Roman territory. She became a perfect mother to the Papal Zouaves and devoted herself to their sick and wounded throughout the campaign in the most heroic manner. At the Battle of Mentana, in 1867, between the red-shirts and a force of French and Papal troops, a bullet penetrated her clothing as she was fetching water for a wounded man, and for this she was decorated by His Holiness with a medal for bravery.

'In the summer of 1860 we proceeded on our way to Paris according to plan, stopping off at Amiens on the Sunday to see the Cathedral, the finest Gothic architecture in France. With the three eldest children, I lionized all the principal sights of Paris, and took them to Versailles *pour la Fête des grands Eaux*, with memories of how my brother

George and I had enjoyed it by ourselves on that day nearly forty years ago.

'During this holiday in France I took the two girls to see my old convent in the Rue des Fossés St. Victor. The nuns were on the point of leaving their venerable old walls, necessitated by the improvement scheme of Haussman, which required the eradication of the notoriously bad Quartier Mouffletard, and the nearby Quartier St. Jaques, where the convent had been built. They had bought a house at Neuilly, and were very distressed at the impossibility of carrying their dead along with them. Considering that the church and cloisters were lined with dead nuns, to say nothing of their little outside cemetery which was full to repletion, the impracticability of doing so, even had they obtained official sanction, was sufficiently apparent. Being moved at their fret, I offered to raise subscriptions for a Mortuary Chapel in their Neuilly abode, and this somewhat appeased their lamentations.

'Accordingly, I took much trouble and, paying for the printed documents out of my own pocket, I appealed to all those Catholic families still extant whose names appeared on the convent death-roll, such as Talbot, Blount, Biddulph, Fenwick, Howard, Stonor, Petre, Widdrington, Fitzherbert, etc., and was inexpressibly shocked at some of the refusals I encountered. Altogether the nuns benefited to the small extent of £15, out of which William sent £5 on behalf of the families of Charlton and Anne.

'But the palmy days of the historical old house had long vanished, and ladies of distinguished birth no longer professed at *Les Dames Anglaises*. Indeed, even in my day, as long ago as 1830, it had become an *Irish* convent, so to say, with the Hibernian accent prevailing. Soon after I left it is possible that a revolution of sorts took place in the convent cloisters, for my dear old Poulette, *Doyenne* of the community, who had in turn taken charge of my mother and us three sisters, left in 1833 when she was eighty-three years old and came to reside in Baker Street, claiming that she had been obliged to leave as she could no longer live with nuns who were not ladies.

'On our way back from Paris dear Eliza Charlton met our train at Newcastle, and again I noticed her flush and her unnaturally bright eyes. A month later I went to Newcastle and found her lying on the sofa, a professed invalid and seeing no one. She confided to me that she had been examined by the doctors and that both lungs had been found affected past recovery, and that, with great care, she had been given about two more years to live. It struck me as odd that her husband, Dr. Charlton, recognized as the first physician of Newcastle, should have allowed his own wife to reach a condition of such hopelessness before discovering the evil that was hastening her into another world, and which the consultants declared to have begun its inroads at least two years before. At that time Eliza's husband had stethoscoped her, and yet had found out nothing serious to be the matter. But then Dr. Charlton had stethoscoped his young brother Henry almost on the eve of that boy's death from rapid decline, and had pronounced that nothing ailed him but a fit of idleness. The stethoscope certainly did not seem to be my medical brother-in-law's strong point.

'On September 10th dear Oswald went back to school at Edgbaston, and on the same day William and I went on a short visit to Alnwick Castle. It was only a small party, but the presence of the Marquis and Marchioness of Westminster, with their youngest daughter, Lady Theodora Grosvenor, made the visit very pleasant.

'In September also there were great doings at Beaufront

Castle, Hexham, when Constance, daughter of the house, was married to Alfred Frederic Adolphus Slade, son and heir of Sir Frederick Slade of Maunsel House, Bridgwater. Although invited to the wedding, we were forced to decline, but had the story of it immediately afterwards from Mr. and Mrs. Hodgson, who came on to Hesleyside straight from Beaufront. It seemed that a staff of Gunter's men had come up all the way from London to do the cake and ices, and other dainties, for which that well-known establishment is famous. Alas! the good fare so provided was too much for Mr. Cuthbert *père* who broke out suddenly in boils, with a proportional boiling effect on his temper. At any rate, the morning after a dance in the neighbourhood, in honour of the Cuthbert-Slade alliance, the guests at Beaufront were informed with Mr. Cuthbert's compliments that he re-quested all his guests to leave by twelve o'clock. There was just indignation at this mandate, to add to which no horses had been ordered to take the guests away. However, horses were eventually procured and everyone left, and the Hodgsons, Mr., Mrs. and Miss, came on to us.

'One bad result of the uncouth education William's gen-eration of Charltons had received was that they were accus-tomed, boys and girls alike, to ride anything, regardless of the animal's half-broken state, neither parent troubling their heads as to whether they broke their necks or not. Frank, for instance, when a mere boy, rode a race on the moor with his face turned to the pony's tail. My husband, true to the tradition, was wont to make his children mount any half-broken animal that came into his stable, until the very grooms cried shame. In vain I remonstrated, always silenced by this contemptuous apothegm: "Why you, you are a mere park rider!" which was far from true. As a matter of fact, all horses fretted under William's hand. When we were at the

Q

Lakes in 1854, we had with us Mosstrooper, a sturdy cob of fourteen hands or more, and Lily, the children's pony. But William, so proud of his horsemanship, could never get Mosstrooper over the narrow bridge at the Ambleside water-mill, certainly a trial for any horse, so that we used to change steeds for that part of our ride. For with me on its back Mosstrooper would step quietly across without the prick of an ear, and I always ascribed William's nervous, jerky hand on the reins, communicating nervousness to the animal he rode, to that early habit as a boy of riding half-broken mounts.

'One morning about this time Fanny, Amy and Ernest set out for a ride, and had only got just past the entrance gates when he came gallopping back to say that Kielder had kicked and bucked, that Fanny had been thrown, and that she had hurt her arm. Dr. Elliot came up at once from Bellingham and found it badly broken, and, after setting it, advised us to send to Newcastle for Dr. Heath. But instead of that, as the Hodgsons in any case were leaving, I took Fanny and went with them to Newcastle, where Dr. Heath put the arm into splints and urged great care about it. To continue the story to the end, Fanny mended, but could never raise her arm above her head, so we took her to London to consult Sir James Fergusson about it. But all he did was to say that it had been a very bad compound fracture and had been very well set in the first place, and from that day to this Fanny has remained unable to use her arm properly. Surgery in 1861 was lamentably lacking.

'The butler Inkley had begun his games and both nurses, Josephine Boudrot and Mrs. Hughes, had fallen violently in love with him.

'William and I were due to stay at Eaton Hall in October, but Lady Westminster wrote to put us off a month on account of the Duke of Norfolk's death, and so we went on invitation to Lady Wolseley at Wolseley Hall, Rugeley, instead. Lady Wolseley was an excitable little widow, hard as any Catholic of the old school can be, but very anxious to amuse us. She took us to see all the places of note in the neighbourhood; such as Blithfield, Lord Bagot's place, in the park of which is the celebrated "Beggar's Oak", whose branches are supported by innumerable crutches. Beaudesert, Lord Anglesey's, was another place we saw, and also Shugborough in Warwickshire where we walked over an ancient foot-bridge on which Queen Bess had set her feet. Trentham, the Duke of Sutherland's house, was, I thought, a very grand edifice. On Sunday we went to Rugeley and heard Mass in the church Mr. Whitgreave had built at his own expense, and after Service we adjourned to the mediaeval mansion he had all but ruined himself in building. Three years before, in 1857, I may mention, Mr. Whitgreave had been instrumental, through the agency of a dream, in causing Dr. William Palmer, the Rugeley poisoner, to be convicted of killing with strychnine his friend, Cook. On this Sunday occasion Mrs. Whitgreave, a beautiful woman, appeared dressed in mediaeval style to suit the house, and took her stand in front of a *pietà* of life-size situated on the first landing of the broad, but very steep, staircase.

'While we were at Wolseley Hall Father Darnell wrote from the Oratory saying Oswald had been kicked at football and was laid up with a bad foot, and that as it was likely to be a long business he advised us to have him home.

'On December 12th we paid our visit at Eaton, where a large pheasant shooting-party was assembled, all giving their golden guinea to the Marquess's head keeper at the close of each day's sport, with William following suit. We

remained on a little after the big party had dispersed. The
Chester Assizes were on, and one night several lawyers came
to dinner, the general topic of conversation being about the
cases to be tried and how the prisoners were mostly Irish
Catholics. Lord Westminster gave his company a reminder,
saying: "Gentlemen, a Roman Catholic lady is sitting on my
right!" "Yes!" I said at this, "but an English Catholic, not
an Irish one, which is all the difference in the world. English Catholics are responsible beings who are taught right
from wrong, whereas Irish Catholics, belonging to a yet
savage nation, know no better and are perhaps excusable on
that account."

'In January, 1861, little Ernest, aged eight years and four
months, was attacked by a most virulent form of scarlet
fever, and at one time his life was despaired of. So near to
death did he appear to be that his uncle, Dr. Edward
Charlton, thought it would be advisable to have him
anointed. Mr. Flint had just left on holiday and a strange
priest had just arrived to officiate in his place who had met
with an unfortunate accident while getting out of the train.
Things were only at a beginning on the Bellingham section
of the line, and no lamp or light of any sort was in place to
assist passengers to alight after dark. As a result of this state
of affairs the *locum tenens* of Mr. Flint stepped into a quick-
set hedge instead of on to the platform, fell, and sprained
his ankle. The carriage had therefore to be sent for him to
bring him to the house with the Holy Oils for Ernest. The
poor little priest could not stand without support, but he
duly anointed our sick child and gave him Communion,
Ernest being conscious all the time. But as soon as he had
taken the Sacrament delirium returned. Meanwhile, on
February 1st, 1861, the Bellingham section of the new railway was officially declared open. William, the children, all

excepting Ernest, the servants, all excepting Mrs. Hughes, in attendance by the sick-bed, and good Mrs. Hunt, who never left her post no matter for what excitement, went in to see the opening ceremony. It was just a toss-up whether Ernest lived out the day, and it was arranged that the stable boy and a horse should stand in readiness to gallop in for Dr. Elliot if a change for the worse took place. Ernest was delirious most of that day and had to be restrained from getting up and going to the island in the river, a favourite playground of the boys. I had in my possession a little phial of St. Walburga's Oil and a beautiful Crucifix blest by the Pope. Bending over Ernest, I saw his nose was sharp and his eyes sinking and a death-like colour on his face. There was not a minute to lose, and I ran for the phial. I sought to fix his wandering attention, and I said to him: "Dear Ernest, listen to me. You are very ill – dangerously ill. But I am going to put a drop of this Oil on your tongue, and if you will repeat with me one OUR FATHER, praying that your life may be spared, God is sure to grant your prayer." He did so, and I clearly saw a change come over his face! He fell into a calm sleep and when he awoke it was certain that a change for the better had taken place. Dr. Charlton came in the evening, said the fever had taken a turn, and gave the little boy champagne and water to help him to recuperate his strength. My brother-in-law may not have been an adept with the stethoscope, but he was clever in his treatment of scarlet fever, and was the first of all medical men to give the patient an alcoholic stimulant at the turn of the tide. Inch by inch Ernest recovered and, very slowly, got quite well.

'The Volunteer movement was in full swing and William's latest toy, the Bellingham Volunteer Company, had now been in existence a whole year, well cockered up by him on the least excuse. Every Saturday the Hesleyside men belonging to it, with the gardener Hodgson foremost in the van, assembled in the pantry and, after partaking of refreshment, would be carted down to the drill ground in Bellingham; but having broken down two vehicles, one of which was my own nice basket pony carriage, it was represented to them that in future they must walk. William used to lavish food and drink on his beloved Volunteers, but whisky would have been to them a much more palatable beverage than the champagne that went down their throats.

'It was in May that I took Fanny to London to have her arm seen to, going into lodgings not far from Grosvenor House. Ernest and the nurse, Mrs. Hughes, came with me; partly because it was my intention to take him on a tour for change of air and scene after his severe illness, and partly for the purpose of separating Mrs. Hughes and Josephine, who were both madly in love with the dissolute Inkley and, in consequence, at daggers drawn.

'The Queen's mother, the Duchess of Kent, had died a little time before and the Queen took her death very much to heart. An uncertain bruit was in the air, and rumour ran that Her Majesty was suffering great mental distress at some untoward circumstance that had attended her mother's deathbed. The Jesuits were putting it about that the Duchess had been *received* before drawing her last breath, though not the least proof to that effect was visible. Father Galwey, who attracted a large congregation at the Jesuit Church in Farm Street on Sunday afternoons, when he commented in his sermon on the facts, tendencies and *on dits* having to do with the world of fashion, was greatly puzzled what to preach on this highly delicate subject. He hinted strongly that the Court had been enjoined to keep religious silence so that no word should transpire enlightening to outsiders. If, he said it was any subject but a religious one that was so absorbing to the Queen, then the public would undoubtedly have been informed of it. Something, he concluded, had evidently taken place which Her Majesty's ministers of state did not desire to impart to the general public. Father Galwey, as a matter of fact, had hit the nail on the head! The Duchess of Kent was received into the Church at the last, and died a Catholic! Her doctor, whose name I think was Merriman, became a Catholic himself and divulged the secret some years after.

'Fanny and Amy had to be put in mourning for Monsieur d'Egville's dancing class, and I got them black silk dresses. D'Egville taught dancing well, but in the matter of deportment he also taught his pupils the art of drawing in their chins to such a ludicrous extent that the result was a grotesque and hideous grimace. Amy, who had joined us in London, travelling in charge of Josephine Boudrot, to have her teeth seen to by Rogers, the best dentist in Town, never learnt to pull these hideous faces; but poor Fanny, who invariably clung to the worst side of things and people, did not get over her facial contortions for a long time. I used to be on thorns when she was introduced to anyone, for a most unbecoming retirement of her chin was an invariable response. Fanny took singing lessons from Madame Anichini, who said she had a lovely voice, but it would require a great deal of culture.

'Ernest was taken to the Zoo, an immense treat for him who was so fond of animals; and he also went to see the terrible gorilla at the British Museum, for the adventures and explorations of Chaillu were then *en tapis*.

'My remaining sister, Mary Fairfax, lay seriously ill at 55 Eaton Place. I went to see her and sent daily to inquire. Undoubtedly she was very ill (she died in October) and

rather ——, but I was then accustomed to measure everybody by the yardstick of dear Eliza Charlton's perfection of
character, a standard to which few mortals could attain.

'As Miss Stevenson wished to leave as soon as we got
back to Hesleyside, I had to look out for someone else; not
for the usual governess instruction, but simply to read with
Fanny and Amy and help them to appreciate good literature. I engaged a Miss Wishart to come to us in July, a
recent convert with the best recommendations, who had
previously been governess to Therese and Olympia Doria,
the daughters of Lord Henry Kerr, and to a large number
of Weld Blundells. Miss Wishart's appearance was decidedly in her favour – and to her disadvantage likewise,
as will be mentioned in its right place.

'At the end of our short London season Amy went back
to Hesleyside with Josephine, while William, Fanny,
Ernest and myself, with Mrs. Hughes and Walker in
attendance, took a trip to Jersey and stayed for a month at
St. Heliers, during which time we thoroughly scoured the
Channel Islands, amazed at their fertility. We left Jersey
finally, partly because of the extreme dullness of the place,
and partly because of the impossibility of procuring a
respectable female servant where we lived, each one that we
tried being either drunken, profligate, or, more generally,
both.

'While in London Mrs. Hughes gave me warning, not
desiring to go back to Hesleyside. Her reason for this, which
did not come to me till later, was that she and Josephine
were still at daggers drawn over Inkley as the bone of contention. The air of Jersey did Ernest, who was slowly getting stronger, a great deal of good; but he was still extremely
delicate and had to have great care.

'We returned to Hesleyside at the end of June, 1861.

having employed that month in a leisurely progress through Normandy via Granville, Caen, Rouen and Dieppe; a most interesting tour, and much more so then than now, for so much of the picturesque has departed with the pulling down of old houses in those historic towns. The celebrated abbey church of St. Ouen at Rouen is to my mind the finest Gothic specimen in Europe, and, once seen, can never be forgotten.

'The morning after our arrival at Dieppe I took Ernest to see the little old town of my childhood's recollection, for the string of grand hotels now facing the *plage* are of the time of the Second Empire. My old town consisted of the Grande Rue running through the centre of Dieppe, the area immediately adjacent to it, and of little else excepting the Casino quarter on the sea-front. The dirty, unhealthy harbour, at the entrance of which stands a huge *pietà*, separates the town proper from its even filthier twin-sister, Le Polais, the inhabitants of which are of different race, speak a different language, and used never to intermarry with the others.

'My last visit to Dieppe was thirty-six years previously, in 1825, when I was only ten, and my footsteps took me towards the house we then inhabited, in a by-street near the harbour, which, for all I knew, might no longer exist. But there it was and, to all appearance, empty. When applied to, the *concierge* was of opinion the *les propriétaires* would object to anyone being allowed to go over it in their absence, but a *douceur* quickly melted her scruples and she showed us every hole and corner. It was a melancholy visit! Not a bed, not a chair or sofa, had been renewed or moved; there stood the bed grandpapa Crathorne had died in, with its coverings folded just as if it had happened only a week ago; there was my little brother Michael's room and bed – not a chair even out of place; my governess and jailer's room was just the same, even to the hateful table sitting at which she used to tyrranize over me at my lessons. It was like a bad dream come true and quite cast me down.

'We got back to Hesleyside early in July, and learnt from Miss Stevenson on arrival that the conduct of Josephine and the infamous Inkley had been scandalous during our absence. It was therefore decided to part with Josephine, and the wicked Inkley ought to have been treated in the same way; but the difficulty was to get a sober and efficient butler in such a house for drink as Hesleyside. When the time came Miss Stevenson was sorry to go, having become very much attached to Amy while we were away. But Miss Wishart was due and had advertised the day and exact hour of her arrival.

'Miss Wishart, her successor, had no accomplishments to offer in regard to music and drawing, both of which had been Miss Stevenson's strong suit, and for this reason I had to have recourse to Hemy, the best piano and music master in Newcastle, who came up on the train once a week for 15s. and who taught both abominably, with a skimble-skamble method and with a strong Newcastle twang which Fanny, of course, with her inborn propensity for hooking on to the least desirable traits in people, soon began to imitate.

'As William and I did not intend to entertain that autumn, I thought it a good idea to take Oswald and Ernest for a short tour in Scotland, during which there was an incursion of Hesleyside by a rabble from Newcastle at the instance of Dr. Charlton, who thought that his prestige would be locally enhanced if the more humble among his patients saw for themselves the grandeur of his birthplace. Most discomposed of all was Hodgson, the gardener, who greeted me on my return with the cheerful information that the ungainly multitude had swarmed in the woods and uprooted every worthwhile fern in them, leaving the place as if wild beasts had wallowed there. It was a sore blow to me, for I had been for some time collecting specimens of ferns to plant out in the woods, where they throve pretty well considering the climate. I had also tried acclimatizing violets, primroses and lilies of the valley in the sunny spots, but even so they refused to take on life.

'During this autumn of 1861 we had the hot-water pipes laid down in the passages in an effort to warm the house in winter. The mistake was that we did not have the heating system in the rooms as well, for what could be more dangerous than stepping from a passage at a stove-hot temperature into an icy cold room; for poor old Wilkinson, who stoked the furnace, had no idea whatever of regulating the heat and under his hands it amounted to a mercy that Hesleyside was not burnt to the ground. We also had gas piped from Bellingham, two miles away, and put all over the house, excepting in the drawing-room and dining-room.

'Christmas came again and, endeavouring to give pleasure all round, I insisted on a tree and carefully selected presents for everyone. Alas! my desire to please fell short in one respect. Miss Wishart had been moody and out of sorts all day, and when I presented her with a French embroidered cambric handkerchief she took it as if it were an insult. Fanny also, although I had given her an expensive birthday present as well, seemed dissatisfied with a pretty garnet brooch and earrings I gave her off the tree. So I hurried through the rest, vowing inwardly that it should be the last Christmas tree I would ever have a hand in. Earlier in the day Miss Wishart had spoken most offensively to William about some of our old Christmas customs and, in particular, about the *crèche*, which she, like all low Protestants, which she had been before her conversion, thought childish. Such people utterly forget that all religions had a picture-reading period, when by means alone of painting and sculpture could the poor and uneducated be taught doctrine and the significances of the Church's ceremonies and feasts. How few, for instance, would know to-day the Stations of the Cross were it not for picture-reading?

'When we parted with Josephine, a person of the name of Farrington took her place as my youngest's nurse, Vèva as we called her for short, and another young Catholic woman named Harris came as lady's maid. But about the end of January, 1862, after the boys, including little Ulric, had gone back to school, Harris suddenly gave me warning and went off in a very low condition. Nothing would induce her to say why she wanted to go, but soon afterwards it came to our ears that she, like others, had been ruined by the atrocious Inkley. Hannah Jameson was then again in Bellingham and William insisted that I engaged her as Vèva's nurse, although I was against it on account of her consumptive tendency.

'It was, of course, ridiculous to send Ulric to school at the tender age of six and a half years. It is true that Doctor Newman had advertised the Oratory School at its foundation as one for little boys, but he did not keep to the letter of that declaration. It was a school for boys, and not for children! But even if it had been it was not the right place for Ulric, who was the idler of the family. But what could I do, living, as I did, so completely out of the world? William took no interest in schools, and himself had known none but Ushaw. He was always a good paymaster to his family, but far too easy-going with the money; paying, as an instance, the full price per head for each of his sons at Edgbaston when, as he should have known, even two brothers are taken at a reduction. But business-like procedure and practical common sense had never been a characteristic of a Charlton.

'In March, 1862, there was a regular exodus, only Mrs. Hunt, the grooms and Dorothy Garford, as maid of all work, were left at Hesleyside. Vèva, just two years old, was farmed out at Bridgeford with Hannah Jameson in charge. The boys were all at school and Amy at her convent; but the rest of us, William and I, that is, with Fanny, leaving Miss Wishart with relatives in London, and taking along Walker as valet and Farrington as lady's maid, took a trip to France.

'In Paris we met again our old friends, General and Mrs. Beckwith, the latter of whom had been converted by Madame Davidoff. They were most kind and with Mrs. Beckwith I became very intimate. At a dinner they gave us we met Mrs. Herbert of Clytha, Mrs. Hamilton and her lovely daughter, and many others. Mrs. Digby Boycott came in after dinner, looking her usual lovely best. Father Darnell had left the Oratory in consequence of the *Oxenham* episode, and was in Paris as tutor to Janette Doria, then merely a youth. He had his evenings free, so we saw a good deal of him and, on fine evenings, would take him to the Bois and give the poor man some fun.

'Dear Eliza Charlton died while we were abroad, on May 10th, 1862, aged forty-six, and her husband came to Paris on professional duty a few days later. I was sitting with Madame D'Agoult in the hotel ante-room when Dr. Charlton was suddenly announced, and I must admit he seemed to be bearing the loss of his saintly and perfect wife with equanimity, and those who saw him at Bellingham on the day of the funeral were, I later heard, of the same opinion. It may have been relief at the pressure of her long and anxious illness being lifted; and yet he must have known that much of the respect shown to him was only reflected from the universal love and esteem with which his angelic wife was regarded. She was, like Frank Charlton, *the theme of honour's tongue*.

'The month of May passed very enjoyably in Paris. We knew a lot of people and, among others, the Vincent Eyres, and his sister Isabella. Isabella and her brother went with us to Fontainebleau, where we made a point of visiting the lake called *Le Bassin des Carpes* opposite the palace and feeding the wonderful fish which had been swimming in its waters for hundreds of years. The *carpeaux* and the *carpillons* and their finny elders fought eagerly amongst themselves for the bread we threw to them, but *Madame la doyenne des Carpes*, a portly old lady of some ninety years dressed in a flowing garment of dirty white, weaved about in the background with dignity becoming to her age and condescendingly regarded the high spirits of the rising generations. She was a venerable figure and riveted attention on herself, but she was in no sense beautiful to look at; in fact, a decidedly nasty looking old fish.

'Charlie Searle, who had been in our star cast when we had the theatrical week at Hesleyside in 1856, developed histrionic mania in consequence of his success on that occasion, and, never having been brought up to anything, took to the stage in real, good earnest. In 1861 he hired the Princess Theatre for the production of Shakespeare, managing the house and acting in the plays himself. As Hamlet he was beautifully got up, looking the part and acting it better than the usual run of Hamlets because he played it as a gentleman, which he was himself and which he conceived the Prince of Denmark also to be. He had a brilliant first night and the theatre was crowded with the élite of London society; but whether it was that he bullied the other actors, or made them conscious of his social superiority, he soon came to grief and had to give up the venture. The truth was that he totally lacked genius! Poor Charlie! He was forced to take small parts in the provinces on poor pay. In 1863 he came with a travelling company to Newcastle under the pseudonym of Allerton. The next year he followed Isabella Eyre to Hesleyside and offered to her, but it ended in fiasco. When my husband was in America in 1873 he came across Charlie Searle, who had just lost the whole of his theatre wardrobe in a fire and had no money at all with which to repair his loss. His parents, Mr. and Lady Harriet Searle, were universally condemned for bringing up their two sons as impecunious carpet knights, having nothing to act as a recommendation to the mothers of heiresses but their own mother's noble maiden name.

'When we returned to Hesleyside we busied ourselves in preparations for the Volunteer bazaar, and I worked incessantly, greatly helped by Miss Brady, the Catholic schoolmistress. Miss Brady was up at the house so often on bazaar business that it roused the jealous ire of Mr. Flint, and again we had to suffer from the tyranny of the priest, who never seemed to bear in mind that but for my husband, who paid so liberally towards the expense of St. Oswald's Mission out of his own pocket, he might never have been there at all. Little by little, Mr. Flint, whose father was an Irish commercial traveller, became a nuisance and most objectionable.

'I have ever had a great belief in prayer, and by teaching my children to offer up their petitions from the earliest years I instilled in them a perfect faith in God. The prayer of a little child so seldom goes unanswered! I remember that when Eliza Charlton came to Hesleyside in May, 1854, she brough with her a very handsome coral necklace as a present for Fanny; and I was sensible that Amy, although she kept silence on the subject, was envious and hurt that she had not one also. The next morning, when I went upstairs to pray in the chapel, I found a letter on the altar, written in a childish hand that I recognized as Amy's, and addressed: "To God, in the Mass." On opening it I found inside a petition that she might be sent a coral necklace like her sister's. I ran down at once to show Eliza the little Act of Faith, who was so pleased with the child's piety that she applied to her sister, who owned a facsimile, and the result was that Amy proudly wore this visible answer to her prayer.

'About five miles from Hesleyside, on the right bank of the North Tyne in the direction of Wark, stood Lee Hall, a picturesque old house which for many generations had belonged to a dimly and distantly related branch of Charltons. William Charlton of Lee Hall was a rough customer, gentle as to birth, but far from being so in bearing, and my husband had lately taken him in tow. In some respect he had become more civilized and had even joined the local Volunteers. Drink was his great failing, and as long as he could be kept from it he could be doing very well, as his appearance was in his favour; an advantage shared by his family in general.

'The "Volunteer" bazaar at Bellingham was a most successful affair, and soon afterwards William and I went for a few days to Edinburgh, taking train from the railway-halt at Charlton, over the river, and travelling on a pass which we had for certain days of the year. On our return we were met as usual by the ever-faithful Mrs. Hunt, who on this occasion had a tale of woe to tell. The infamous Inkley, it appeared, had lured Charlton of Lee Hall to Hesleyside by the bait of drink and had caroused with him the whole night through, so that he had become completely drunk. Inkley himself, who was not a drinking man, had kept quite sober, his only intention being to annoy Mrs. Hunt, with whom he had a feud of long standing. Nothing daunted, the poor old woman resolutely declined to go to bed until Charlton had left the house and she could shut it up. But he, very much in drink by then, refused to leave and might have carried out a threat to strike Mrs. Hunt had not Inkley interposed, who knew well what the result of that would be for him. Charlton and Inkley had kept up the carousal till the early light of dawn, when the former, slightly sobered up by then, felt some shadow of compunction and left the premises, escorted solemnly and silently to the door by Mrs. Hunt, who had kept watch all night long without a wink of sleep. No one ever had a braver or more true-hearted servant. Mrs. Hunt was never not on duty and, although herself a Protestant, would attend family prayers as an example to her fellow servants. Inkley this time had gone too far and was given instantaneous dismissal, while a letter was promptly despatched to Charlton of Lee Hall, couched in very proper and well-deserved language, wherein he was informed that henceforth all friendly intercourse must cease. He wrote a most truly contrite letter in reply, but from that day he gave himself entirely to drink and by that means brought on an early death. So Inkley went and Walker, the footman, reigned as butler in his stead. Indulgent as my husband could be in giving bad servants good characters and, in general, overlooking their shortcomings, Inkley got no character from him. Walker, who had come to us as footman about September, 1854, had so far given every evidence of being both honest and sober, but the sequel will display him as lamentably deficient in regard to both those qualities, so needful in a servant. At

R

Hesleyside, as concerns butlers, our footsteps were dogged by dismal fate.

'During September all three boys went back to Edgbaston and William and I went on a visit to Bretton Park, near Wakefield, one of Mr. Wentworth Beaumont's houses. I there taught his wife, Lady Margaret Beaumont, how to spin. Her parents, Lord and Lady Clanricarde, were staying there and also Lord and Lady Houghton, Mr. and Mrs. Headlam, and Mr. and Mrs. Morritt of Rokeby, the husband being the worst style of impudent man I ever met, and so acknowledged by all who knew him, even those who professed to be his friends. Luckily, they were a childless couple, so that no one would inherit his impudent vulgarity. Lady Clanricarde got me in a corner one morning and poured forth no end of Court secrets, about Lady Flora Hastings and the Duchess of Kent, and about the petty affairs of the Queen's palace. But of the *great* secret she knew nothing, viz.: that the Queen's mother had died a Roman Catholic fortified by all the rites of Holy Church. Many visits did I pay that year in the northern counties, wishing to cultivate friendships for Fanny's sake, who, now in her seventeenth year, would soon be coming out.

XVII

AN UNFORTUNATE ADOPTION

I N this section of her memoirs Barbara confines herself
entirely to the year 1863, in the spring of which, it will
be remembered, the Prince of Wales married Princess
Alexandra of Denmark. It was also the year of Frances
Charlton's debut, at the age of not quite seventeen, and the
two events, however remote in social space, react on one
another, almost to the exclusion of other interesting matter,
in the pages that follow.

First there is a little season in Paris, and then a grand
season in London, in both of which, under an anxious
maternal eye, the debutante daughter appears at every ball
and rout of note, and dances to her heart's delight.

It is while in Paris that the fateful figure of Rosanna first
appears on the scene, henceforth to form a theme on which
Barbara most willingly dilates. The curious story of this
young female scatterling, as Barbara would depict her, is
unfolded fully as one turns the pages and cannot help but
read between the lines; but to lay the blame for all the
bitterness entirely at Rosanna's door, as Barbara insists on
doing, is perhaps unfair. It was against Rosanna that
Barbara, earlier in her writings, was inveighing when she so
heatedly referred to the waif and stray who repaid with ingratitude the kindness lavished on her for two long years at
Hesleyside by Mrs. (Cholmeley) Charlton. There was, in
fact, a certain similarity between the cases. In each, with the
fond connivance of the principals concerned, a lodgement
had been obtained in the Charlton family, which duly
developed in the lodger a sense of possession and superiority,

of self-assertion and preponderance, and became in due course an infliction and a sad regret.

The concluding pages of the section deal with an outbreak at Hesleyside of that dread visitant, smallpox, her extremely noble part in which Barbara describes in simple language without the least desire to pose as a sick-bed heroine.

'In February, 1863, taking the two girls with us, William and I took up our old quarters in the Hotel Windsor, Paris, and, while in London on our way, I lunched with Lady Margaret Beaumont at 144 Piccadilly. Our friends, General and Mrs. Beckwith, spent every winter in Paris and, luckily for us, were still there. Worth made Fanny a most lovely débutante dress to wear at the Embassy on the occasion of the Prince of Wales' marriage at Windsor with the most beautiful Princess Alexandra of Denmark, aged nineteen, eldest daughter of King Christian IX, which took place on March 10th. There was no ball, on account of the Court being in mourning, but there were illuminations and a grand display of fireworks. Fanny looked sweetly pretty and, if only she had not been lacking in *savoir faire*, would have made a great sensation. She was about the same age as my sister Fanny, sixteen years and seven months, when she was presented at our Embassy in France, but Oh! what a difference between the two. My Fanny had more of beauty, talent and intellect than her aunt, but far less worldly wisdom and discernment. My Fanny was always easily led, too often on a wrong path, and now, to accentuate this evil tendency, she came under an influence which might have led her far astray:

'There was a Monsignor then in Paris whom I accepted at his own valuation, not knowing till too late that he was dangerous, unworthy and disedifying, and had been involved in a clerical scandal which came to the ears of the Vatican. This priest of bad repute, actuated on this occasion, let it be hoped, by a genuine desire to perform a charitable deed, induced us to proffer friendship to an unhappy Irish girl, whose father was Sir Arthur B——t of an ancient and honourable name, but whose mother was a drunken, low-born Irish peasant whom he married and departed life some fifteen years before the time of which I write. This woman, Lady B——t, had made a second marriage with a man of no social standing, and who, while deploring his wife's open habit of drinking, indulged himself in the same fashion in the privacy of his home. I never came across the second husband, but the mother and Rosanna, her daughter, were domiciled in Paris. Rosanna was young and, naturally, did not drink. She hated it in her mother and had just fled from under that inebriate roof, to wander over Paris in search of work in order to support herself, when I was prevailed on by Monsignor to befriend her; little reckoning what an unsafe companion, from a social and religious point of view, I had found for my own girls, and for Fanny in particular. I will say, however, that Rosanna, in dread of her mother's con-stant state of intoxication, behaved herself with perfect composure during our stay in Paris, and that, neither Fanny nor Amy being ever left alone with her, she as yet exerted a bad influence on either.

'We took Fanny to a dance given by Lady Bethune, whose husband, Sir John Bethune, later became the tenth Earl of Lindsay. He was a remarkably handsome and distinguished man, but she, Jeanne Eudoxie Duval of Bordeaux, was one of the vulgarest French *bourgeoise* I ever met in society. What mystery caused him to blur his escutcheon with such low blood? Honour, perhaps! Mrs. Digby Boycott had issued the invitations on behalf of Lady Bethune, and there I saw Mrs. Philip Miles in all her beauty. Mrs. Digby Boycott had recently taken her up and was introducing her in the Faubourg, when Mrs. Round, the daughter of Horace Smith, let loose her *mauvaise langue* at Lady Bethune's dance and put a stop to the poor lady's social progress. Mrs. Round, the reverse of popular in Parisian society, had made but little way herself. Fanny was really too young to appear at such a function, and yet her namesake, my sister, was a distinct success at the same age.

'Lady Margaret Beaumont came to Paris and we had great fun shopping in each other's company. William and I gave a musical party at the Hotel Windsor, at which were present among others: the Beaumonts, Beckwiths, Montbrisons, Blennerhassetts, Digby Boycotts and Mr. John Ogle. A *cantatrice*, whom the priest who brought Rosanna to our notice wished to push into the ranks of opera, sang for us at his recommendation. Mrs. Beckwith strongly advised her not to attempt such a career, whereupon the *holy* Abbé, an Englishman by birth, vomited forth his pent-up gall on Mrs. Beckwith and on me, who was her friend. Lady Cowley sent us her opera box and Madame de Bouillé an invitation to a deadly dull evening party, a few days after which duly came the usual *quête* 20 *francs pour les pauvres*. Most French evening parties are not worth twopence half-penny, but their balls are always well worth going to. Poor Madame D'Agoult died in childbirth while we were in Paris, and by mischance we sent to enquire an hour or so after she had breathed her last. We alighted at the invitation of Madame de la Chère, who took us in to see the poor dead woman laid out with her still-born infant in her arms; a most touching sight. We were bidden to the funeral and attended.

'Dear Mrs. Beckwith, the kindest and best of women, was my constant companion; but she did wear a most comical style in dress. Although a married woman, she had always been ascribed the character of an old maid – which, *par parenthèse*, she really was – and, with not so bad a figure, had the particular cut and *tournure* of *une veritable vielle fille*. The odd thing was that if she sought to choose a garment, whatever it might be, for any young girl, that young girl at once acquired the old-maidish appearance that belonged to Mrs. Beckwith. Sometimes it was excruciatingly funny, but not when it came to one's own door. Fanny, of course, must take it into her head to be dressed by Mrs. Beckwith, the immediate consequence being that at the age of not quite seventeen she put on the appearance of being fifty, all in Havana-coloured silk, a *rotonde* that no young person ever wore, and, of all styles in head-dress, a bonnet! A white bonnet, twice too big for her, garnished with a profusion of dark violets. She walked a perfect guy, but it was more a melancholy, than a comic, sight to see anyone so young and so misguided. What could I say? My tongue was tied! For how could I tell the kind woman, my devoted friend, that she had made of Fanny a figure only fit to frighten crows? Even William, usually unnoticing about dress, said to me: "Why do you allow Fanny to dress in that ridiculous fashion? She looks as if she had already been out ten years." Even Lady Margaret Beaumont spoke seriously to me on the subject, but it was to no purpose that I passed on what she said.

'We came over to London towards the end of April, travelling with the Beaumonts, and strenuously busied ourselves in looking for a house; a difficult task in that season of seasons when London was full to overflowing as a result of the royal wedding so short a while ago. Finally, we discovered a very small house in Chesterfield Street to be still unlet, probably because the exorbitant price of 32 guineas weekly was being asked for it by Mr. Montgomery, its owner. But William, with his large heart and never-failing generosity, gave that thievish sum rather than that we should suffer disappointment, having for himself a closet of a bedroom, my own being not much bigger. He had been very suffering during the latter part of our stay in Paris and was still far from well. He had all my pity!

'Mrs. Hunt and other of our Hesleyside servants came to Town, and we had hardly been a fortnight in London when Sir Roland B——t, Rosanna's brother, took lodgings in Half Moon Street a minute or two away and brought his sister up to live with him; really intending, as we had good cause to know, that she should live with us. In a day or so Rosanna was seldom out of our house! She was a pretty girl of eighteen, just two years older than Fanny, with a very large head and thick figure, but with pretty hands and feet inherited from Irish peasant blood.

'I did not think at the time that everything the priest in Paris told me was worthy of belief about the B——ts, so I took steps to ferret out the truth for myself from a poor Irish family who also came from near Churchtown, Co. Cork. Rosanna's grandmother, they told me, was very much addicted to drink, and her daughter, then a child, used to feed the poultry. Sir Arthur B——t, Rosanna's father, took a violent fancy to the little poultry-feeder, had her separated from her drunken mother, and placed her in a convent to be educated; stipulating she would not learn to play on any musical instrument so as not to spoil the beauty of her hands. She was still a mere child when Sir Arthur married her, and her uncle kept the toll-bar. Her brogue had been educated out of her at the convent, and her daughter Rosanna, who had been put to school in England, never had it. With all her faults and one great failing, I must do Lady B——t the justice to say that, as far as I could judge, she always seemed a frank and guileless creature. But what struck me at once, and so forcibly, with regard to Rosanna, was that, having got the run of our house in Chesterfield Street, and with it the over-trusting confidence and affection of Fanny, she immediately began to treat the latter as her inferior in a bullying kind of way. This she never did to Amy, whom she respected more and liked the better of the two. Nor did she dare to inoculate Amy with the seed of disbelief, as she had tried, she told me years after with regret, to do with Fanny.

'The May Drawing-room was held that year by the Princess of Wales, and it was the last occasion, on account of the crush of carriages, it was held in St. James's Palace. It was the largest Court ceremony of its kind that had ever taken place, and we just got in in time. Fanny was beautifully dressed, and beautifully *coiffée* by Cavalier, but in her silly, uncontrollable manner she huddled herself up in a corner of the carriage and went to sleep; so that when she emerged on arrival at the Palace her head looked as if the cats had been at work on it. Ellena, Duchess of Northumberland, presented me, and I presented Fanny, and the next night we went to the ball given at Northumberland House by Charing Cross in honour of the royal marriage. The Bride looked lovely, and the youthful couple danced a quadrille together quite close to where I sat. When the set was over the Prince strode across the room without taking any pains to see to his lovely partner, who took this lack of courtesy in her royal mate with perfect good humour and walked, unattended, back to her seat. Princess Mary of Cambridge, afterwards Duchess of Teck, a perfect balloon of fat, danced away as lightly as an india-rubber ball.

'There was a great bazaar held in Willis's Rooms, King's Street, St. James's, by the tip-top élite of society. Lady Tankerville invited me and Fanny to go and sit at her stall, saying that she knew it was the intention of the Prince and Princess to stop and buy at it. They did so, and she chose some china jars which her husband, greatly to my surprise, took exception to and insisted on her choosing others.

'Willis's Rooms were also used for the Yorkshire ball, a celebrated event in those days, and Lady Ripon had arranged a fancy quadrille in which Fanny had a part, paired with Captain Stewart. Mr. Herbert, an artist, had dined with us previously and, after dinner, had made a sketch of Fanny's costume which was considered the prettiest and most artistic in the quadrille. She was looking lovely that night, but was out of sorts because of Mr. Twyford's attentions, who had fallen in love with her at Lady Houghton's evening party and was now pursuing her to desperation at the Yorkshire ball. He would send her opera boxes which could not be accepted, as Fanny would not accept him and snubbed him on all occasions. And yet he was a handsome, gentlemanly, well-to-do young man; certainly the nicest looking of all her admirers, though being a Protestant was against him. That Fanny had conceived a budding passion for Sir John Acton there is little doubt; but as that highly intellectual baronet, twelve years her senior, was already more than half engaged to the Countess Marie Arco-Valley, whom he married two years later, it was hopeless from the first. Others besides myself opined that Fanny's monomaniacal affection for so deceitful and uncertain a personage as Rosanna was largely on Sir John's account, as her brother, Sir Roland B——t, was the former's toady, trying – the silly fellow – to match his brain against Sir John's, and making himself intensely ridicuous in the attempt.

'Altogether Fanny had about twenty good, swell balls that season. Lady Belper's ball was very smart, and the two given by the Countess Torre Diaz were both good. Lady Margaret Beaumont gave one, and with my invitation to it came six extra cards for partners of Fanny's choosing. She danced the whole evening. The Dowager Lady Townsend gave two balls, and Fanny did not miss a dance at either. Lady Blackett's balls were very good, but rather mixed. Those of Lady Goldsmith, in her beautiful Regent's Park house, were beautiful affairs. We went to other Protestant balls, and at most of them we were sure to meet Lady Lothian chaperoning her daughters, Lady Alice Kerr and Lady Henrietta, who became Madame Kerr of Roehampton.

'During the season we gave many round-table dinners for twelve at our little house to the best *partis*, both Catholic and Protestant, all on Fanny's behalf, which were acknowledged to be the most *recherchés*, in respect of food and company, that were given by people of our standing. We also gave two dances, and the best proof that they pleased was the fact that a lot of the young men, obliged to show their faces at a sweller ball, soon came back to us really to enjoy themselves. One night we dined with Lord Herries to meet Cardinal Wiseman and Monsignor Searle, his *Prime Minister*. One was as repulsively coarse to look at as the other. The Cardinal was purple in the face, a colour that imparted to him an ignoble appearance. After dinner there was a reception in honour of the birthday of the Pope.

'We went to a large Catholic gathering at the Star and Garter, Richmond, which was followed by a dance. Lord Houghton gave us an introduction to Mrs. Norton, one of the *Three Graces* of London society in the reign of George IV, and the model for Diana in George Meredith's *Diana of the Crossways*. She lived in the same street, and when she first came face to face with Fanny in our little drawing-room she exclaimed: "Oh! So you are the pretty girl with the cameo-cut face I saw at the opera the other night!" She spoke truth. When Fanny was prettily turned out, with her hair done like that of a rational being to show the beautiful contour of her head, she did look like a cameo, as did my dear mother. How blest was Fanny that in her my mother's gem-like features effectually counteracted the Brobdingnagian visage of the Cholmeleys! I cannot enumerate all the balls and parties Fanny went to on the memorable occasion of her first season, for all of which we had to thank the Duchess of Northumberland, her mother, Lady Westminster, and, above all, Lady Margaret Beaumont, at whose house, 144 Piccadilly, we dined several times in addition to a smart ball and two smart drums.

'As the season advanced, Rosanna, the Irish waif, impressed on Fanny's too pliable mentality that her head was too small to give an appearance of containing brains, insisting that to have a large head was an infallible sign of intellect and that all clever people had them; she herself having as large and as vulgarly shaped a head as any peasant girl in Kerry. Fanny drank this twaddle in and thenceforth she went to all ends to enlarge her beautifully shaped head, hampering it with butterflies, bows, false hair, lace, and everything imaginable and unimaginable, until she looked, to use her father's own expression, like Madge Wildfire. He attacked Farrington, the maid, on the matter, who frankly admitted she could do nothing with Miss Charlton. One evening, when we were going out, Fanny came down dressed for the party, but, as regards her head, looking like a guy. So I delivered an ultimatum, saying I would send the carriage away unless she went upstairs at once and divested herself of the foolish frippery; having set her heart on going to this particular dance, she went up and did as I had told her. And this craze of hers, this *idée fixe* imparted to her by Rosanna, continued until she went to Naples in 1867, and was taken in hand by the Duchess of Cirella. If only there had been a strong hand to back me, I could easily, at that early period in London, have suppressed Fanny's injurious *Rosanniacal* gullibilities. Alas! it was too sadly otherwise. True, the heads of both Sir John Acton and Algernon Swinburne were abnormally large, and the former was Fanny's dream of what a man should be. As for Algernon Swinburne, his head was so large his brains came through in an *indecent* manner!

'Alterations had been going on at Hesleyside while we were away – one reason why we left for Paris in February – and when we returned home from London on August 1st they were completed. The old dining-room was made into a sitting-room, the old library became the new dining-room, and the interior courtyard was roofed by a skylight and used, first as a temporary library, and afterwards as billiard-room. It was not a good piece of work; in fact the flooring, without drainage or cellaring, had been done *anyhow*, that opprobrious word being the sign and symbol of how things were carried on at Hesleyside. In consequence of this higgledy-piggledy way of doing things, the damp got in to rot the bindings of the books, many of which were of considerable value.

'The main alterations, as I said, were complete when we returned from London, but there were several painting and papering jobs still on hand, and in the midst of them my poor husband sickened of the smallpox! It had broken out in several places in the northern parts of England. Mr. Beaumont had it at Bretton Park at the same time as William, and notes of enquiry were constantly passing between the two places. While our own bedroom on the ground floor was in the hands of Crace's decorators, William and I occupied the large room at the north end of the east wing, and, so firmly convinced was I that I should not catch the obnoxious complaint, I never left my husband's sick-bed once. Luckily, he had it very favourably. The epidemic broke out in Bellingham too, and there were one or two fatal cases. Such a visitation had never been known before in the healthy North Tyne airs, so it was understandable that a panic resulted.

'I at once got Dr. Elliot to come up and vaccinate every person at Hesleyside, beginning with myself, for the sake of example, and followed by dear old Mrs. Hunt. Only one servant refused, a hopelessly obstinate Presbyterian housemaid who said that it was wicked and a sin to thwart the Will of God. It was God's Will, in that case, she should catch it; which she did, and of a most virulent kind. She was put to bed in the night nursery on the top floor, and not a creature would go near her; so until I could get hold of Betty the mugger to come up from Bellingham I had to sit with her, by day and night, myself. The maids had no objection to waiting on William during his attack, but they absolutely refused to go near the sick housemaid. When old Betty came I handed over my watch to her. The housemaid recovered slowly, but was so disfigured that she was not recognizable. Everything requisite was done for her, but when she was well enough to go I refused to see her. So William saw her off and gave her his plaid to wrap up in, for she did not possess the requisite clothing for a journey. September saw us free of the epidemic, and William out and about. The children, of course, had been kept severely apart, and I had all my meals sent up.

'The date of the smallpox epidemic at Hesleyside is fixed by the two following letters from Doctor Newman, the first of which is dated: The Oratory, Birmingham, September 7th, 1863.

MY DEAR MRS. CHARLTON, – I must throw myself on your mercy and ask a question which I feel to be necessary;

but I am obliged to act in the interest of parents generally. A report has reached me that you have small-pox in your house. I most sincerely feel the anxiety you must be under if it be true; and I trust it is either a mistake or, at least, that the complaint has shown itself in a mild form. I know too how extremely careful and thoughtful you are in such cases, and that if there is any-one whose prudence claims our implicit confidence, it is you. But, knowing all this, still, as a matter of form, I think it right to trouble you with this, in order that I may be able to assure anyone who enquires that your boys, whom you and Mr. Charlton have been so kind as to commit to us, have been in no risk of receiving the infec-tion. Excuse this freedom, which I sincerely hope will not add to your trouble, and believe me to be most truly yours,

JOHN H. NEWMAN.

'On the receipt of the above letter I wrote to Doctor Newman minute particulars of the safeguards I had adopted to keep my children free from risk. My letter seems to have quite satisfied him, and on the 10th I received the following re-ply, dated: The Oratory, Birmingham, September 9th, 1863.

'MY DEAR MRS. CHARLTON, – Thank you for your most kind and satisfactory letter just received. I hope we shall see your boys, as you propose, on Thursday. I shall directly telegraph *Yes* to you. My best respects to Mr. Charlton, and my true congratulations on his easy riddance of what might have been so anxious an attack.

'Very truly yours,

JOHN H. NEWMAN.

'So the boys went back to school, and I went to Edin-burgh to get some easy chairs and a table or two with which to furnish the new morning-room, having already sold some old, rubbishy stuff to make place for them.

XVIII

A ROMAN VISIT

IN this section Barbara is occupied with the year 1864 and the first five months of 1865, during which the misdoings of Rosanna continue to be recited at some length.

Her second daughter, Amy Mildred Mary, makes a provincial début in Newcastle, being at the time sixteen and a half years old.

There is a long Italian interlude. William and his two daughters, leaving Barbara at home, proceed to Rome, and Amy sends letters back descriptive of the journey and of the society in which she mixes on arrival.

Illness descends, and Barbara flies to the succour of her family, only to find that the truth had been exaggerated by report and that her anxiety was needless. But she stays on and treats her readers to a spirited and gossipy account of things and people in the Eternal City, which is concluded by an instructive, though lightly rendered, history of Doctor Manning's appointment to the archiepiscopal see of Westminster, consequent on the death of Cardinal Wiseman in February, 1865.

For Barbara the years now roll on apace, and the scenes of her activity change with that advance. With two débutante daughters on her hands it is no more than natural that the match-making side of her nature should develop at the expense of the simple motherly aspect of her disposition. She is in fact, at this stage of progress in her memoirs, gradually loosening herself from the frame in which she was set, amid picturesque and old-world surroundings, as a Victorian wife and mother. It is the natural effect of time advancing; but she has not yet quite begun to step out of the picture.

'The year 1864 was an ill-omened one for me, and the forerunner of several such not unaccompanied with sorrow. I should not revert to certain incidents of this miserable period of my life were it not to caution others against the sad effects of a misguided kindness. The blame, if blame there be, must lie on us, on William and me, for admitting to our family circle so ill-conditioned, false and recklessly extravagant a girl as Rosanna B——t, now fast becoming utterly insupportable, turned out to be. The entire burden fell on me, for William was out all day and, besides that, was of an extremely good nature, especially to pretty women who, like Rosanna, both witty and amusing, were a source of entertainment. He was blind to the evil she was doing Fanny, and so I had two against me – my husband and my eldest daughter. Amy was certainly very young, but before the year was out even she had sense enough to see that Rosanna was not the right kind of which to make a close friend.

'On March 2nd, under pressure from Fanny, Rosanna was invited to Hesleyside to stay a month; but she managed by her wily ways to hook herself on for six uninterrupted months, until September 5th. Soon she began to look upon everything in the house as her own, bringing about disorder all around.

'While we were away in London Rosanna was at Hesleyside with Amy, and seems to have behaved fairly steadily and rationally during our absence. Some time previously I had bought a dozen pairs of gloves for the boys to wear when they came home for the summer holidays, and now, on return from London, I searched for them high and low. "Oh!" said Rosanna on being told about the loss, using her special put-on childish manner, "I am so sorry; but I came across the box while you were away and, as the gloves were just my fit on trying them on, I've been wearing them." It was sheer impudence and I found it hard to disguise my

S

anger at such disregard for the law of *meum et tuum*; but her behaviour in that sort of way was all of a piece, and the boys had to go without their gloves. As Rosanna was by now looked on by our friends as more or less of a fixture at Hesleyside, she gradually got to be intimate with such people as the Beckwiths, Ogles and so on; and as we took her with us on occasion to various social gatherings, in that way she soon began to learn her way about. Amy was due to come out in the autumn at the Newcastle county ball. Although only sixteen and a half years old she was as fit to make her début as any steady, well brought up girl of twenty. Cautious in every respect, she was not to be turned aside a hairbreadth by any ill-mannered Irish waif and stray.

'Some time in September there was a dance in the Bellingham Town Hall, to which we, and a lot of our neighbours, went, bringing friends. It was a very ill-managed affair, but Amy was looking lovely at it in pink silk. A few days later she came out in Newcastle, wearing white, and we made up a party for the ball at the Station Hotel. Her Uncle Frank nicely came to see her make her début, and others present were Rosanna's brother, Sir Roland B——t and Major Longley. Major Longley was the son of the then Archbishop of Canterbury, and he whispered to Maria Mosely that he would have proposed for Fanny had his father not been who he was.

'The next day William, Fanny and Amy, together with Sir Roland and Rosanna, but without me as the party was so large, went by invitation to Felton to pay a visit on the Riddells. Naturally, the Hesleyside party only stayed the customary two nights and said adieu on the morning of the third day; but the B——ts, brother and sister, found the quarters comfortable and showed no sign of leaving. However, when the Felton omnibus drove up it was intimated to them civilly that they were not expected to stay on, and so they had to depart then and there, leaving their baggage to be packed for them and sent on by a later train.

'Sir Roland and Rosanna, the latter of whom had now been for six months living on us, went off south to pay a visit at Coughton. We were to meet again shortly in York at a grand bazaar and ball, with other festivities, during Hussar week, and the B——ts engaged themselves to procure lodgings for us in the crowded city. Rosanna's manner towards us when we met at York was so heartless and unfeeling, and so unmarked by any form of gratitude, that it even stirred the quiet Amy to remonstrance. Rosanna took Amy's admonition with the utmost composure, and freely acknowledged that neither she nor her brother had ever had the smallest heart. She spoke quite sincerely on this occasion, telling Amy that, owing to her mother's sad propensity, she and her brother had always been forced back on to themselves and obliged to scramble for the bare necessities of life. "But whatever Mama's faults may be," she added, "we quite freely acknowledge that she has the best heart among us."

'It appeared that Rosanna, while away, had fallen desperately in love with Sir William Throckmorton at Coughton Court; and that his sister, having ascertained that Rosanna, at her mother's death, would come into £600 a year, thought she would be a suitable match for one of her younger brothers. So there began, in that beautiful old Warwickshire house, a fine intrigue and play of cross-purposes which brought out in full relief Rosanna's natural duplicity, such as I knew well by now but was to know even better in years to come. For Fanny, in spite of the snubs and kicks bestowed on her by Rosanna, would still cling to her false friend, for only by so doing could she remain in sentimental touch with Sir John Acton, in some sort the patron of Roland B——t.

Fanny's infatuation went on for a long time, and her father, entirely without guile himself, was often put into a false position over it. William was no intriguer and was utterly without understanding of the deceitfulness of others; he was himself thoroughly *bon enfant*, and born alas! with a mind destitute of the power of observation.

'Before I close the record of the year 1864 I have a most amusing incident to relate. William, the two girls, and I had been away for one night, and when we got home on the evening of the following day our good, faithful Mrs. Hunt met us in the entrance hall to tell us that a stranger, a man, had arrived overnight, asking for Mr. Charlton. Hearing Mr. Charlton was from home, the man next inquired for Mrs. Charlton, and, receiving the same answer, begged he might be given supper and a bed. Mrs. Hunt, however, would not allow him to remain in the house while the family were away. "But," the stranger said, "I am a Roman Catholic priest, and your master will be very much displeased if you turn me away." So, at this, the poor, good, faithful creature gave in, although she felt certain that the man was really a thief in disguise with confederates in hiding in the woods. She cautioned Walker to put the silver carefully away and double-lock the pantry door, and she arranged for all the men on the estate to come running directly they should hear the big dinner bell ringing an alarm in the night. But nothing had happened, and Mrs. Hunt's supposed thief, having sauntered about the grounds all day, was even at that moment in his room. When he at last emerged, he did so in the bodily shape of Father Belany, only slightly known to us, who had made a special journey to offer his priestly services as a marriage-broker on behalf of my two daughters. William received him very coldly for his impudence!

'On the 23rd January, 1865, William, Fanny and Amy, with Annette and Walker in attendance, left Hesleyside on a long projected expedition to Rome. I stayed behind, myself, for several reasons. Firstly and foremostly on account of Vèva, not yet five, whose nurse, Hannah Jameson, was in very bad health, and who, once my back was turned, would never have been out of Bellingham, planting Vèva in her sister Polly's stuffy cottage while she went gossiping and gadding about the little town. Secondly, I did not like to go abroad and leave my three young boys at school, where anything in the way of illness could happen. Thirdly, I own I sought to lighten the expense as it was constantly borne in on me that William was inclined to spend more money than was necessary.

'The travellers spent some time in London and a few days in Paris, thus creating a delay that was not well judged, for their main object was to be in Rome by Holy Week.

'On their arrival in Rome Fanny and Amy found that all their jewellery, including the gold necklace and Cross Lady Margaret had given the latter for Christmas and a bracelet of some value I had lent them, was missing. While in London they had had the jewel-box out, and it seemed certain the theft had taken place there. Annette was much to blame for being so flighty and careless, but she was not suspected of being the thief, and soon another incident occurred.

'Our party arrived in Rome on the 8th February, just in time for the Carnival before Holy Week, and attended at the great ball. The Hugh Cholmeleys were then living in Rome, and Isobel, Hugh's wife, arranged for the girls' fancy dresses for it. Amy was in Mrs. Plowden's *Marchesa* quadrille, partnered by Sherburne Weld; both so tall that there was a universal laugh when it came their turn to pass under the gauze canopy in one of the figures of the dance.

Bouquets were showered on both the girls, but unfortunately Fanny, who had been a little out of sorts, started a bad headache halfway through the ball and was taken back to the hotel by Katty Bellasis, who, with the greatest kindness, stayed with her for two hours until her father and sister came home; Annette being out at a dance of her own somewhere. On arriving at the hotel Katty Bellasis had laid her lace pocket handkerchief and a handsome fan of ivory and painted chicken skin on a table in the outer room, and thence had gone through into the inner apartment to help Fanny to bed. Gloves, handkerchief and fan all disappeared and were never seen again, which did at least prove, much to her own satisfaction, that Annette, however wanting in prudence she might be, was not the thief. Not until ten more years had elapsed was the real thief discovered; a wonderful thief, a sly, plausible and cautious thief whom we always put above suspicion and who, by then, had been with us for twenty-one years. It was Walker! Drink, that deadly poison so prevalent at Hesleyside, finally threw him off his guard, and in 1875 his wickednesses were discovered, though not before he had robbed his generous and unsuspecting master of £40 in cash and several valuable articles besides. For years he had been most cleverly disposing of stolen goods, and was so skilful at the trade that he must surely have been educated to steal. Even Mrs. Hunt, forced to the admission that she knew Walker drank, was dumbfoundered at hearing he stole.

'On Ash Wednesday Fanny sickened for gastric fever, similar to an attack she had suffered at Hesleyside three years before. It is probable that this time she brought the seeds of it from home as there were no symptoms of Roman fever in what she had. She had a nun to nurse her. And then William sickened of the genuine Roman malaria, then considered a dangerous complaint, and so two of the party were *hors de combat*. While this was going on so far away, the Beckwiths came and stayed some days with me at Hesleyside and urged me to travel out to join the sick in Rome. But on March 23rd I got a letter from Amy, which reassured me and convinced me that William and Fanny were in good hands.

'The Papal States were so *arrières* that stamps for letters were unknown, and every envelope cost 3 francs 75 centimes each way to and fro. No wonder the Progressive Party in the Vatican could no longer stand such foolish backwardness.

'Amy wrote one more letter, dated March 28th, but I did not receive it, for in some mysterious way bad news from Rome filtered through to Newcastle, and thence rapidly traversed the valley of the North Tyne, to the effect that William had suffered a relapse and was very ill indeed. Walker was still in bed with erysipelas and what probably happened was that a servant of the Silvertops had written home to some Newcastle friend or relation a letter containing a distorted and exaggerated account of the three invalids at the Hotel de l'Europe. At any rate, the rumour so alarmed George Dixon that he rushed down from Mantle Hill and begged me to start for Rome without delay. So I got a few clothes and necessaries put together and, on April 2nd, set off on the six o'clock train, with £50 on me, given me at the last minute by George Dixon. At Newcastle I had a long time to wait for the night train to London, and Dr. Charlton, who was at the station to keep me company, begged me not to break my journey for any reason all the way to Rome. The rumours had by then got quite out of hand and, although my brother-in-law kept it from me, were now to the effect that William was dead and Fanny on the point of death. Arriving at Charing Cross early in the morning, I left by tidal train for Dover, Calais, and the South.

'That night I slept in Paris, where I saw Isabella Eyre before leaving for Marseilles by the 11 a.m. train, April 4th. I slept that night at Marseilles, after a long, tiring journey, and sailed the next morning for Cittavecchia. I was lucky to meet on board two nice people, a Miss O'Hale, quite a young girl and a Catholic, and her aunt, Miss Gill, who was a Protestant. They were very kind, and when the steamer stayed some hours at Genoa we took a carriage and drove about to see the sights – the cathedral, the Doria Palace and the Church of Santa Maria dell' Anunciata. The next morning we arrived at Leghorn and, making up a party of four with a German fellow traveller as our fourth, we went by road to Pisa to see the Leaning Tower, Campo Santo and the Baptistery. Before going on board again, we went to see the large synagogue, founded in 1581. The Duc and Duchesse de Persigny had joined the boat while we were lionizing; she a very childish person, playing "*Ah! vous dirai-je Maman*" on the saloon piano, eating bonbons and throwing them about. The next morning – Sunday – we heard Mass at Cittavecchia, a short fifteen minutes' Mass and a novelty to me. We arrived in Rome about mid-afternoon on April 8th, six days after leaving Bellingham.

'Amy and Hugh Cholmeley came to meet me in the carriage, and the first thing I learnt was that the invalids I was prepared to find at their last gasp were convalescent and doing very well indeed, and that my sudden emergence on the scene was thought by them to be a superfluity. Fanny and Amy were lodged in the Corso Roma with the kind Hugh and Isobel Cholmeley, while William, recommended by the doctor to seek country air, was in occupation of their villa at Frascati, fifteen miles away. At first I had a room in Major Darell's lodgings near to the Corso Roma, but soon I moved over to the Cholmeleys, whose kindness can never be matched, and all four of us lived in their house for nearly a month. When William returned from Frascati he was nervous and irritable; according to his English physician, Dr. Small, a certain consequence of Roman fever. Before he fell sick I had it from him in a letter that he burned with adoration of the beautiful and accomplished Isobel, but now his illness had worked a change, for which I was very sorry, and his admiration had turned to petulance. How the false report of William's demise and Fanny's alarming state of health percolated to Northumberland will never be known; but I was astonished at the almost universal satisfaction my arrival gave to the English colony in Rome.

'Before Holy Week the Cholmeleys gave two evening parties at which Isobel sang, and, for an amateur, I never heard such beautiful singing before; it was quite up to a professional standard. In many ways she typified Corinne; painting and modelling like an artist and declaiming in French and Italian with the voice and easy delivery of a first-class elocutionist. There was nothing Isobel could not do better than most. She talked fluently in three languages besides her own, and she was never known to utter an uncharitable or unkind word, not even of those in Roman society who virulently attacked her. It must be admitted she dressed in an eccentric style, but what artistic personality is not apt to do the same?

'Hugh Cholmeley, her husband, always known to us as Hugo, was the nephew of my mother-in-law and, therefore, William's first cousin. He had gone into the banking profession, established himself at Rome and was now a very prosperous man. Isobel was a Miss Curtis, a purser's daughter, who appeared in Rome at a very youthful age carrying a letter of introduction to her future husband in which he was requested to advance her prospects as a teacher of drawing; but she had not then made up her own mind as to what profession to adopt. Hugo saw this young, beautiful and accomplished girl and fell desperately in love with her, knowing she was not his social equal and of a genuine Bohemian class. A Bohemian, in fact, she remained to the end, which was her great sin in the eyes of the well-born among the Roman sisterhood; and yet I aver that whatever Isobel's imperfections might have been her perfections were such as to outweigh them completely and make her of those in life whose like we shall not look upon again.

'Hugo, Isobel, and Harry Darell of Cale Hill, near Ashford, Kent, who was Hugo's cousin, lived a perfectly contented *vie à trois* at No. 234 Corso Roma, concerning themselves with the affairs of nobody. It is to her credit that, for Hugo's sake, she did not press for the dissolution of her marriage. Great must have been her temptation so to do, for Harry Darell was no saint, but in spite of all she remained the *Casta Diva* of Rome, although a section of society turned their backs on her. Poor, dear, kind Hugo keenly felt such a social setback, but did not falter in affection or in studied courtesy towards his honourable little wife.

'One day Isobel informed me that Harry Darell admired my daughter Amy extremely and would like to marry her, but admitting that the Cale Hill property was so entangled and tied up he would be unable to make provision from it for a wife and children, and thinking that the problem might be settled in some other way. On that occasion she never alluded to Harry Darell's love for her, which, simply owing to her honour and virtue, had not brought her to grief. She said quite naturally that she wanted Harry to marry and that my Amy was the nicest girl for the purpose she could imagine. I put the proposition to Amy, who took it, as she did everything, with assured calm, though hardly thinking that this suitor, more than double her age even if still very handsome, was quite the husband she had dreamt of.

'Holy Week came and Easter followed after, attended by all the gorgeous ceremony of the Church. I quite thought it a sight to see the glittering equipages of the Cardinals and the cloth of gold in which they dressed their servants, but it was to me a sight that made the mind revert to the poor fishermen of old. And now Amy, who had been so well all the time William and Fanny were sick, began to complain of a sore throat; so much so that Dr. Small was called in, found her throat ulcerated and her pulse weak, and ordered her to leave Rome as soon as possible. So it turned out a lucky thing after all that I had journeyed to Rome in pursuance of a false rumour to find a rather less than half-hearted welcome on arrival.

'William, Fanny and Isobel Cholmeley were just on the point of departure to Florence for the Dante fêtes, and so as soon as they had gone Amy and I busied ourselves with our own preparations in accordance with the doctor's orders. The morning William and the others set off, he took me to Castellani's and bought for me a beautiful mosaic cross, and on it the head and monogram of Christ, which had been recovered from the crypt of San Clemente Church. How well I remember our last evening drive along the Via Appia. Hugo and I got out to walk a little way and so leave Amy and Harry together in the carriage to have their bit of talk. The next morning we were up at 4 a.m. and all four of us drove down to meet the boat at Cittavecchia, and then came the parting! It was indeed sad quitting the dearest, kindest, most hospitably generous relation in the world, which is what Hugo had become in our eyes. How could we help loving him and Isobel?

'While in Rome I spent much of my time with Miss

Hare, who lived by herself in the Palazzo Parisani and, being an invalid, hardly ever went abroad. Wiseman was defunct and an archbishop had to be appointed to Westminster in his place. Doctor Manning was in Rome for that Easter of 1865. His Holiness forbade all mention of Doctor Errington's name on the voting lists. Monsignor Talbot, who was the Pope's right hand, was constantly running in and out of the Palazzo Parisani telling Miss Hare in strict confidence of the goings on, and it is thus that I became acquainted with some of what went on behind the scenes. The Bishops, almost to a man, had acted contrary to the expressed wish of Pope Pius IX and cast their votes for Doctor Errington. They knew the ins and outs of the matter a good deal better than the Pope, who had not a word of English and who, politically speaking, knew less than nothing of conditions in the United Kingdom. His Holiness, in fact, was merely a tool, as concerned those affairs, in the hands of certain leading priestly spirits in the English and Irish Colleges in Rome. Pius IX was naturally severely irritated at his injunctions being thus disregarded and, by what he wittily described as the Lord's *coup d'état*, appointed his own mannie, Manning, to the vacant see. There is no doubt that the Pope made the right selection in nominating Manning, who at first was very unpopular with his clergy as he tried to restrain their childish talk and silly manners, and so raise the Catholic priesthood in the public estimation. Manning always held aloof from the Jesuits, perhaps on account of their questionable system of education and forgetfulness that boys of Spanish and other foreign parentage answer to a very different treatment than do English boys. The new Cardinal-Archbishop plainly showed by a splendid personal example that to be a good Catholic it is first necessary to be a good citizen, twin virtues that ought to be inseparable. Manning was the very contradistinction of Wiseman, inasmuch as he was the personification of an anchorite of old, and his high-born, handsome face was marked with spirituality. He lacked worldly pride and sought not the honours due to a prince of the blood royal; he did not exact that everybody in a crowded room should rise when he appeared. Above all, he did not toady converts as his predecessor had done, and lost caste in so doing. He raised the status of English Catholics as no priest of the Church in modern times had ever done before. Finally, he was a perfect father to the poor and oppressed. He had manners!

'When Cardinal Wiseman once went north to visit his old school of Ushaw, in Durham, it was announced that he would take the opportunity to make a Visitation to Newcastle. Hearing this, my brother-in-law Edward and his wife, being the most prominent Catholics in the town, wrote him a personal note of invitation to luncheon on the day of his visit; and this they did in ignorance of His Eminence's strict injunction that all such communications must reach him by direction to his Prime Minister, Monsignor Searle. But the Edward Charltons had only intended honour to the great man and were sadly disconcerted when no answer came; for they had planned to give him and his clerical entourage a first-rate reception, placing at disposal for the day their carriage and servants, besides the mere incident of hospitality. The day of the Visitation came and, excepting for the local Catholic clergy, there were none to meet the Cardinal at the station; Dr. Charlton, himself, having carefully departed the town on a professional visit to a country patient. Wiseman and his train ate a luncheon of an improvised character at some house and shook the dust of Newcastle from his feet, never to return. Poor Eliza Charlton in her devoutful way took the matter very much to heart, though claiming that she and her husband, the victims of such discourtesy, could not have acted otherwise, and averring that a last-minute acceptance, or even acknowledgement, would have been sufficient. And it was this *punctilious* Cardinal who, to the astonishment of every right-thinking Catholic, toadied old Lizzy Cookson, a convert and a vulgar, worldly old maid, who had *come over* at the instigation of Mrs. (Throckmorton) Riddell of Felton. Old Lizzy had had no proper instruction; her religion was that of farm-yard poultry who pick up anything that catches the eye, which in Lizzy's case meant worldly advantage and social puff. Latterly Wiseman's Sanctum Sanctorum at Westminster was open to a few prominent converts for midnight Mass, among which old Lizzy was always to be found. But at his death in 1865 she re-attached herself like a watch-dog to the Duchess (Drummond) of Northumberland, threw aside the Catholic precepts which she had never really understood, and embraced the religious folly of Henry Drummond with its angels and apostles. Lizzy Cookson died at Felton, but she did not die a Catholic.

'During June Isabella Eyre often came to see us, and one day, when she and Amy were talking over Harry Darell's offer to the latter, Isabella said, half in fun, "Well, Amy, I should not have refused such a man!" It happened that Harry Darell came to London from Rome about that time, and asked Amy to help him to search for a wife, seeing she would not marry him herself, as he wished to settle down, and end his days, in England. The *vie à trois* in the Corso Roma had come to an end after nine years, and perhaps it was a pity that the purity of that unconventional connexion ceased. For Harry's spiritual love for Isobel had kept him sober and good, and through her persistence, although herself a convert only, she had made him practise his religion.

'When Harry Darell pleaded thus with Amy, she thought at once of Isabella Eyre, and, he heartily approving, my services were enlisted in the good cause. I wrote to Isabella's mother and received a letter in reply thanking me most affectionately for assisting to bring about so good a marriage for her daughter, and I was given *carte blanche* to act in the affair according to my judgement. It was therefore only a matter of bringing the two willing ones together. Curiously enough, Fanny had her first offer at that interesting time; from a Mr. McDonnell, who was straightway rejected.

'Early in July Amy and I left London for the North, and were followed by William and Fanny four days later. Major Darell came to Hesleyside by special invitation on the 17th, and Isabella Eyre, by a curious coincidence, put in an appearance on the 18th. The stage was set; the proposal was duly made and, as duly, accepted. But the business arrangements over settlements proved not so easy on account of the tangle of the Cale Hill estate, and the Major was obliged to make frequent journeys to London. It was looking bad when the two rich Eyre aunts, known in Paris as *Les Misères*, came forward in a handsome manner. Two more dried-up old maids could not be found anywhere, one of whom, Mary Eyre, has been commemorated by George Sand in her *Histoire de ma Vie*. With this valuable help added to Isabella's own £15,000, and with the would-be bridegroom's life insurance on top a settlement was at last arrived at, and on September 4th William and Fanny, and George Errington, who was staying then at Hesleyside, went to London for the wedding. Something was in the air, for on the way down Mr. Errington proposed to Fanny in the train, and we all felt great annoyance at her for not accepting such a very highly favourable offer. He took his refusal much to heart and did not think of marriage for another twenty-seven

years. Our Annette, who could not recover from the theft of
the jewels as long as the thief remained at large, left us and
became maid to Isabella. Archbishop Manning married the
happy pair. At the wedding reception an accident threw a
transitory depression on the newly married couple. One of
the young Eyres, perhaps too full of champagne, removed
his sister's chair when she rose to cut the cake, in consequence of which she sat down heavily on the ground. It was
a typical piece of Catholic horse-play.'

And here, for the time being at any rate, we take our
leave of Barbara. She herself merrily writes on, almost to
her dying day, but this first instalment of her life has
reached a full-length volume size and must unavoidably be
lopped. The moment of farewell, moreover, is not ill-chosen.
She and William, at the ages of fifty-one and fifty-six respectively, are well-advanced across the spacious tract of middle
age. Her two eldest daughters – the youngest being a
nursery child of six – are out and about in the world of
fashion, receiving and refusing offers of marriage. Her three
boys, ranging in age from sixteen to eleven, are safe at school.

On other counts as well it is time to say goodbye. An
ordinary routine of life has succeeded to the liveliness and
sparkle of her younger married state. Her days are over of
movement and momentum and things no longer happen to
her as they did. She is still socially inclined, paying visits and
entertaining guests; but she has to trot her daughters out and
round, so that the former activity partakes more and more of
chaperonage, and the latter less of cheerful hospitality. Amid
the maternal cares and wifely solicitudes of which the
passing hours are now composed her distinctive personality
begins to fade, and, regarded as the subject of a nineteenth-
century portrait study, her 'period' value diminishes with
the advancing years.